Flaubert

FLAUBERT

WRITING THE MASCULINE

MARY ORR

OXFORD
UNIVERSITY PRESS

OXFORD
UNIVERSITY PRESS

Great Clarendon Street, Oxford OX2 6DP

Oxford University Press is a department of the University of Oxford.
It furthers the University's objective of excellence in research, scholarship,
and education by publishing worldwide in

Oxford New York

Athens Auckland Bangkok Bogotá Buenos Aires Calcutta
Cape Town Chennai Dar es Salaam Delhi Florence Hong Kong Istanbul
Karachi Kuala Lumpur Madrid Melbourne Mexico City Mumbai
Nairobi Paris São Paulo Singapore Taipei Tokyo Toronto Warsaw

with associated companies in Berlin Ibadan

Oxford is a registered trade mark of Oxford University Press
in the UK and in certain other countries

Published in the United States
by Oxford University Press Inc., New York

British Library Cataloguing in Publication Data
Data available

Library of Congress Cataloging in Publication Data
Orr, Mary.
Flaubert: writing the masculine / Mary Orr.
Includes bibliographical references and index.
1. Flaubert, Gustave, 1821–1880—Criticism and interpretation.
2. Gender identity in literature.
3. Masculinity in literature. I. Title
PQ2249.O77 2000   843'.8–dc21   99–048440
ISBN 0–19–815969–2

1 3 5 7 9 10 8 6 4 2

Typeset in Sabon
by Cambrian Typesetters, Frimley, Surrey

Printed in Great Britain
on acid-free paper by
TJ International Ltd, Padstow, Cornwall

A mes amis:

BILL H., CHRIS W., DAVID K. and DAVID W., GRAHAM F., IAN H., and IAN H., JAMES K., JOHN M. and JOHN T., JOHN DAVID R., LUC B., NEIL MACK. and NEIL MACN., NICOLAS J., PAUL C. and PAUL D., PETER A. and PETER S., RICHARD S., STEVE M., TOM H.,

for their various contributions to this book in conversations and on hikes up mountains.

Acknowledgements

THIS book could not have been written without the support of the University of Exeter Research Committee, both in the granting of research leave for Lent Term 1998, and in financial assistance for residence costs in Paris during this period. The School of Modern Languages Research Fund provided for assistance with the index. I would also like to thank the Director of the Institut de Textes et Manuscrits Modernes, Prof. Jacques Neefs, and Odile de Guidis for their interest in the project, and generous help, not least for permission to use the Centre Flaubert's resources over the summer of 1998. To the students in my Flaubert Special Subject and my many colleagues for their feedback and comment on various sections of *Flaubert: Writing the Masculine*, a very special thanks.

Contents

Abbreviations and Sources

QUOTATIONS from the works of Flaubert discussed in this book are all from the respective volume of the Conard edition of the *Œuvres complètes*. Reference matter is largely within the main body of the discussion and follows Harvard style, with full publication details of all works cited included in the Bibliography. Where a specific critical debate on one of Flaubert's works is reopened, readers will find wide-ranging coverage of secondary literature from various perspectives in the footnotes. Throughout, the following abbreviations are used to refer to the works of Flaubert covered in this study:

BP	*Bouvard et Pécuchet*
CS	*Un Cœur simple*
DICT	*Le Dictionnaire des idées reçues*
ES	*L'Éducation sentimentale*
H	*Hérodias*
LSJ	*La Légende de Saint Julien l'Hospitalier*
MB	*Madame Bovary*
SAL	*Salammbô*
TC	*Trois Contes*
TSA	*La Tentation de Saint Antoine* (Third Version, 1874)

Introduction

GUSTAVE FLAUBERT, writer of a diverse and inimitable small *œuvre* of published fictions and the enormous *Correspondance*, has been the subject of much speculation with regard to both his sexual or gender bias, and the ways in which his views on art and his famous style are reflections of concepts that might be described as masculinist at best or misogynistic at worst. Psychobiography, important as it is — and the *Correspondance* is usually cited as the proof of, or key to, Flaubert's views behind his novels — is not my approach in this study. Excellent work has already begun to reread the copious *Correspondance,* not least by ensuring that the previously censored letters are included in the complete works. The vexed question of the gendered nature of Flaubert's writing to his *correspondantes* has been treated by Tricotel (1978) and more recently Reid (1995). This approach none the less leaves intact concepts such as 'authority', 'intentionality', or critical *idées reçues* about 'great novelists' (m.) and their right to the final word over their fictional works. The same applies to genetic approaches to Flaubert, and perhaps even more to the ironic, back-door approach to the fictional *œuvre* which is DICT. In addition, all of the above lead to a certain self-referentiality that evades or covers its own blindspots, a self-referentiality that has been at the core of the challenge from feminist and gender criticism. It is therefore the fictional works themselves, Flaubert's published novels and short stories, that will be the main source of my investigation of the subtle and complex representations of the masculine, revealed in the imaginary rather than the documentary or epistolary realm. The challenge not to ground the fictions in Flaubert's biography, or letters, or compare them with his early works, permits a reading in a double time-frame. Weight will be given to the real historical and cultural world of Flaubert's times, which informs explicitly and implicitly the characterization, settings, and themes of the fictional landscapes that constitute 'the masculine'. I will be paying particular attention to the codified social roles and rights for men within the legal framework of the *Code Napoléon* as these emerge in fictionalized form via Flaubert's male characters. They reveal various negative power- and social relationships with men, as well as with women, to demonstrate that, while law is on their side, not all men are equal or unaffected by the laws of Patriarchy.

The second time-perspective is the late twentieth-century revisionary optic of criticism and theoretical method that allows a term such as 'Patriarchy' to be evaluated. Retrospective theorizing allows the many previously occluded ambiguities in any set of realities to emerge, and maps the transformations across time and space of imaginary and social constructions. Shifts in gender value, the codification of what is 'feminine' or 'masculine', are significant markers of such changes. Fictional representations, especially 'realist' novels, have the necessary complexity of sexed and gendered bodies, in relationship with one another and society more widely, to provide a hypothetical, but no less relevant, corpus for the study of gender. The close readings of such fictions then provide a space for the informed theoretical rereading of the blindspots of one's own acculturated perspectives about what is 'masculine' or 'feminine'. Flaubert's Bouvard and Pécuchet would have been perplexed if faced with the discipline of gender studies, but *DICT* is a clear example of its formulation in a previous manifestation and set of discourses, even if ironized. While politics and national alliances change, sex and gender power-relations have maintained a constant force with variations. Hence the study of a writer so entrenched in male value-systems (white, middle-class, male, educated), even overt misogyny, provides a platform from which to debate the very dominance of such criteria and their outworkings in his fictional representations, as well as the defence strategies that such strongly biased writing will employ. Feminist criticism and feminist work in masculinities theories are two theoretical bases from which to operate and will be used in this book. However, the potentially biased and anachronistic assumptions these largely Anglo-American theories may also carry with them will be counterbalanced by the socio-historical approach mentioned above, by close readings of the non-standard in Flaubert's fictions, and through this, a reading of the historical context of sociology and gender studies themselves, arising as they did out of the mid-nineteenth-century subdivision of scientific disciplines. Literature of this period seems, then, an ideally 'scientific' base on which to work, as all truth is relative and Flaubert's works are abundantly so.

In fiction's complexities, unrepresentable truths none the less find expression alongside represented ones, particularly in a writer who put such a premium on style and the *mot juste*. Time is what is required to reveal the relevance of both sets of representation. Their truth-value stems from the durability, and multivalency, of the 'real' to which the representation points. Schehr (1997: 210–18) assesses the wide variety of critical approach and response Flaubert's writing has generated, from 'existentialist psychocriticism, structuralism, semiotics, and the various strains of poststructuralist thought' to make of him the 'founder of modernism' (210). Summative descriptions of the effects of Flaubert's writing include disruptive hermeneutics (Derrida, 1984), uncertainty (Culler, 1974), even homelessness (Schehr, 1997): all describe a discomfort in the critic that Schehr also highlights. In spite of Schehr's excellent work to recuperate gay readings of French fiction (1995*a* and 1995*b*), the critical discomfort is not perceived as male gendered. The 'figure of the feminine' for Schehr disrupts the universe of the novel, but because 'the position of the woman as commodity happens also to be sociologically true in the world that the novel represents' (1997: 232), her effects are limited. The same is true of displaced male characters, such as Frédéric—'figures of feminine desire' (ibid. 233). Thus even the best gay-studies criticism may reveal its own blindspots. One of the wider aims beyond *Flaubert: Writing the Masculine* is to provide critical tools to counter naïve gender criticism itself and to dislodge the weighty valorizations of received critical opinion (mostly male). The chapter on *MB* will be opening again the debate about Emma's alleged 'masculinity', not least because Baudelaire saw it as such. The study more widely will then assess Flaubert's canonicity and whether this can be categorized by criteria as various as the writer's 'realism', 'difficulty', or 'modernity'. The conclusions will open up these terms, particularly the last, with respect to Flaubert's fictional and critical legacies.

Williams and Orr (1999) provides the most recent and thorough evaluation of approaches to Flaubert studies, both through the collected articles and the exemplary and pithy survey by Williams in the introduction. Here, unequivocal appraisal of the importance of gender studies and in particular feminist criticism speaks back to Schehr's blindspots, such as those above. Most ground-breaking has undoubtedly been Czyba (1983), in her cogent elucidation of patriarchal power structures in Flaubert's representation of women in his novels. Other feminist critics such as Schor (1985) or Kaplan (1991) have endorsed and expanded this work to demonstrate the running thread of misogyny in Flaubert's writing. Yet to follow this avenue—whether as a stylistics or linguistics study of masculinist discourses, the analysis of the gendering of writing itself *à la* Cixous (1975) as 'écriture féminine' or écriture masculine', or as a study of misogyny *tout court* (either from a feminist or a gender-studies perspective)—renders writing, or, indeed, reading 'the masculine', an essentializing endeavour. This kind of recuperation of either the feminine or the masculine oversimplifies the highly complex historical, legal, educational, medical, and institutional contexts of gender in the nineteenth-century France of Flaubert's times, and in a Europe out of which France was emerging as a major industrial nation. It is the formation and reformulation of 'masculinity' and 'manhood' in its complex and evolving nineteenth-century and French contexts that this study of 'writing the masculine' seeks to analyse through Flaubert's fictional representations. Its critical impetus is current feminist work on patriarchy (see Walby, 1990) and strategic use of masculinities theories as 'practised' by Seidler (1989), Connell (1995), and Collier (1995). The last is of particular relevance because of its critique of law as seat of patriarchal domination and it fits with my investigations within the French context of the straitjackets of the *Code Napoléon*.

The methodology of this book is directly informed by gender theory, in all its branches, but might be described as 'feminist within masculinities theory', combined with close readings of the fictions within their own socio-cultural context. The advantages of shuttling between the two historically determined timeframes allows a critical warp and woof, but weaves a reading which is also cognizant of the misappropriations of Anglo-American gender studies when applied to France, and the appropriateness of gender theory more generally to the historical and ideological context that precedes it, with all the different codifications this may entail. Masculinities theory by its very nomenclature demonstrates an already pluralized form calqued onto the prior work of feminism and its own endeavours. Overriding are issues of gender rather than sex. Consequently, it can only go some way to uncovering the socio-political and economic factors which produced the templates, codes, roles, and functions for men in the mid- to late-nineteenth century.

Gender is a term that has psychological and cultural rather than sexual connotations; if the proper terms for sex are 'male' and 'female', the corresponding terms for gender are 'masculine' and 'feminine'; these latter may be quite independent of (biological) sex. Gender is the amount of masculinity or femininity found in a person, and, obviously, while there are mixtures of both in many humans, the normal male has a preponderance of masculinity and the normal female a preponderance of femininity.   (Stoller in Oakley, 1985: 158–9)

In fact, gender is itself a very recent concept, behind which lies the concept of sex, and even this has only had a very short and modern history emerging with nineteenth-century medical discoveries and scientific research on the body.

In terms of the millennial traditions of western medicine, genitals came to matter as the marks of sexual opposition only last week. Indeed, much of the evidence suggests that the relationship between an organ as a sign and the body that supposedly gives it currency is arbitrary, as indeed is the relationship between signs.   (Laqueur, 1990: 22)

While the latter quotation would seem at first glance to reiterate current notions of 'gender trouble' (Butler, 1990) emerging out of Derridean *'différance'* and postmodernism and its concomitant theories of language and the interchangeabilities of signs (and gender), an opposite stance will be taken up in this study. Sex as category needs to be revisited by gender theory made more aware of the complexities of race, class, or national (legal) identity. The major point which will re-emerge with each chapter is that the construction of sexed and gendered identities is both historical and epistemological. To impose late twentieth-century modes of discussion about the masculine on Flaubert's novels, without careful consideration of the very terms of reference themselves (which are far from neutral or politically correct), leads often to anachronism and kinds of research which are culturally naïve and often culture-blind. Emma Bovary, for example, has been assessed as an anorectic or a shopaholic. What Laqueur is making clear in his comment about the sexing of bodies is that it was the emergence of biology as a discipline in the nineteenth century that contributed to the division of production from procreation. Before it was established as a science, in the Renaissance for example, ideas about persons were based on neither gender nor sex. Bodies were seen in a macrocosmic order of which they were a microcosm, or designated a fixed place within a social pecking-order (Laqueur, 1990: 8). 'Naturally', all three quantum leaps — orders based on macro–microcosms, sex, or gender — position women to one degree or another as the bits men have left over from their own self-definitions, or negativized as 'a problematic, unstable female body that is either a version of, or totally different from a generally unproblematic, stable, male body' (ibid. 22). As feminist scholars have made abundantly clear, it is *always* women's sexuality that is being constituted: woman is the empty category.

However, this leaves open the very real question of how to constitute the necessarily 'full' category, and within the parameters of 'sex' prioritized, though not exclusively, over 'gender'. One major source are the codifications or institutionalizations of norms. In France, the *Code Napoléon* provided the blueprint, and set up the bourgeois, enfranchised, male as norm, subject, and citizen. Concomitantly, woman was disenfranchised second-class citizen, denied economic or legal status in her own right. Her only value was in providing the secondary or negative pole of the binary to his positive self. Such institutionalizing of the sexual division of labour, capital, status, and rights, with its downgrading of woman as tantamount to her legalized womb within marriage, occurred in France to a degree not found elsewhere in Europe or in the other developing democracy of the epoch, the United States of America. As Joan Scott reminds us:

gender is the social organisation of sexual difference. But this does not mean that gender reflects or implements fixed or natural physical differences between women and men; rather gender is the knowledge that establishes meanings for bodily differences. These meanings vary across cultures, social groups, and time, since nothing about the body, including women's reproductive organs, determines univocally how social divisions will be shaped.   (1988: 2)

Nineteenth-century concepts and notions about masculinity, about what 'being a man' might mean, were very clearly shaped by gender and sexual division—a classic case of two separate spheres. However, although there may be similarities in how such 'patriarchal constructs' predominated in both France and the United States, there were big differences between nineteenth-century American constructions of manhood and French 'manliness' after the emergence of Napoleon I. Among these were the very different religious, legal, and educational factors such as Protestant or Catholic moralities, and access to higher education or school curricula. A further variation was the context of Victorian Britain. (See Mangan and Walvin, 1987, and Pugh, 1983.) While all three nations shared the common feature of dichotomizing the public and private spheres as the preserve of men and women respectively, institutions were produced variously in the three countries because function, role, and inheritance laws among others determined specific parameters. While all three, too, were in the throes of massive industrialisation, scientific advances, and medical research developments, and based knowledge and power on reason, there was a timelag in France. Here also, there was almost no access for women to medicine or science.

The nineteenth century was the medical epoch *par excellence*, producing 'scientific proof' and evidence in the new disciplines of biology, psychiatry, pathology, gynaecology, craniology, and criminology; anatomy was indeed destiny. Deemed male were action, reason, rationality, physical strength; and female the unruly, irrational, sexual yet passive part, to be disciplined and controlled. Where France stands out more strikingly in comparison and contrast to Britain and the USA is in the codification of these inequalities to the unprecedented degree in the *Code Napoléon* of 1804. To add to Scott's quotation above, it was not only gender that 'establishes meanings for bodily difference', but also sex. The most blatant example is the division of every aspect of the *Code* along the line of paternity versus maternity, whereby the two categories could never overlap. Hence production was set over reproduction, economics over housekeeping, manufacture (heavy industry) in opposition to 'light' industry or home-making. The paradox was of course that sex as pleasure was also harnessed to split femininity into a further two parts along the same public–private divide: wives and mothers at home were 'protected' from the 'filles publiques', yet men (public figures and ordinary men) had access to both. The reason is clearly that both categories of women have the seamless male 'active' sexuality as positive standard against which female sexuality is receptive, passive.

Flaubert's novels, even the eponymously women-centred ones, are unusually dichotomized in terms of male and female spheres, even in the context of the nineteenth-century realist novel. In spite of the ink spilled on Flaubert's 'femininity' through the person of Madame Bovary, or rather the muscular androgyny in which he allegedly cloaked himself, this study will not equate the characters of either sex with Flaubert. Such gender 'bending' obfuscates the nub of the issues in his novels: their dynamic is always the circulation of bodies and power. The 'masculinity' of Flaubert's various strong women protagonists apart from Emma Bovary—the Queen of Sheba, Hérodias, Salammbô—will be treated as highly problematic even if they are among the most active, powerful, or charismatic figures in their various contexts. There is never any range of female parts in a given work. No main female protagonist remains alive to tell her own tale. Certainly the very powerful Hérodias is doubled in her daughter Salomé and lives, but as a kind of reincarnated Jezebel she is the butt of Ioakanann's curse and prophecy because of her incest, prostitutions, and magic charms. These 'overfeminizations' are really stereotypes of the feminine: the implication is that woman is essentially prostitute and manipulator, sex pure or impure. At best she is a foil to the men, and any wiles she might successfully employ because of her native intelligence are always relegated to bodily impact. Hérodias needs Salomé and her nubile body to complete the deed: Salammbô's courage in retrieving the veil is negated by her submission physically to Mâtho and by her father's use of her in the diplomatic game of securing his empire. While Félicité fills most of the textual space in CS, this is undermined completely by the patronizing title, her menial and passive status, and the narrative stance towards her 'imbecility', that a parrot might be mistaken for the Holy Spirit. And the late Flaubert increasingly metes out only menial, servant, or domestic roles to the very few women characters who figure in works which are largely men's worlds. Madame Bordin's concern with acquiring property in *BP* is another facet of this domestication of striking women in Flaubert's *œuvre*, following the footsteps of Emma or Rosanette.

Flaubert is too much the upholder of sex as *destiny* in perfect accord with the Napoleonic vision and *Code* and the concomitant valorization of his 'half' of humanity in France 1821–88 to accord the concept 'masculine' (although he would have couched it in his own terms as 'dur et musclé') to a woman, because of the dishonour this would then entail for men. Less problematic are any 'feminine' attributes the major male characters may have. With regard to Flaubert's men, 'feminine' seems always a term 'under erasure' in that it is overwritten by a preponderance in the same protagonists of strongly virile markers: obduracy, very male bodies, strong sense of self, or mastery in their world. Even Charles has all of these in modified form because his bear-like presence at the end of *MB* does make him a force to be reckoned with. Antoine, Mâtho, Ioakanann have a dignity and *amour propre* in spite of death or abnegation of self. Frédéric's platonic bisexuality vastly surpasses Cisy's sissiness. And although they inhabit an almost female-free world, and hence evade performance anxieties in their retired state, away from public-order masculinities, Bouvard and Pécuchet dally with 'the feminine' because everything around them is in a potential state of erection. Their 'foyer' replicates the public/private spheres in an exchange which only shuffles the process of the Copy. The very fact that they are a self-bolstering pair or couple (as Frédéric and Deslauriers also returned to hearth and home) only further underpins the paradoxes and contradictions of the gender enterprise. Individualism remains properly male.

How does one become (a man) and then stay individual? How does one separate from the models of patriarchy without stepping into other such models? In a close reading of Beauvoir's famous adage for men as well as women in *MB* (Orr, 1999*b*), I addressed these issues, analysing how all-essential 'success' was—in business, love, the household, the Comices—

with failure to be avoided at all costs, in order to ensure one's place of advantage, endorsement, authorization, and legitimization. This study opens the questions of male success and failure to wider spheres: politics and war, philosophy and integrity, morality—all spokes round the hub of exploit or action-in-the-world.

In the scientific and positivist age of nineteenth-century France, Flaubert's works certainly show women as powerless. More surprisingly, they uncover how men are disempowered, made impotent, even if they have all-powerful positions. Equally disconcerting is the fact that the novels do not centre on heroes' exploits either. Action is itself largely dispensed with both as criterion of masculinity and as mode of narrative intrigue. Plot—the activity, and thrusting nature of the hero— which is so pivotal to the novel genre in its nineteenth-century form in the hands of either a Balzac or a Dickens, is often reduced to static inaction or aborted action. Flaubert therefore challenges action as causality and progress, key tenets of the realist novel tradition, by either un-manning or de-heroizing his main male protagonists such as Frédéric. Variations of this are doubled male protagonists or overmasculinized secondary male figures, as we will see in *SAL*. Hewitt's investigation of current debate on hypermasculinity, fascism, and homosexuality (1996) has a strange pertinence to this novel with its exploration of ethnic cleansing and 'aryanism' a step away from holocaust or the Bosnian crisis. Actions lead to dénouements. Flaubert equally problematizes this privileged site in the ways in which his male protagonists meet their ends in pseudo-elevation, or pseudo-decrease.

Flaubert's novels and stories are therefore concerned less with the differences between men and women, as these are pre-given, than with what differentiates men from other men. Their various power-relations, rivalries, and antagonisms will be central to the chapter in question. In their specific contexts and as individuals in their respective texts, Flaubert's male characters illustrate the ideological and epistemological ramifications of an all-male public domain, and, as we will see, its faults, failings, and impasses. Not least of these is the tautology that if politics equals men, then all men equals politics, but via a politics where men are not in fact equal. This will become the overriding conundrum in *ES* but is implicit in various guises throughout Flaubert's *œuvre*. The masculine therefore is not democratic. By cutting society in two along lines of sex and gender, the flaws in the valorization of certain qualities as masculine is not only a feminist problem or one for women. What I will be uncovering in Flaubert's novels are the implications for men of these valorizations when they do not conform or fit in. Is the only other position left available for them one tantamount to that of women (as Schehr, 1997 suggests above)? Mâtho, for example, becomes 'feminized' in its most negative connotations as victim and sacrifice. *BP* will reveal that homosociality as chosen paradisal world has its own male dystopian snakes. The knotty problem is how distinctions between same-sex equals may be made, which the solution of mirror-image copies does not easily resolve. Flaubert's novels, then, reveal an unusually high preponderance of unlikely male figures when compared to the works of other nineteenth-century realist novelists, and are almost overmasculine in this statistical regard.

The representations of various kinds of homosocial relations also bring to the fore different codes and rules for male behaviour, status, and manners which make Flaubert's works so rich in their investigation of the masculine as constructed across societies, generations, professions, events in history, and in their negotiations with women. The highly problematic, tenuous, shifting, and fragile divides and borders between male categorizations emerge clearly, whether this is within the antique world of Carthage, or Paris and Normandy in the nineteenth century. Without a properly historical contextualization of these codes, however, it would be too easy to read male–male relations or friendships erroneously or only superficially. My 'Reading the Other' (Orr, 1992) negotiated a coded homosexuality, when this term was not available at the time, alongside codes of male friendship and manners which are not now in current usage. The so-called civilized, rational, male behaviours of Flaubert's France are therefore opened to question, but so too is the dichotomy civilized–uncivilized, because Flaubert problematizes the superiority of universal human/maleness: 'Ah, Quelle immorale bête que la foule! et qu'il est humiliant d'être homme' (Letter to George Sand, 31 March 1871). Many critics argue from this Flaubert's misanthropy or mandarinism

(Tricotel, 1978: 156). Yet as man, Flaubert is also part of this same 'foule' in the public sphere and shares with his male contemporaries certain ideas which transcend class or rank. Herein lies the blindspot of patriarchy's hierarchical constructions, throwing into question how men become individualized and in which male spheres. The representation of these processes lies at the heart of Flaubert's investigation of masculinity, its freedoms and constraints judged against categories and norms.

Reading his male characters as they interact directly with the models and expectations for manhood, its duties, institutions, and roles is an obvious starting-point, but does not reduce reading the masculine only to reconsiderations of the outer man (gender). How one is to become a man 'of character', distinctive through inner qualities like Antoine, puts 'character' as critical term back on the agenda in renewed form. The masculine analysed in each chapter will be taken into the different territories whereby its connections with sex, gender, social function as stereotype or classificatory model, or person in the singular emerges. Knight (1985), the most concentrated study of Flaubert's characters, and her aims, make a starting-point:

> In taking character as the pivot between formal and moral values in Flaubert, I shall challenge both structuralist devaluations of the general role and status of character in his work, and traditional readings of many of his well-known protagonists. By arguing that the use of unintelligent reflectors of experience is part of a positive intention, I shall show that the very characters dismissed by both the moral and formalist approaches as 'weak vessels' should be viewed as *exemplary* since they acquire privileged aesthetic status and are central to the operation of Flaubert's value system.' (6, author's emphasis).

This will be particularly clear with regard to how protagonists situate themselves *vis-à-vis* Family and State or one another in various ways in each of the novels. Conformists are many and seem to be rewarded, whereas men 'à contre-courant' are killed, destroyed, or self-destruct. These are the men who fail to be 'outils' or 'utiles' within the prevailing power-struggles, *arrivisme*, economic and industrial expansion which constitute the prevailing ethos in Flaubert's France across the period of production of his novels. Utilitarian man is as apparent in the seeming anachronism of Carthage with its elaborate war-machines as in the scientific world of Les Chavignolles or in Homais's pharmacy. Yet Flaubert's biting irony in the promotion of such figures of useful masculinity he most detests— Homais, Sénécal, Spendius, Gorju—only underlines their uniformity and lack of imagination, not their individualism. There is no poetry in their souls. As Kelen (1994: 23) puts it, 'Ce n'est point hasard si l'homme de l'époque industrielle et technologique a été standardisé à l'égal de ses machines; si l'homme a été considéré comme utile, comme utilitaire et donc fabriqué en série; l'homme utile est remplaçable, tandis que l'individu libre, l'homme de gratuité, l'homme créatif est unique et irremplaçable.' Whether one is a man in the new-world industrial workplace (*ES, BP*), or undertaking the ancient-world jobs of 'guerrier', 'sage', 'artiste', what counts is a personal dynamic, charisma, or even their negatives—ridiculous difference, indifference to society at large—to counteract the *bêtise* of crowd mentalities and entrepreneurial behaviours. 'Seul les êtres libres sont capables d'engagement. Les individus cohérents, troublés ni par les idées à la mode ni par les conduites moutonnières, sont inévitablement les guerriers parce qu'ils sentent le besoin irrépressible et vital de s'impliquer . . . le guerrier intellectuel ou artiste peut se définir ainsi: de tout temps, *il prend risque de déplaire*' (Kelen, ibid. 111 and 113, author's emphasis). We will see the particular problematics for masculinity of this criterion of 'making a difference', because its collective force for change only leads to a new formation of similitude, and individuality congeals into conformity. By contrast, it is the mad, the peculiar, and the marginal to corroborated collective masculinities that are Flaubert's key heroes, protagonists who have been discounted as feeble, boring, or inarticulate by the critical machine. Kelen (ibid. 121) names four characteristics—love, poetry, mystery, prophecy—which she sees as markers of the exceptional (male) individual, all interestingly in operation in Flaubert's novels in his counter-characters, Charles, Mâtho, Frédéric, Julien, Loulou, Antoine. Such traits would seem to run with the grain of romanticism and against the grain of industrialization and the nineteenth-century realist novel. How far Flaubert's whole *œuvre*, via these strange chief male protagonists, takes on a prophetic function about the spirit of his age will be assessed at the end of the study. Flaubert is perhaps the father of a neo-romanticism, rather than the father of realism.

Flaubert's male counter-protagonists, however, also fail to become anti-heroes. The paradox that I will be contending throughout this study is that, in Flaubert's works, both hero and anti-hero fall short as terms to describe his 'exceptional' individuals, male or female. What seems constantly to be the case is that artistic intervention 'rescues' the potential anti-hero at the point when he would transcend a singular mediocrity to join a brigade of 'noble' anti-heroes. It is the thunderbolt of vituperative ink that holds the character always in mediocrity (or baseness) of a certain kind and begs the question why Flaubert should constantly seek to prevent any potential for anti-heroism. Suffice it to say here that Charles Bovary dies inexplicably *in extremis* of emotional disorder; Frédéric Moreau, as young man of many prospects and privileges, is a list of listlessness; Mâtho is overtly and overly scapegoated as he is sacrificed on the altar of patriarchy; Antoine's monumental despair is his bid for sanctification, yet his elation is a stodgy silence. *TC* illustrates all-too-mortal manhood in the grip of vice of different kinds, offsetting any counter-virtue to cancel out both sides, let alone furnish criteria for suitable sanctification. Bouvard and Pécuchet hold the two ends of one and the same metonymical chain of male links and logical connectors, so that which character is which in the end signifies nothing.

Flaubert's chief male protagonists not only fall outside the norms, categorizations, and classifications of 'successful' masculinity and male roles in nineteenth-century France of the Napoleonic Law of the Fathers, and according to the 'laws' of realism; they also hark back to other formations and practices. Such 'avant-garde anachronism', also heralding a kind of *fin-de-siècle* decadence, is so dangerous to the codes and specifications of the 'new man' (*homo economicus*)—Homais, Lheureux, Spendius—that Order and Law intervene to annihilate any dissenters and promotors of alternative lifestyles. The censorship of masculinities not deemed appropriate has largely remained hidden thanks to the overt promotion of certain hegemonic male authorities largely at the expense of women (see Figure 1, p. 20). The secondary and minor position of women without rights to vote, to control their own bodies, to own property, or have their own money, has frequently been documented as part of the essential division into two spheres that the *Code Napoléon* engineered and institutionalized. Critics have not focused on the detrimental effects of this same codification for men. My study shows this society as divisive for men also outside its institutionalized 'rights' to autonomy and democratic equalities. These are the illegitimate son, the orphan, the homosexual. As Annalise Maugue puts it so succinctly:

la Révolution de 1789 et la révolution industrielle ont transformé les status et les rôles, bouleversé les valeurs, remodelé les identités . . . Contraint de se re-situer relativement à une femme en mouvement qui bouscule les plus anciens repères, l'homme se voit contraint de confronter sa propre praxis à la liste supposée de ses mérites et de s'interroger sur sa place dans le monde. Il n'en vient pas pour autant à remettre en question sa prééminence . . . ni à faire de la masculinité l'objet d'études spécifiques; il reste très généralement l'Un dont l'évocation vient seulement aider à cerner et définir l'Autre.   (1987: 8)

It is this aporia which I will investigate in its many forms through Flaubert's male protagonists, the search for identity both by those legally endorsed (such as Frédéric) and the 'enfant trouvé'. Becoming a subject, as one seamless set of criteria, ideals, and behaviours within a codified pecking-order, is, in Flaubert's hands, fragmentary and contradictory. Through sex and gender lenses, Flaubert's individuals can be read as markers of the many problematic jostlings and highly changeable socializations which mid- to late nineteenth-century manhood was confronting in both the domestic and public spheres (whether this was in the division of domestic and social French configurations, or of France in relation to its colonies or the wider world). Power and competence remained none the less sex- and gender-specific as terms and concepts. Flaubert's works, then, provide a nineteenth-century fictional example of recent masculinities theory; 'while there is certainly societal domination by men, this isn't reducible to one societal system of process; instead there are effectively lots of patriarchies, dominated by different types of men, operating simultaneously' (Hearn, 1992: 3). *SAL* will be discussed in Chapter 2 for its deadly critique of extreme, public, and powerful intersecting patriarchies. How far Flaubert also puts in place radical and necessary counter-checks to such authoritarianisms will be opened to debate in relation to both this novel and his *œuvre* more generally.

Authority, power, and right to speak go together and would seem to endorse the tautologous situation of manhood as public because it has eschewed the private sphere. Through characters such as Frédéric, Flaubert reassesses the notion of 'public men'. 'The notion of public men as "public figures" or individual men "in the public eye" is itself an ideological elaboration of the general construction of men in public ... The powers of men and of public men applies especially to the power of *able-bodied*, heterosexual, "middle-aged"/older, middle/upper class white men' (Hearn, 1992: 3–4, my emphasis). Spendius offers a different example of quick-witted, linguistic, and strategic superiority, even if he is a slave. Hannon, Antoine, and Monsieur Aubain all demonstrate public men unable ultimately to dominate because of their failing bodies. Other male characters have been silenced by critical 'authority' because they use words sparingly or take 'passive' roles. It is arguable that in fact all the male protagonists are written out of their respective stories by the 'public' authoritative third-person narrator. Flaubert's famous indirect style itself must then come under scrutiny. It is far from being objective or atonal and reveals the further aporia of language as neutral. Is the impersonality of style for which Flaubert strove a master discourse, or one for both masters and slaves? Is rhetorical authority innate or made?

By employing contemporary feminist and masculinities theories, the plurality of patriarchies is everywhere made visible. This has the further advantage of underlining those specific to nineteenth-century France which the Revolution did not in fact destroy, but merely altered. Flaubert's novels have not been properly positioned as historical fictions at this level, although some useful work has begun: Green (1982) on *SAL*, Lambros (1996) and Orr (1998*b*) on *MB*. The *œuvre* shows the seamless expression of a certain kind of patriarchal dominance with local or temporal variations from the Rule of the Fathers in pre-Roman Carthage, in Egypt in the third century AD, in the Paris of 1848, in Normandy in the mid-nineteenth century. If one were to investigate these masculinities only along gender lines, then some of the important questions about constants (rather than geographically or historically specific constructions, and developments) would be lost. Through the screen of sex, the biological aspects of maleness can be revealed and investigated as recurrent, even ubiquitous, patterns. One may not escape the issues confronting masculinities theories spearheaded by Jungian and mythopoetic approaches concerning 'essential' masculine traits or characteristics. However, as we will see, Flaubert's unlikely male protagonists open up possibilities for theorization of the masculine outside either sex or gender optics, in those elements which are largely neither biological nor sociological functions of being male/masculine. Gender theory needs categories beyond those of biology, politics, medicine, sociology, psychoanalysis, or archetypal binaries. One is the ethical. This, rather than the transfigurative as aesthetic (see Orr, 1995) will be taken up in *TC* as a triptych of alternative masculinities in their reaction to social and personal responsibility.

These 'adult' fairy-stories also put in pictorial modes the universal questions that the novels all address in various ways. Thematic criticism therefore returns to the scene. In particular, there are the two forces of Thanatos and Eros. Rather than reading them as Freudian drives, this study will analyse them as threshold experiences for the male protagonists in question. They are nodal points in each of the works considered. They also trigger issues that constitute the stuff of 'grand narratives'—cruelty, violence, war, the battle between the sexes and between Culture and Nature. What seems constantly written out is a valorization of nurture, wonder, creative energies, children. Is the powermongering that predominates over love a 'given' of (male) nature or an overcompensatory strategy to maintain one order of reality rather than another?

Children do have their place in Flaubert's works but in disproportionate number as only children, aborted, ill, prematurely dead, orphans, bastards, outside the family. They also collocate with the sacrificed other of the *Code Napoléon*, for they share the same status as women. Hannibal, Victor, the sacrificed male children in *SAL* highlight the potential individual nipped in the bud, or lost in the crowd. Zola's depiction of crowds is often seen as the acme of naturalism. Flaubert's male crowds are peculiar *loci* and act as thermometers for the body politic. On the battleground, in the competitive commercial ring, on the barricades, the nameless are a gauge for the named heads of power and show the paradox of the latter's dehumanization and depersonalization. The 'Barbares' in *SAL* are dumbstruck by the 'civilized' practices of Carthage. Hérode in *H* has become a puppet. *ES* offers a clear example in its representations of the crowd in its constant regroupings but inevitable bloodshed and antagonisms against the individual. Flaubert's equal lambasting of peacetime crowds, the mediocrity, bureaucracy, and the industrialization of man in the name of progress will show 'bêtise' with a universal face. While his novels promote a clear criticism of bourgeois France and such herd mentalities, they also show how the inchoate can return in all-too-frightening (male) guises as the wheeling crowd at the barricades in *ES*, or the force of the armies on the march or being massacred in *SAL*.

One of the bleak messages of Flaubert's novels is that patriarchies are fundamental and inevitable and affect both men and women. Reaction against one brand enmeshes one in another, an impasse not fully recognized even in current masculinities theories. On the personal front, this may lead to madness, suicide, or withdrawal from conventional modes of behaviour to become a hermit or prophet. But this impasse is coupled with the more provocative, potentially essentializing, facet of Flaubert's *œuvre*: that manhood is necessarily separate from womanhood. *TSA* perhaps displays this 'superman–antiwoman' most starkly, that quest for sexual and social autonomy outside the private–public economies, yet valorized by higher authority and thus lending an aesthetic and moral weightiness concomitant with a lightness of being. '[M]anliness could best be attained through sexual autonomy from women' (Pugh, 1983: p. xx). Essential, even elemental, manhood is being sought here, but outside Nature as all-too-feminine. The second striking feature of this impasse for models of patriarchal systems is that it reproduces ideological variants of the same structure. It locks 'essential' features of the sexes back into an immutable frame of reference. Thus the flight from the nineteenth-century family model, the paterfamilias ruling over his own kingdom like Homais, to find a homosocial universe (as *BP* explores), results in an inevitable harking-back to previous, even pre-revolutionary versions of social order. If the bourgeois is then eradicated as *mentalité* in one easy move (as *SAL* demonstrates), the problem remains: manhood remains always on the one side of the male–female binary divide. David Pugh's study of the 'Sons of Liberty' and the 'masculine mind' in America in the nineteenth century compiles an important list of post-revolutionary qualities as against pre-revolutionary qualities (ibid. p. xxii), the former positioned as the first term: 'equal v privilege; liberty v domination; honest work v idle exploitation; natural dignity v factitious superiority; patriotic conservatism v alien innovation; progress v dead precedent'.

This classic positioning of the positive term of the binary first actually underlines the double-binds and contradictions of the model (for American and French masculinities) if male characters in Flaubert's fictions are used as sources of comparison, along lines of both gender and innate sexual characteristics. Flaubert, by dint of his hatred of those bourgeois values exemplified by the left-hand, 'positive', terms comes down on the 'right'. Politically speaking, this terminology is also revealing of a potentially right-wing Flaubert: 'democrats' to the left, 'aristocrats' to the right. However, because no cross-over to any feminizing attributes is possible—we are locked within political, legal, and other institutionalizings of power where women are non-persons—not only are reproductive concepts disallowed, but patriarchy (list left) or patriarchy (list right) cut off 'otherness' to their advocated system and thus produce constantly *reductive* positions. If women's disenfranchisement is returned to the picture, that is, in the doubly negative position at the base of Pugh's binary structure, then the two terms are no longer delineating and opposites, but complementary and appositional.

A man can be equal *and* privileged under the *Code Napoléon* and the American Constitution when women have no vote, and so on down the list (Fig. 1). We will be uncovering Flaubert's trenchant investigations of these problems with 'democracy' in *ES*. The global problem with his own penchant for the 'aristocratic' values is that any social reformations or reorganizations (such as his dystopian *BP*) are but a shifting of the deckchairs of masculinity on the *Titanic* of evolving patriarchy. And the arbitrariness of the 'values' also becomes apparent if Flaubert's characters are matched up to them, for there is no ultimate scale

MEN'S HISTORY		
Pre-1789		*Post-1789*
privilege	v.	equality
domination	v.	liberty
idle exploitation	v.	honest work
factitious superiority	v.	natural dignity
alien innovation	v.	patriotic conservatism
dead precedent	v.	progress

WOMEN'S TIME

FIG 1. A redefinition of the masculine at various stages of the development of patriarchal power. Derived from the list of post-revolutionary versus pre-revolutionary qualities given by David Pugh in his study of the 'Sons of Liberty' and the 'masculine' in nineteenth-century American (Pugh, 1983).

whereby their 'proper maleness' can then be judged. Frédéric is the character of idle exploitation; Charles Bovary does honest work; Julien exemplifies liberty *and* domination; Ioakanann is natural dignity and factitious superiority and alien innovation and so on. The classifications simply break down when the fictional figures are introduced. An imagined male figure constituted from all the elements to produce 'Universal Man' would be the contrary possibility. However, Flaubert eschews any such configuration even with Bouvard and Pécuchet. His individual characters might seem to fit more on the left in this list, and his stalking-horse caricatures on the right in the place, in David Gilmore's words, of the 'Ubiquitous Male' based on the criterion of performance: 'We might call this quasi-global personage something like "Man-the-Impregnator-Protector-Provider"' (Gilmore, 1990: 232). Ironically, Gilmore's hyphenated term could hardly be more consummate a description of the triple function for manhood under the *Code Napoléon* in post-revolutionary nineteenth-century France with its obsessive codifications of heredity and inheritance laws. Again, Flaubert's anti-family heroes (or hyper-family orientated ones, like Charles), who are both unproductive and unreproductive, pit individual male persons against the deindividualizing functionality of this universal social man. The price, however, is cynicism, emotional penury, death, often at the hands of their very creator, trapped in the impasses of Flaubert's own hyper-masculine artistic ends, seeking to put his individualizing mark on fictions, not infants.

Further problematic issues emerge even if, as a rule of thumb, Flaubert's most individual protagonists express a form of manhood appearing in the left-hand column. Whence come suitable models to identify with and react against? Julien is an interesting case in point, for his genes and upbringing should not make him turn out a crazy killer, whereas Charles remains totally unaffected by direct interventionist gender-training from both his parents. The intense anxiety about personal normality as male in issues such as potency, public power, authority, and personal self-validation in 'healthy' personhood and fatherhood was replicated in and promoted by the scientific treatises and concerns of the age. Nye (1993) quotes among others Dr Jean-Alexis Bellois's 'Conseil aux hommes affaiblis' (1829); Gobineau's 'Essai sur l'inégalité des races humaines' (1854–6); Dr Prosper Lucas's 'Traité de l'hérédité naturelle' (1847–50); and Bénédicte-Augustin Morel's 'Traité des dégénérescences physiques, intellectuelles et morales de l'espèce humaine' (1857). These titles point at the Achilles' heels of a masculinized society, which Badinter frames more generally within sexology:

Tout compte fait, le discours médical du xixᵉ siècle a transformé les comportements sexuels en identités sexuelles. Les pervers succédant aux libertins une nouvelle spécificité. Alors que le sodomite, note M. Foucault, n'était que le sujet juridique d'actes interdits, «l'homosexuel du xixᵉ est devenu un personnage: un passé, une histoire et une enfance; une morphologie aussi, avec une anatomie indiscrète et peut-être une physiologie mystérieuse. Rien de ce qu'il est maintenant n'échappe à sa sexualité . . . L'homosexuel est maintenant une espèce.» Succédant à l'âme platonicienne et à la raison cartésienne, le sexe est devenu l'ultime vérité de l'être.   (Badinter, 1992: 156)

None of Flaubert's problematic protagonists is a 'normal' functioning male in either the domestic or the public spheres. The culturally condoned masculinity of the vagabond (the blind beggar in *MB*), the free agent (Rodolphe), the provocateur (Dussardier), has freedom only for a season provided they are not cripples or outcasts like Hippolyte. All are 'monsters in the mirror' of 'proper' masculinity. The plethora of 'célibataires' and 'marginaux' provokes questioning of heterosexual models (like Homais), a deep fear of the fatherhood of the Fathers. Flaubert's problematic protagonists are, perhaps, least 'normal' when it comes to male sexuality and experience of sex. In the last chapter I will turn to this subject which has been ignored by critics eager to endorse the cerebral, the aesthetic (the male) sides of the mind — body split.

The ensuing study investigates the many facets of masculinity signalled above by considering each of Flaubert's works in the order in which it was published. At the end, any evolution in nineteenth-century forms of the masculine may then become apparent. Through close readings, I will focus on particular structures or roles, themes or relationships, or tackle critical *idées reçues* as appropriate to the work in question. Each chapter remains an autonomous study, for readers interested in only one work, but cross-reference will enable readers familiar with the complete works or interested in gender theory to build up a fuller picture. For gender-studies sceptics, each chapter offers a new reading of old debates over and above any specific theoretical approach.

For each of Flaubert's major works, the fragments of fractured and split masculinities, particularly traits which are so ubiquitous, or so pushed to the edges of the male sex and gender map, will be considered. In *MB*, Charles Bovary will be explored as a figure of male emotional and private life within marriage and the life of the couple. Abundantly, for Charles, the personal is not the political. Chapter 2 on *SAL* is the longest and the closest to what might seem a set of character studies of the male protagonists precisely because so little has in fact been written on these individuals. It will demonstrate that the political is not the personal. The over-polarization and hierarchization of masculinity at all levels, social, political, international and cosmological, recurs even as rhetorical figures in this text. This is patriarchy on the left in Figure 1, whereas *ES* considers the set of criteria for democratic masculinity, on the right of the diagram. This chapter will show how far the impersonal is, in fact, the political through Frédéric, Deslauriers, and the other 'célibataires' and 'solitaires' who are juxtaposed with crowds of new men made so through their right to vote. In Chapter 4, Antoine struggles to maintain the personal in the face of the 'metapersonal'—Hilarion, the figures of the Heresies, other gods, and God. His is the problem of how to be *and* act the *imago Dei*. In Chapter 5, *TC* uncovers the contradictions of the interpersonal within political, legal, or religious frames. I undertake a new reading which investigates the morality of *TC* not through the religious or ethical, but through its anthropological strata. I look at the three male body-parts which signify 'life' in order to investigate the public conscience of man, not his subconscious. In Chapter 6, for Bouvard and Pécuchet, the political is completely personal, made in the image of one's own private (e)state. I will concentrate on the private lives of this bizarre couple, including their private parts. The Conclusions will then evaluate the representations, patterns, forms of the masculine *à la* Flaubert which match with the drawing on the front cover of this book. Nicholas Eastwood's contemporary recasting of the severed head of John the Baptist (after Moreau, contemporary of Flaubert: see jacket) sits independently of even Salomé's hand to hold it, yet radiates light. This severed head as iconic representation of the aporias of Flaubert's epoch, or rather the aporias of vaunted male individualism, underpins my study, which argues for Flaubert the writer- vivisectionist of the male body, political and private in prose which conceals and reveals the method and madness of production, including that of a self-styled pathologist of literary language. The double-sided pen-scalpel cuts into representations of France and French history, literature, and culture, to reveal its interconnecting tissues, malignant growths, disease, but, like Canivet, may not be able to record anything but 'rien' in the autopsy of male emotions.

'Uncertainty' has served too long to occlude the polyvalency of meanings in Flaubert's works, albeit veiled in complex rhetorical strategy and counter-strategy. Reading 'the masculine' through contemporary gender theory combined with 'masculinity' as codified in his times is one way to remake not a 'postmodern' or even a 'modernist' Flaubert, but a writer of *his* times. This makes his *œuvre* a rich source for new theorizing about the current 'crisis in masculinity', for fiction is no less constitutive of a cathexis of realities past and present than previous criticism. This book is indebted, as the wide-ranging but not exhaustive bibliographical references underscore, to other approaches which set up signposts to this one. 'It is of course a measure of Flaubert's inexhaustible greatness that he has to be invented anew for each successive generation' (Raitt in Williams and Orr, 1999: p. x). My hope is that readers engaging with Flaubert from very different angles from this one will find something new in his works revealed by the ensuing analyses. For specialists working on literature and gender, I hope that *Flaubert: Writing the Masculine* may offer another pearl on the string of understanding identity in representation.

Madame Bovary

FLAUBERT'S Normandy novel, while subtitled *Mœurs de Province*, is much more than an exploration of those customs and reactionary agrarian mores of society which are suggested by its provincialism. Certainly Yonville is compared and contrasted unfavourably by Rodolphe, Léon, and Emma, and favourably by Canivet and Homais, with Paris. Yet its international and universal dimensions—'[il] vaut bien Constantinople'—constantly rise up from its dislocated centre: the couple, Charles and Emma. They embody Normandy and a 'once upon a time'. The provincial focus is a crystallization, a reworking, of a wider and universal grand theme, the tragedy of unrequited love set in the banality of the everyday. Such universal appeal has caught the imagination of numerous critics who have read *MB* as a landmark in nineteenth-century fiction, *the* novel of adultery, female adultery, realism, the female condition.[1] This chapter has as its starting-point not adultery, but its legal context, marriage. As Heath (1992: 1) has put it so succinctly:

Flaubert's novel has an intense social reverberation. Brought to trial for offenses against the family and religion, it gained notoriety that focused it at once as part of a questioning of marriage, sex, and the role of women. Its achievement was to transpose those given social elements into a new configuration that captured and articulated a fundamental experience of the post-romantic, commercial-industrial, democratic period.

---

[1] Individual critics of international excellence would take too long to list. See among others Fairlie (1962); Heath (1992); Lloyd (1990); Neefs (1972); and Orr (1999*b*) for monograph studies of *MB*. Tanner (1979: ch. 4) and Overton (1996: ch. 4) read *MB* as exemplary of the novel of adultery and female adultery respectively. Czyba (1983) remains the best study of women in Flaubert's works.

It is precisely the impact of the questioning of marriage and sex for men that this chapter will examine. How does Flaubert treat the male side of the family romance, ' "[l]e grand jeu du mariage", pour reprendre les mots de Claude Lévi-Strauss, [qui] condense toute la dialectique du "Nous" et du "Eux", de l'identité et de l'altérité, de l'ordre et du désordre' (Mauran, 1996: 7)? How do sons become lovers, husbands, fathers (the public, legal male roles), and develop sexually and emotionally (the private, individual person)? How do they negotiate the public demands of the institution of marriage and the often contradictory private demands of intimacy? Two quotations here serve to outline this contradiction which replicates the split caused by the *Code Napoléon* (along sex and gender lines) of the two spheres: public (rational) for men, private (emotional) for women. The blueprint of the institutional dictats and treatises is found in Balzac's *Physiologie du mariage* of 1829:

Le mariage peut être considéré politiquement, civilement, moralement, comme une loi, comme un contrat, comme une institution: loi, c'est la reproduction de l'espèce; contrat, c'est la transmission des propriétés; institution, c'est une garantie qui intéresse tous les hommes; ils ont un père, une mère, ils auront des enfants. Le mariage doit donc être l'objet du respect général.   (quoted in Adler, 1983: 17)

The other face of marriage is the romantic 'happy-ever-after' which 'contient en germe la négation radicale du mariage comme institution. La femme devient maîtresse et, corrélativement, le mari, comme ensorcelé, subit une forme d'aliénation liée à la dépendance affective' (Mauran, 1996: 45).

It is Charles Bovary who tries to combine the two as he works out his changing part in not one marriage, but two. His affectivity and position in the married couple as 'Nous' provides the central focus of this chapter and opens up in a different way the question of the famous incipit of the novel. Charles is abundantly the male figure for whom the personal is not political. Elsewhere I have discussed Charles as a son of his generation, a pale reflection of the representatives of the previous one in the public domain, but husband/widower *par excellence* in the private sphere (Orr: 1999*b*). The paucity of role models in *MB* who might exhibit manly and adult emotions to all the novel's sons is striking. Both Rodolphe's and Léon's fathers are dead, leaving them no one to imitate, identify with, or rebel against, while Charles's father is a figure *in absentia*. Justin is an exploited ward-servant in the Homais household, while Hippolyte is no one's son, only a misshapen stable boy.

The model of the happy nuclear family, as promulgated by the *Code Napoléon*, and Balzac, seems to be epitomized by the Homais family. Madame Homais is suitably secondary, the fecund female genitor of two children of each sex to replace both parents doubly; the paterfamilias rigorously rules and monitors, provides for and sustains, his brood. However, the realities behind the shell of virtuous citizenship—the slovenly, disordered, emotionally prudish, hidebound and authoritarian domesticity behind closed doors—undermine the model at all points. *Chez* Homais is the fictional ramification of the horrors of such an unemotionally constructed model. Fathering and mothering as affective bond are absent, as too is conjugality. Based on legal, laicized, and civic duty designed totally to serve male interest ('c'est une garantie qui intéresse *tous les hommes*'), every adult French man and woman under the *Code* was to honour, obey, beget children for the State and pass on property and legitimacy to empower the Nation and keep it 'clean' from moral corruption, impotence, and disease. The latter stem implicitly from uncontrolled chaos, embodied in unruly, rampant, female sexuality which corrupts and adulterates the mechanics of law and order, citizenship, patriarchal authority and power. Marriage as institution was an ideological coup, for it regulated such diverse forms as the passions, feelings, and high emotions of romance (marriage for love rather than material advancement), with marriages of convenience arranged round dowries and family inheritance or advancement in an entrepreneurial world to guarantee social control. Couples were the essential powerbase to produce children for the State:

Le couple est une invention nouvelle, Le Couple comme solitude personnelle, refermée sur elle-même, apparaît au xixe siècle. Avant, comme l'explique Philippe Ariès, le couple n'était ni intimité, ni espace privé, ni lit clos, ni alcôve conjugale. Le couple et la famille étaient ouverts, immergés dans un milieu plus vaste: la communauté ... Il appartiendra à la bourgeoisie de faire passer l'amour passion dans le mariage, où il était inconnu, sinon interdit.   (Adler, 1983: 11–12)

Proof of this theoretical pudding are the Homais, where there is no evident 'amour' or even the word used euphemistically for regular, pleasurable, conjugal sex aside from procreation. Léon cannot imagine Madame Homais as lover. She can only be the 'épouse', 'mère', 'ménagère'. The copy of *L'Amour conjugale* in Justin's possession is therefore not only the source of Homais's apoplexy concerning his children's innocence but also a cause of deep-seated anxiety for his own sexual and emotional identity. Homais in fact bungles his way into relationships quite without noticing on three occasions, twice with Léon and once with the Bovarys as a couple when he intrudes into their conjugal privacy and bedroom.

By contrast, the Bovary household is in fact the avant-garde outworking of the new coupledom, formed not principally for money, nor children, but for 'love'. Berthe of course appears as the due outcome of the regular intercourse Charles and Emma enjoy. Sartre is among few critics to pick up on Charles's sexuality from one of Flaubert's notes: 'Vie sexuelle avec Charles: très important (note: ça lui donne envie de baiser avec d'autres). Cela devient: les caresses conjugales à désirs d'adultère' (Sartre quoted in Sicard, 1980: 39). However, this marriage too is a failure, unworkable not because of Charles's but because of Emma's false expectations, which lead to her adultery outside it as codified institution:

[Flaubert] décrit les aspirations d'une femme incapable de trouver un homme digne de former avec elle le couple qui constitue la revendication minimum que les romantiques aient formulée à l'encontre de la société bourgeoise. . . . Pour les hommes que rencontre Emma Bovary—et pour Flaubert ils représentent bien la société de l'époque—l'amour n'est qu'un supplément de leurs préoccupations bourgeoises. (Bloom, 1992–3: 786)

Most of the prominent men in the Yonville community also evade institutionalized marriage completely (in spite of the fact that it is advantageous to their interests) or destroy other men's marriages for their own ends. Rodolphe and Guillaumin are the bachelor philanderers who take advantage of women including wives, because sex can be got without financial commitments or upkeep of an 'épouse'. Lheureux, on the other hand, lives parasitically, and legally as I have argued elsewhere (Orr: 1999*a*), on wives as sources of revenue, whether as bringers of dowries or spenders of marital incomes. Thus the idea of marriage as codified by the *Code Napoléon* is criticized and satirized in *MB* on three major counts. First, there is the hypocrisy of the State and the Church as institutions of marriage for their own ideological ends. Implicitly, by dint of being a *célibataire* as celibate cleric, Bournisien is put on the impossible spot; he is unable to diagnose Emma's marital malaises, let alone counsel couples for the sacrament he must uphold and administer without being allowed personal experience of it. Marriage as sacrosanct bond is then in constant danger of being put asunder by other men outside any Church context. These may be the bachelors of the novel or its married womanizers like Père Bovary who 'jests' with Emma at Charles's expense. Second, there is indictment of the State institution of marriage for money. 'On se marie rarement par amour. . . . On se marie surtout par intérêt. Pour la grande majorité de la bourgeoisie, le mariage est la grande opération financière de la vie. Les romans aux héros coureurs de dot, bien plus que de jupons, fleuriront' (Adler, 1983: 69). Bovary (father and son) and later Léon will marry for money and the dowry the wife will bring, a normal, albeit callous, calculation for financial not personal interests and thus a contract by arrangement. Finally, by contrast, marriage for love, or the Romantic ideal as embodied by the Charles–Emma couple, is doomed because the daily round fails to match the false image promulgated by Emma's reading of romances.

Yet there is more at stake if we come to the question of marriage in *MB* from Charles's point of view. He does a lot of marrying in the novel and intensively in its first part. In an updating of the famous question put to Tiresias about whether sex is more enjoyable as a man or as a woman, Charles is in the unprecedented position of being able to compare marriage for money (arranged by his mother) to the ironically named 'nouvelle nouvelle' Héloïse, anti-model of Rousseau's secularization of Abelard's famous love-match, and marriage for love (arranged by Emma's father). His second wedding may seem to epitomize provincial marriage customs. However, its stereotypical conformism to rituals is ironically and paradoxically overturned by the narrative account from Charles's experience of his (second) wedding night. This turns out to be a singular and intensely emotional experience, one that transforms him and which is an implicit testimony to an attempt to forge relationships on persons not property. As Mercier has noted, Charles's second wedding has further singularities because of its position in the plot:

Noce au singulier comme le veut l'usage, et, cependant, noce singulière par la situation au seuil du livre, c'est-à-dire à contre-courant de cette tradition qui veut que les romans se terminent par des mariages. En commençant par la fin, en renonçant au romanesque de l'idylle, pour ne retenir que le prosaïsme de la vie conjugale, Flaubert ouvre une des voies du roman moderne. Or comme l'hiérarchie des mariages va decrescendo de l'*hymen* des dieux à la *noce* paysanne, le mot borne d'entrée en jeu l'ambition d'Emma. Croyant échapper aux Bertaux, elle retombe dans Tostes. La noce, terme d'une évasion ratée, inaugure ses malheurs et consacre officiellement son échec.   (1978: 47)

This critic rightly links the wedding procession with Emma's funeral cortège as a matching pair at the end of the novel, but has not seen the other striking parallel, Charles's hyperemotional state on both occasions. In Charles, Flaubert not only reworks the stock character of the cuckold (Sinclair, 1993), he also adulterates the novel of adultery by making the adulteress's husband an exemplary model of married lover (Orr, 1999*b*), and faithful husband, not once, but twice. Charles has genuine mementos of Emma which contrast with the vain cupid as synecdoche of Guillaumin's philandering or Rodolphe's box of 'souvenirs' or, indeed, Emma's keepsakes.

Moreover, Flaubert challenges the two conflicting models of marriage itself—financial *ménage* and happy-ever-after conclusion of romance—by making *MB* the novelistic attempt to write the story of the after the 'happy-ever-after' which closes romances with 'l'amour conjugale'. Justin's reading of its intertextual source pamphlet while living in an 'ideal' *Code Napoléon ménage* and the terrible anger it provokes in Homais counterpoint Charles's lived attempt to find a blueprint. Neither his parents' mismatched alliance for money with its ensuing domestic violence (Orr, 1999*b*), nor his first marriage, provide Charles with a model for his conjugal bliss with Emma. Charles thus is the vehicle whereby Flaubert offers an alternative to the dominating 'époux civil' and the mushy 'époux romantique' who will always ride off into the sunset. As simply 'l'époux', faithful right to the bitter end, generous and unauthoritarian, he is also the 'époux manqué'. Whilst he stammers in his entry into the classroom of life (where male gender roles are shaped), and stammers into love (test of male sexuality), his highly emotional and male response to the extreme experiences of joy and sadness, calculated not for private effect (like Rodolphe) nor public honour (Homais), emerge only in his authoritative commands concerning Emma's funeral arrangements. Here he is doubly the 'époux manqué' because his 'épouse', Emma, is dead and has deceived him, being unable to match or reciprocate mature acceptance of the 'conjugal'—that equality, self- and other acceptance, mutual and often silent conviviality, difference within unity, the routines of togetherness varied by the occasional party. Emma can only see in Charles everything opposite to her desires because these, not the person, are the problem. In the remainder of this chapter Charles's conjugality as a model of adult (anti-Romantic) and male love will be investigated to highlight the ways in which he is the underrepresented part of a couple configured more as democracy than *Code Napoléon* autocracy. He is also powerfully the ironic, failed, but none the less reality-centred re-embodiment of the most famous precursor models of romance, Prince Charming and Romeo. By holding up the mirror of Charles's more 'unmasculine' sides, the much-rehearsed question of Emma Bovary's so-called 'masculinity' can then be reopened. Finally, the chapter will consider the 'époux' as co-partner in a third kind of ideal marriage, 'd'affinités'. Because Charles and Emma conform neither to standard male and female sex and gender characteristics, nor are androgynes, *MB* offers some understanding of the couple as *coniunctio*, the concept of the transformational process in a union of opposites.

It is the false dichotomizing of male and female roles and destinies, traits, and capacities, as well as all the assumptions automatically made about Charles because of his ludicrous patronym, that have obscured his nobler sides. Critics of both sexes have accused Charles of idiocy, bovine boorishness, and have laid Emma's search for love elsewhere firmly at his door. The problem has been that the name does not necessarily match the person: patriarchy's obsessions with line forces the male bearer of the name to suffer it for life, whereas the woman has at least an opportunity in marriage to change hers.

ce qui en est cause ici, finalement, est le sexe de l'anatomie attribuée, celui de l'État Civil. Et cette anatomie fonctionne socialement comme le lieu même de la clarté et de l'évidence. Tout le monde est supposé avoir l'un des deux sexes et être certain duquel des deux institutionnalisés. C'est même, et cela est bien surprenant ou comique si on s'y arrête un moment, la définition fondamentale de l'État Civil. Obligatoirement et toujours mentionné, bref la base de l'identité et ce aussitôt après, le nom patronymique et personnel. Donc, d'une part le sexe anatomique socialement assigné. Et de l'autre part, les concommitants de cette anatomie ... le privilège de masculinité. (Guillaumin, 1984: 70–1)

The very attributions of sex and power with name have in fact been applied too unquestioningly to the unambitious, plodding Charles, as anti-model of the masculine. Charles's destiny is perhaps to be misunderstood by Emma, by critics, as that of a prophet in his own land and therefore reviled. The cross he bears in his name does, however, become transfigured into a name, Bovaryism, posthumously, and by his belated passion. He is Passion, not quite in the manner of the divine 'Époux', but because of the death and figurative resurrection in his mind of Emma. His 'saintliness' is folded in the shroud of the everyday, the ordinary round of the common man, and revealed in his agony at the end of the novel, prior to his death in the garden. This Gethsemane experience in the secular realms—neighbours interpret his rantings and grief in the garden as due to drink— none the less goes to the heart of male despair, the sense of complete abandonment by the Universe (God) and by reason. Charles does follow his 'destiny', which is to have no regard for what society deems correct, or that which is predestined in accordance with the dictats of the *Code Napoléon* with its bullying, single-sex schooling, and training for 'proper' manhood. Charles follows his free will with Emma, and more importantly allows her fully her own. This is his strength and his undoing, for his altruism, total trust, and generosity as regards giving her money is unprecedented in a world where wives could not have access to money without the authorization of the husband. Charles's democratic idiosyncrasy in marital affairs is therefore singular, and even more so after her death.

His free will becomes captivation to all that was hers, especially her tastes. His final decisions for her burial are the mark of his one mind with her, for she would undoubtedly have chosen to be buried in her wedding dress. Her egotism is thus transformed into his altruism, a peculiar merger of the two opposites they seemed to embody in life: Emma is the law of 'take', Charles the law of 'give'. I shall return to the standard, reverse, order of these norms in Chapter 5.

The impossible democratic marriage Charles forges between the State institution and the romantic myth of matrimony is achieved because he does not fulfil his allotted role in either model. His is a solution by default and by synthetical double negation. His bungling attempt at conjugality as consent between adults fails, but it points up by contrast the adolescent qualities of the romantic love propaganda as fed to women by the State in order to mask its aim to hoodwink them into marriage and second-class citizenship, and highlights the role of parents for promoting this fate. The snare is to make women believe in marriage as the *point culminant* of female existence, as apotheosis of femininity. What happens in the daily routine before sunset is obscured by both romantic and social tales told to girls (and boys) and never revealed. The chief end of the romance—the first tinseltown kiss at the altar—is allowed no alternative corrective story of 'the next chapter' to put it in its proper place. Even nowadays, 'there just aren't very many really convincing positive images of heterosexual relationships, despite (or because of?) the enormous glamour industries' (Tristram in Seidler, 1991: 42–3). Thus the active hero versus passive heroine model at the heart of fairy-tale and Napoleonic ideologies is kept in view, not the ubiquitous reality of day-to-day relationship. Giddens (1992: 39–40) puts his finger on why the propaganda works:

Romantic love introduced the idea of a narrative into an individual's life—a formula which radically extended the reflexivity of sublime love. The telling of a story is one of the meanings of 'romance', but this story now became individualised, inserting self and other into a personal narrative which had particular reference to wider social processes . . . The complex of ideas associated with romantic love for the first time associated love with freedom, both being seen as normatively desirable states.

Emma exemplifies someone constantly inserting herself into her tale of love, and she openly embraces this as a desirable state for its emotional fulfilment and for the freedom 'true love' brings to the straitjacket of unglamorous circumstance at Les Bertaux. Giddens, however, does not spell out how such a divergent view of love could be meshed with the practical constraints within marriage. It is precisely the potentiality of improving one's lot through marriage, but as seemingly free choice, that 'falling in love with the handsome prince' provides, for it is an 'action' which bridges the divide between the constraints and social parameters for women and their training for such a narrow and passive role. Everything is therefore focused on the process of love, not its outcomes, to hide the real arrangements that are going on behind the scenes. This gap in (un)realities is at the heart of Emma's *mariage d'amour–mariage de raison* which her father negotiates with Charles without her knowledge. Père Rouault is the practical operator who secures a suitor who will not cost him very much as regards dowry. Unlike the magical generosity of good fairy godmothers, the godfather Rouault is a pragmatic, canny, and calculating provider who wants to get this expensive daughter off his hands to a suitable suitor who can pay, and who loves her. Emma's answer, then, to the realities which puncture the 'happy-ever-after' is not to confront reality at all, but to retreat further into the Ideal by replaying the falling-in-love over and over to make it produce the fairy-tale result. This can never mesh with Charles's desire for a quiet, banal conjugality which totally accepts the everyday reality— indeed, embraces it.

Critics have often cited Flaubert's famous parody through para-phrase of all that is romantic and clichéd in Emma's reading:

Ce n'étaient qu'amours, amants, amantes, dames persécutées s'évanouissant dans des pavillons solitaires, postillons qu'on tue à tous les relais, chevaux qu'on crève à toutes les pages, forêts sombres, trou-bles du cœur, serments, sanglots, larmes et baisers, nacelles au clair de lune, rossignols dans les bosquets, *messieurs* braves comme des lions, doux comme les agneaux, vertueux comme on ne l'est pas, toujours bien mis, et qui pleurent comme des urnes.   (*MB*, 50–1)

However, they have not connected this with the centrality of the investigation of marriage in *MB* or Flaubert's use of all these elements rewoven ironically into his own version of love story/marriage plot, Emma and Charles's (after-)romance. As well as the timeless structure, Flaubert also reworks particular intertextual variants. While Frølich (1977) and more recently Green (1999) have suggested convincingly 'The Sleeping Beauty' fairy-story as an intertext of the novel, 'Cinderella' seems the more fully reworked. The allusion has been picked up *en passant* by Philippot (1997: 71) and Zenkine (1996: 114) in the context of Emma at La Vaubyessard Ball. With Charles primarily in view, this intertext is dismantled in *MB* on two levels. The first is subversion of the original model to show its ideological inappropriateness and implications for adult heterosexual conjugality. The second is to dovetail it with an equally powerful alternative model to reveal the impasse of the false binary of *mariage d'amour* (romance) and *mariage de raison* (the system of dowries), that a happy-ever-after is impossible. Thus the tragic double demise of Charles and Emma is rewoven as the ironic Yonvillais equivalent of *Romeo and Juliet*: suicide by poison and a stab in the chest.

While love is the power that transcends class, rank, social expectation, or family honour in both intertexts, it is the idea of progress and social advancement through marriage that is the clearest ideological propaganda of the Cinderella story in its Louis Philippe context. For those not born into the upper classes, beauty is the passport to transcend class or circumstance: love can then blossom in the remotest corner because 'fairy godmother' *fatalité* intervenes. This *arrivisme* in the feminine is further promulgated and glamorized by the fashion magazines that Emma reads. For men, the beautiful (and good) 'princess', not the ugly sisters, will secretly be trained in all the domestic duties behind the scenes, but this is kept invisible behind her ball-dress. It was *dépassé* for the prince, as a role-model of manhood, to sweep the lady off her feet; all that was required was to find a woman whom the shoe would fit. Clearly, even Charles Bovary has what it takes to discern the daintiness of Emma's slippers, the sign that this is the woman for him. By contrast he has already noted the footwear of the ugly sister (whom his mother, not a magic godmother, picked out for him). Héloïse's large feet and heavy *sabots* mark her out as of peasant stock, not a lady. The irony is of course that Emma is equally of this class and race but has hidden her origins well by disguise and dressing up.

The hidden catch and power of the Prince Charming myth is that Cinderella not only goes to the ball and captivates, captures him. She then importantly submits (her free will) when he comes to claim her, thanks to that fetishistic token he already possesses: the slipper. Her free choice is of course not a choice, for who would choose to return to the drudgery of the kitchen? Choice into marriage, then, is a non-choice for women under the *Code Napoléon*, but this is disguised by the trappings of fate, the unique meeting with a special 'other' which changes the course of circumstance. This place of brokerage of ideological worlds is the ball, where public and private are ritualized in highly codified and hierarchical ways to ensure that both parties make their match and a deal can be struck where rationally there are no real interests on either side. The legitimized sex and the heir the man gains—that is, the erotic and procreative side of the bargain—is hidden to his partner. In return for her prize, the woman gains security of status, but only for a day.

'Insofar as immediate attraction is part of romantic love, however, it has to be separated quite sharply from the sexual/erotic compulsions of passionate love. The "first glance" is a communicative gesture, an intuitive grasp of the qualities of the other . . . to someone who can make one's life . . . "complete" ' (Giddens, 1992: 40). For Charles and Emma, the differences of the 'first glance' are overt. For the latter, the experience, because it is one of the essentials of romance, is repeated, with Charles, with Léon, with the Vicomte at La Vaubyessard, with Rodolphe. Its repetition empties it of its meaning and purpose as the unique moment. On the other hand, Charles is smitten by the foot and the slipper, the aura of home and hearth surrounding Emma when he goes to attend her father, the charm of delicacy and madonna-like femininity he has lost in childhood and in his first marriage. First glance, for Charles, is the 'one and only', but less in romantic terms than in circumstantial ones. Flaubert thus doubly deflates the high and false idealisms of the 'happy-ever-after' glance, and writes the original story of Cinderella back into the marriage, not the courtship, of this couple. Emma and

Charles do indeed go to the ball, but as a married couple after their marriage at the beginning of the novel. This is the incident of Emma's illusion and delusion: she pretends to be a Cinderella for the night by refusing to allow Charles to dance with her, as if she were single once more. This night will indeed shape her subsequent days but with the effect of undoing her marriage, not creating it. The tragedy is further compounded because the 'bad' fairy-godmother of fate allows her this experience once she is married, not before. So brainwashed is she by romances, that she forgets where her story does not fit the original fairy-story plot.

But there is another twist in Flaubert's intertextual restitching; with a transsexual transformation in the negative. Charles is the person who is invited to the ball, but who is not allowed to dance; nor does he get a carriage even for a night, or to keep the girl whose slipper becomes a riding-boot in other liaisons. Pumpkins remain pumpkins in Charles's world. The cigar case which Charles finds after La Vaubyessard may be a masculinization of the slipper, but there will be no woman to buy him one. It is Emma who sweeps him off his feet on his (second) wedding night but into the mayhem of an unravelling of his whole being, financial, professional, private, and ultimately personal as he enters the excesses of grief, not love.

Charles as Cinderella-in-the-masculine doomed to the kitchen status of reality puts the other side of the story for critical effect. Moreover, his unmasculine contentment with lot and hearth, mundane tasks and place in society designated by the ugly 'sisters' of patriarchy, overturn implicitly the goals of the male face of the model. As the good character with the emotional sensitivity which is normally rewarded in fairy-tales or romances, Charles is a loser in the grasping, calculating, opportunistic public and personal real male worlds which surround him. Flaubert is too subtle to recast Charles as the negative Cinderella, however. The role, sex, and gender reversals only go so far. More important, though, he falls short of the ideal prince-husband, not once, but twice to two impossible women who nag him to be more the man of their dreams or false images. Completely faithful to them and to himself to the last, even when the scales fall from his eyes concerning Emma's affairs, he is transfigured by love.

Le cœur simple n'a plus de moi; sa bêtise, ignorant les limites de la personnalité sentimentale ou vaniteuse, est l'infini; . . . C'est ce que démontre l'innocence sublime de Charles dont la 'pesanteur sereine' honnie de tous renvoie à la sérénité et à l'impassibilité désolantes des grands animaux (Bovary, bovin). [. . .] la candeur merveilleuse de Charles qui est tout parce qu'il est tout *amour*. . . . Charles *est trop*, trop empli d'Amour, trop absent à lui-même et trop présent à l'Autre, pour continuer à *être*.   (Philippot, 1997: 411–20, author's emphasis)

This is less love as sublime 'bêtise' than love as passion. A secularized 'époux divin', his faith, hope, and love take fully on board the 'for worse' of his marriage vows. Charles's love is 'l'amour conjugale' which includes passion, loyalty, fidelity, and generosity to the other. Emma's romantic love, even with the masculinizing twists of her passion and proactive control, is hollow. Charles's unassuming male emotionality emerges, but only if the screens of ideological expectation in the reader are set aside. His delight in touching her dresses is perhaps an equivalent 'stammer' of intimate expression which is rooted in the day-to-day. His marriage is a stumbling attempt to integrate public and private separation of male activity in a union whose principal end is relationship, not the begetting of children. Charles fits none of the male stereotypes of his age and thus 'falls' into an individuality all his own, beyond inversions of potential models or anti-models. In the dark about his potential masculinity as lover and husband, his first name is the half he can stammer out of Le Prince *Char*mant. Almost a 'Char(a)mant', Charles is groping towards his own kind of (h)éro(t)isme, for he remains unmistakably male throughout the novel, a paradoxical model to the men of his age of complete 'husbandness' away from the public eye.

The question of being special for an 'other' also raises the issue of election, that sense of being a creature of tragic destiny whereby one achieves a kind of elevated status, albeit posthumously. It is here that Flaubert combines the 'unhappy-ever-after' reworking of Cinderella with the tale of tragic love *par excellence*, not *Orpheus and Euridice* as Gallina (1992: 84) has suggested, but *Romeo and Juliet*. Instead of the antagonists being warring families, *MB* recasts the two oppositional camps as the sexes, ingrained in positions underpinned by sexual myth.

As is the case in the original intertext, reconciliation of difference can only be achieved through the transforming power of
love, even if the outcome is tragic. Charles and Emma fulfil the
dual destiny of post-Shakespearian tragedy: poisoned romance
and failed medical, rather than heroic, intervention in the
other's suicide attempt cause the double death. The twists which
render this couple no copy, stereotype, or kitschified version
derive from the careful knotting of banality into the new
version. Charles could not be less a Romeo in Emma's eyes,
except initially and before their marriage, because he is a
husband. She mistakes the false Romeos, Rodolphe and Léon,
because they conform in her mind to the mythic one. Emma,
too, is no Juliet, except that she takes poison. Although often
seen at her upstairs window (balcony), she actively searches for
love. Thus both protagonists fall outside or reject or rebel
against religious and social constraints on their allotted sexual
roles, in Charles's case by default, in Emma's by design in accordance with her literary notions. Both are caught in the
internecine bigotries of their times, where money and status are
dominant, and to which personal values and love are to be
sacrificed. Those who go against the grain do so at their own
personal cost: life and money are constantly interconnected in
MB.

Flaubert, however, does not spare, any more than does the
original play, the powers of horror at work in the depths of love.
The lovers' pact and ultimate union is encrypted, so that the
dark side of the sublime—madness, obsession, desire, and self-
annihilation for the other—is represented in its modern male
and female versions in Charles and Emma. The original metaphysical madness or poetic extreme in the teeth of impossible
reality is transposed by Flaubert into the medical, anatomical
world of a Canivet—amputator and autopsy specialist who can
find nothing in Charles—juxtaposed with the medical universe
of hysteria brought to the public theatre by Charcot. What has
not been properly recognized, but what the amplification of
Romeo and Juliet in a modern medical key reveals, is that hysteria too is sexed and gendered. Flaubert succeeds in drawing the
tragic portraits of the beautiful hysterical woman (dead) in
public at Homais's and Bournisien's feet and Charles, the hysterical man, whose diagnosis at all costs must be hushed up or

given a more 'male' diagnosis when Canivet can find 'rien' after the autopsy.[2]

Flaubert's banalization of one of the greatest love tragedies in literature in Charles and Emma paradoxically elevates the sublime mediocrity of this couple and their failed loves to the status of modern tragedy. They have indeed become watchwords for failed grand passion, but this, compared to the real mediocracy of Homais and Yonville, is still of infinitely greater value than a *croix d'honneur*. Charles and Emma are not so much predestined to try, but fail, to love happily ever after. Rather, their internal and external sex and gender programming causes them to react in ways which mismatch at the wrong points in spite of the fact that both, fundamentally, are a match of complementary ideals for the other. Ironically, too, they do have a unique marriage: it is the only one in Flaubert's fiction. It is their other sexual experiences within and outside marriage which are the platitudes, as Emma discovers too late. It is most of all her marriage which ironically provides the enormous freedoms and trust she needs.

Myth has therefore tremendous power to shape and inform representation and re-representation, and this is no less true of critical myths. If Charles's masculinity has been largely dismissed, because it is passive, Emma's so-called 'masculinity' is a prime critical *idée reçue*. Problems in identifying her as woman or man have stemmed, first, from readings of the apocryphal, 'Madame Bovary, c'est moi' taken too literally: the sex of Emma and the sex of Flaubert are elided with gender inversion, compounded with a critical confusion based on merging author and character. Only recently has the *fictional* nature of this statement which has been the basis of much critical 'argument' been stated (Biasi, 1994: 24–5). The second problematic approach has been to read *MB* through the autobiographical or semi-biographical reworking of the Louise Colet–Flaubert liai-

---

[2] For a fuller discussion of Emma's death and medical symptoms, see Siller (1981).The literature surrounding Emma's hysteria follows in the wake of Baudelaire's famous review of *MB*. Among the many critics who have taken up the issue and in some depth, see Heath (1992); Sartre (1980); Beizer (1993: ch. 4); Matlock (1994). For most critics, if they envisage male hysteria in *MB*, it is in relation to Flaubert and thus it is channelled doubly through Emma. I have foregrounded male hysterical traits in Homais and Père Rouault as well as in Charles in Orr (1999*b*). Literary critics recently are reassessing male hysteria in fiction. See for example Showalter (1997).

son and their copious exchange of letters on the subject of sexuality and the writing of *Madame Bovary*. Recent feminist criticism, most notably Champagne and Daly (1983) and Beizer (1993), has overturned many of the earlier sexist assumptions; and these stem largely from the main critical culprit, Baudelaire, who first saw Emma's smoking, wearing a waistcoat, a lorgnon, and so on, as masculine or androgynous. Critics, male in the main, have subsequently followed suit, to recuperate both the strongest character in *MB* and her creator for 'active' masculinity. Subsequently, even less gender-blind criticism still rehearses many of the vexed questions around gender raised by Baudelaire's view of Emma's androgyny, the debate ranging from this to her 'masculinity', her scandalous femininity, or even a switch of the two.[3] By returning to the text, and asking how

---

[3] There have been several excellent explorations. Among the best extended appraisals from male critics is D. A. Williams (1992). For examples of the other positions, see Czyba (1983: 39), 'chez Emma palpite intimement le désir d'être homme [elle] donne souvent à sa toilette une touche masculine, elle porte des vêtements d'homme, ce qui, d'ailleurs, constitue un attrait pour les hommes qui l'entourent,' and 'Ce personnage *féminin*, toutefois ne constitue qu'une image *dégradée* ce que fut Flaubert . . . l'écrivain recrée *la Femme* et rend . . . lisible son propre conditionnement idéologique' (ibid. 112). Auerbach (1982: 180) states that 'the fallen woman is captured in various stages of abasement, proneness and self-laceration. . . . By excising love and passion from the fall, and by subtle modulations of power in the fallen woman, they encompass both the pity of the woman's fall and the transforming power, not of her redemption, but of her will to rise. They mediate between abasement and exaltation, hiding images of woman's triumph in representations of punishment'. Heath (1992: 95) says that 'In the writing of Emma, Flaubert achieved something as radical as it was scandalous: a new conception of the feminine, of woman'; '*Madame Bovary*, in the middle of the century, condensed and expressed a new conception of the feminine, of woman. *Bovarysme* is gender neutral, a condition affecting both sexes, but at the same time above all a matter of women, of Madame Bovary in this—*her*—drama of hysteria' (ibid. 140). LaCapra (1982: 180) finds that 'Emma herself is in character neither for the traditional man nor for the traditional woman, for her desires both exceed and fall short of the expectations of both'; whereas for Vargas Llosa (1975: 137 in the section entitled 'Madame Bovary, Homme'), 'Emma est un personnage fondamentalement ambigu, chez lequel coexistent des sentiments et des appétits opposés . . . Mais son indéfinition n'est pas seulement morale et psychologique; elle renvoie aussi profondément à son sexe. Parce que sous l'exquise féminité de cette jeune femme, s'embusque un homme résolu.' Danahy (1991: 126) claims that 'In Emma, Flaubert encounters his shadow . . . a collection of anti-social tendencies, opposite or wicked self, himself as self-hater, social rebel. . . . Shadow changes sex, merging alarmingly with his buried feminine side, who must be absorbed, mastered so that he can come out "whole" '. Androgyny *and* conflict of male and female are taken up by Wetherill (1993), while the many contributors to Buisine (1997) present the whole gamut of Emma's 'gender trouble', to use Judith Butler's term (1990).

Emma seeks to define *her*self—necessarily an appositional term
and binary opposite to self meaning himself—and by looking
more closely at the contexts of her various donnings of male
attire, I will argue that Emma's very femaleness is clearly on
display. This embodiment then fits totally with her reading,
exemplified in the 'amours, amants, amantes' passage above (a
pastiche of a potted version of the *œuvre* of George Sand), and
in the cameo of her understandings of the demarcations of sex
and gender in society, in her wish for a son:

Elle souhaitait un fils: il serait fort et brun, et l'appellerait *Georges*: et
cette idée d'avoir pour enfant un mâle était comme *la revanche en
espoir de toutes ses impuissances passées*. Un homme, au moins, est
libre; il peut parcourir les passions et les pays, traverser les obstacles,
mordre aux bonheurs les plus lointains. Mais *une femme est empêchée
continuellement. Inerte et flexible à la fois, elle a contre elle les
mollesses de la chair avec les dépendances de la loi.*   (MB, 123, my
emphasis)

Emma's thoughts express extremely cogently the contradictions
for women inherent not just in the institution of marriage under
the *Code Napoléon*, but more importantly in the romance itself,
as crystallized in the Cinderella story. A woman may not have
sexual or erotic desires of her own, before or even during
marriage and therefore certainly not outside it. Emma's rescript-
ings are her attempt to define her frustrated self-identity as
erotic woman *à la* Sand; hence, perhaps, her choice of name for
her 'son'. Like Charles's stammer, her obsessive iterations of
selected bits of this script, but inability to complete the whole,
are articulated through her body, or rather parts of it. While her
bodily symptoms or reactions can and have been read as hysterical posturing through clothing (Gengembre, 1990), manifestations of her anorexia (McEachern, 1997), or shopaholic
reaction (Pedraza, 1997), she is trying to find a way to individ-
ualize herself. The paradox, as in her affairs, is that all she can
achieve is a provincial copy. It is when she has on her own
everyday clothes that she becomes tantalizingly attractive to
Charles and Justin, to name two.

   Thus, in her accoutrements, Emma borrows the trappings of
otherness, including masculine modes, to reinforce her difference from the female herd, so as to redefine her femininity as

freedom. Her dressing-up in seraglio garb is another face of the same desire and underlines that such behaviours are not masculine or feminine but female investments in what the items stand for, eroticism and desirability to men. D. A. Williams (1992: 137–8) is right in saying that 'Emma's adoption of masculine modes of dress . . . do not displace feminine modes'; and equally correct in stating that it would 'be wrong to think of Flaubert as a champion of the androgynous ideal that attracted many nineteenth-century writers. This is because so-called feminine and masculine traits are not brought into a state of harmony'. However, there are issues at stake other than her dressing in male attire as 'yet another example of role-playing' or the contention that it 'suggests a take-over or exchange and has as its counterpart Charles's assumption of feminine modes' (ibid.). Emma's so-called 'masculine' attire and smoking is a marker of her deeper desire to be all-woman, utterly desirable *à la* George Sand, writer of romances for the modern woman. Her desire to be desired everywoman, *actively*, is her solution, externalized by dress, to the dilemma of the Cinderella myth, the continuation of the power of attraction after the ball. This fits completely with Emma's sartorial preferences in general. While she delights in any occasion where she can play 'dressing up', as at her wedding and the ball, she consistently wears clothes that are almost too feminine. Hems always too long (her wedding dress and her riding skirt), signify the ultra-ladylikeness of a medieval maiden for her: 'Emma se comparait aux grandes dames d'autrefois . . . qui, traînant avec tant de majesté la queue chamarée de leurs longues robes, se retiraient en des solitudes' (*MB*, 298). The material is also always more luxurious than is practical for her status either in life on the farm as Mademoiselle Rouault, or at Tostes as Madame Bovary, or at Yonville, where she wears Lheureux's scarves as if she were a courtesan or in a harem. It is the 'amazone' (as riding costume, not masculine warrior-woman) which convinces her to ride out with Rodolphe. Given such consistency of female sex and gender identity in Emma's dress, her sartorial choices when she dons overtly male attire can only be read as a further ramification of her desire to explore female identities. And the donning of so-called male attire occurs precisely at moments of either very low self esteem for Emma or of transition, where she is reassessing her desirability as one lover fades and another appears on the horizon. A second question has never been asked in the debate. In front of whom does Emma sport her 'masculinity'?

There are two occasions when Emma flaunts herself in 'male' guise. In both cases she has been with the respective lover, Rodolphe or Léon, for some while. Subconsciously, she may be aware they are tiring of her, so the bold dress, attracting attention to herself, is designed to shock them again into seeing her as a desirable woman able to refuel the liaison. This is blatantly the case with Rodolphe in that famous 'example' of her so-called masculinity, the wearing *à la* George Sand of the waistcoat:

Par l'effet seul de ses habitudes amoureuses, madame Bovary changea d'allures ... elle eut même l'inconvenance de se promener avec M. Rodophe une cigarette à la bouche *comme pour narguer le monde*; enfin ceux qui doutaient encore ne doutèrent plus quand on la vit, un jour, descendre de l'*Hirondelle*, la taille serrée dans un gilet, à la façon d'un homme; et madame Bovary mère, qui, après une épouvantable scène avec son mari, était venue se réfugier chez son fils, ne fut pas la bourgeoise la moins scandalisée.   (*MB*, 266, Flaubert's emphasis)

Critics have in fact read this only from the viewpoint of the 'shock' of Madame Bovary *mère*, 'little more than the shocked spokeswoman for the virtues of conventional housewifery' (Heath, 1992: 69). The real context, however, is the previous scene where Emma has not only prostituted herself, but put herself in the most servile female position of all, at Rodolphe's feet:

—Oh! c'est que je t'aime! reprenait-elle ... je me demande: 'Où est-il? Peut-être il parle à d'autres femmes? Elles lui sourient, il s'approche ...' Oh! non, n'est-ce pas, aucune ne te plaît? Il y en a de plus belles; mais moi, je sais mieux aimer! Je suis ta servante et ta concubine! tu es mon roi, mon idole! tu es bon! tu es beau! tu es intelligent! tu es fort!

Il s'était tant de fois entendu dire ces choses, qu'elles n'avaient rien d'original. Emma ressemblait à toutes les maîtresses; et le charme de la nouveauté, peu à peu tombait comme un vêtement, laissant voir à nu l'éternelle monotonie de la passion ...

Mais ... Rodolphe aperçut en cet amour d'autres jouissances à exploiter. Il jugea toute pudeur incommode. Il la traita sans façon. Il en fit quelque chose de souple et de corrompu.   (*MB*, 264–5)

As a textbook version of sado-masochistic gender stereotyping, Emma's 'masculinity' has to be rejected. She does not don symbols of her 'master', by adopting his waistcoats, smoking. Rather she replicates in a different style Héloïse's paranoias about losing Charles to other women. Her 'exhibitionism' is a rebellion against the passive role, the sedate and decorous dress of matriarchy, which is on the back of the chief female person in her audience, Madame Bovary *mère*. The waistcoat therefore shows off her erotic female body more strikingly—it fits tightly to her upper body—and defiantly demonstrates her now-recuperated, 'special', femininity to the world. The pose of defiance Emma wants to strike is rebellion against female norms, yet unique femininity *vis-à-vis* other women who are usually seen as rivals in love (sexual or filial). Madame Bovary *mère*, who censures Emma, is paradoxically rather too like her daughter-in-law deep down, thwarted in her femininity also. If one is still determined to guard a 'masculine' Madame Bovary in Flaubert's novel, it is not Emma but Charles's mother who is the candidate. Her active business dealings, her stringent self-discipline and autonomy in spite of an abusive husband, her ability to provide for her son, are all male qualities in her socio-historical context. One can now read back to the other oft-cited example of Emma's 'masculinity', the 'lorgnon d'écaille'. It is firmly fixed 'entre deux boutons de son corsage' and is designed again to show off to better effect an extremely feminine toilette and hairstyle. It may also have the subconscious design of attracting the 'intelligent man' to her as woman.

When Emma dons masculine attire for the second time, she is with the much less macho Léon, but in so similar a place in the relationship that it should forewarn us that her dressing-up will take a masculine form:

Il s'ennuyait maintenant lorsque Emma, tout à coup, sanglotait sur sa poitrine; et son cœur, comme les gens qui ne peuvent endurer qu'une certaine dose de musique, s'assoupissait d'indifférence au vacarme d'un amour dont il ne distinguait plus les délicatesses.

Ils se connaissaient trop pour avoir ces ébahissements de la possession qui en centuplaient la joie. Elle était aussi dégoûtée de lui qu'il était fatigué d'elle. Emma retrouvait dans l'adultère toutes les platitudes du mariage. . . .

Le jour de la mi-carême, elle ne rentra pas à Yonville; elle alla le soir au bal masqué. Elle mit un pantalon de velours et des bas rouges, avec une perruque à catogan et un lampion sur l'oreille. Elle sauta toute la nuit, au son furieux des trombones ... elle se trouva le matin sur le péristyle du théâtre parmi cinq ou six masques; débardeuses ou matelots, des camarades de Léon.   (*MB*, 401–2)

What Emma has chosen to wear is a *carnavalesque*, ironic, variant of the dandy's waistcoat, cap, and particular wig, but one which borders on brothel attire. It is the immediate and female company that she now finds 'du dernier rang' (*MB*, 403), and she faints when she smells the punch and the cigar smoke. The reminiscences of Rodolphe, the Vaubyessard Ball, produce this final extreme of caricatural behaviour, copying in extreme form. As M. Lowe (1984: 26) notes, 'Emma is more like a female Don Juan ... another soul in search of purity, seeks it perversely and exclusively in sexual adventures, which swamp and pervert some of his magnificent rebelliousness and passion for liberty.' She will end her relationship with Léon by copying Rodolphe's behaviour to her, worn as a 'badge' of her sexual prowess, superiority, and availability to other men. Webster Goodwin (1986: 199) notes the singularity of her dance: 'Here there is no question of knowing or not knowing how to dance, no question of a proxy. She leads the dance herself; she makes it her own.' In addition, it is her inner, almost bacchic, fury that is encapsulated in this solitary dance, climax of the solitudes and rancours felt at the Vaubyessard Ball and the opera, where she was so near and yet so far from being the heroine adored by men. However, the distance between reality and fantasy is also made manifest by the realization of the low company around her, her frightening similarity with them, the opposite of the elevation to which she has been aspiring, for '[b]y reflecting a blend of passion and heroism, Emma's fantasies correspond to her two inseparable aspirations ... emotional fulfilment and ... eminence' (Collas, 1985: 64). The 'mi-carême bal masqué' sets the social limits of the images Emma has fed on from her early convent reading of courtly love and its milieu. She is also at the limits of her experience as female lover, or of its costumes. There is nothing else to copy, so she removes her costume to return to the dress of the *Madame* Bovary who goes next to confront Lheureux. It is not the figure of Madame Bovary *mère* who intervenes in this scene to disapprove of Emma's dress, but Léon's mother who plays a similar social role. She has procured the promise from her son that he will break with this dangerous 'femme mariée'. Emma has no more costumes to pretend in and from this point in the novel is the female victim of the breakers and brokers in society —Lheureux, Guillaumin, Maître Hareng, Rodolphe—but ultimately of herself. The irony is that the man who was but a transitory means of escape from Les Bertaux, Charles, understands so intuitively that femininity which is her core self that he orders that she is buried in her wedding dress, satin slippers on her feet. He thus dresses her as the 'épouse'—his, and like the divine one she dreamed of becoming back in the convent.

This ironic return, because secularized and bowdlerized, to the image of the (pseudo-) biblical 'époux–épouse' points to what I see as Flaubert's hypothetical yet cynical exploration of marriage as a symbolic union, a kind of marriage of affinities, in *MB*. Rather than reading Emma and Charles through Freud, the screen of Jung seems much more interesting, because his work offers a psychological reinvestigation of concepts surrounding masculinity and femininity. While there is a small body of criticism that hints in the direction of the numinous (D. A. Williams, 1973: 47) or suggests that 'Emma is Flaubert's shadow *anima*' (Danahy, 1991: 126), it is the alchemical and Jungian concept of *coniunctio* which has double pertinence, as Flaubert certainly knew about it through his reading of the Gnostics and myths in Creuzer among others. First, it speaks of relationship as two different yet interrelating parts, a union of different substances. Second, it reopens the question of androgyny from a different perspective to Baudelaire, that is, the symbolic rather than bisexual meaning of the alchemical term.[4] Each of Flaubert's novels returns in different ways, as we shall see, to the problem of union, the couple, to male and female principles. These as *animus* and *anima* reopen the delineations

---

[4] Useful introductory works on Jung and helpful definitions of *coniunctio* are Schwarz-Salant (1995: ch. 7) and Beebe. (1989: ch. 5, 'The Masculine in Women' and ch. 6, 'The Anima'). Steinberg (1993) offers a Jungian psychological overview of the basic split which too male or too female behaviours create and which require transformation through counterbalancing parts. For a detailed and clear discussion of alchemical androgyny, see the special number of *Cahiers de l'Hermétisme* (1986) on *L'Androgyne*. New psychological studies through Jung of *MB*, and indeed, Flaubert's *œuvre*, are ripe for consideration.

of male and female qualities which have been institutionalized and socialized as sex and gender stipulations for men or women. Schwartz-Salant (1995: 8) gives a definition of *coniunctio* which gets to the nub of the unrealized potential in Charles and Emma's relationship: 'This union process, the alchemical *coniunctio*, was a marriage that, at its highest level of completion, the so-called stage of the *rubedo*, was filled with desire.' Opposites confront and attract one another, mutually transform the other. The key is desire, which both Emma and Charles have in abundance although in differing forms.

The process of change does occur in Charles and Emma's marriage in its mundane, provincial, parameters. It does shift and flex, even though it ultimately fails through too much tension being applied by one partner and the belated catching-up of the other. The passion factor is, however, central to both parties, but it is again at variance with true mutual attainment of desire *à deux*. Emma's selfishness and narcissism get in the way, as does Charles's passivity. Both bring to the other the other in themselves: Emma's *animus* qualities have nothing to do with her 'masculinity', but everything to do with desire for complementarity in sexual and non-sexual terms. Charles's *anima* characteristics do not undermine his masculinity, but offer a non-macho figuration for his whole personality. Emma is in fact aware very early on that change is necessary. Her mistake is to see a change in address or marital status as the answer, rather than the need to change her self, which she takes unchanged into each new relationship. Ultimately, the experiment only goes some way, and is represented as a possibility with hindsight in the bathos of the ending of the novel. Flaubert will, however, pick up and develop alchemical concepts, including *coniunctio*, in his next novel, *SAL*, explore it further in *LSJ*, and pick up on it in *BP* in male–male form.

In this chapter, I have discussed how Flaubert's reworking of the *Cinderella* and *Romeo and Juliet* stories unequivocally highlights the false heart of the Romantic ideal of 'le Grand Amour', that is 'la chose la plus merveilleuse de la vie', 'unique', 'un idéal monogame strict', 'dure toute la vie et parfois éternellement', 'est exclusif, fondé sur la possession', 'absolu et total' (Falconnet, 1973: 26–7), with its impossible standards and dictats for both men and women. Mocked directly by the little statue of Eros in the garden of the philanderer Guillaumin, Flaubert's exploration of Emma's existential dilemmas, given that there was so little else apart from marriage for women to aspire to under patriarchy's *Code Napoléon*, is a biting attack on the inflexible gender-models fed to women and also to men, as we shall see in more detail in *ES*. Divorce (even remarriage) or an independent lifestyle after admission of failure of *'le Grand Amour'* were simply not possible. It is the set of prison doors of female domesticity without the Cinderella option that Emma most radically hammers on, exposing the double standards of the epoch and patriarchal myths about marriage in general. She stumbles on the truth of the platitudes of both affairs and marriage because of the bankruptcy of intersexual congress which denies anything but totally rigid behaviours, hierarchies of power, and pre-given expectations and desires. Marriage myths and dictats, structures and ways of living are rarely discussed in relation to men, which is what makes *MB* such a daringly innovative exploration of a twice-faithful husband. Marriage will never, after *MB*, be anything but transitory or uncircumstantial: it is irrelevant or unnecessary in Flaubert's late works. The inherent point is that men cannot be men in marriage as set up by the *Code Napoléon*, institutionalized religions, or economic arrangements. This direct social criticism has a positive and a negative aspect. In the dipping into the symbolic union (Jung) in *MB*, the evidence of both 'masculine' and 'feminine' in Charles and Emma, Flaubert toys with some of the implications of unconventional marriage. Yet he floods these with the 'real' of social structures and strictures, a return to old patterns as inevitable after the sacrifice of those who would rock the boat because they refuse to rock the State cradle. Flaubert's problem with the *anima* in himself may be the reason, but such speculation lies outside this study. However, his difficulty with too much 'feminine' in men, except in strictly controlled circumstances (*BP*), points to the negative outcomes of his critique of marriage. In the Real, marriage is incompatible with the essential freedom in man to be an individual. Therefore, it seems better to pursue male singleness and single-mindedness with only the occasional brush with the heterosexual union for pleasure not procreation. This indictment, rebellion, and rejection of the institution of marriage has the further advantage of avoiding the lot of the common man. We shall see in subsequent chapters how Flaubert's men fare. Suffice it to finish here with Charles as Man for all seasons, unaffected by the fashions of what his 'manhood' should be or how he ought to express his masculinity in the public or private spheres. In a paradox so typical of Flaubert's representations, he is prevented by his creator from fulfilling a much greater destiny of neo-Romeo dimensions, stabbed in the heart by his author's 'stylo-scalpel'. In order for the Creator to become the greater, the despised prophet-fool needs to diminish and die.

2

Salammbô

'THERE is no document of civilization which is not at one and the same time a document of barbarism' (in F. Jameson, 1981: 286). This quotation from Walter Benjamin is particularly pertinent to *SAL*, the novel of violence as 'raw desire' (Kennard, 1978: 53), but not as 'the quintessential characteristic of female sexual attraction in the male' (ibid. 56). This novel presents the politics and desires of patriarchy in its most overtly hierarchized state. I will read its violent religious and political homicides on international and cosmic planes through the paradox of Benjamin's assertion. This is a world of extremes: gods and rulers on the one hand, soldiers and plebs on the other. In a nutshell, Flaubert presents in *SAL* a fictional 'theorizing' of the master–slave relationship predating Nietzsche. *SAL* is also an extension of *MB* in its reworking of the principle of the couple as linchpin in the dynamics of social order and stability. In the previous chapter I discussed the harmonization potential of masculine and feminine in Charles and Emma, set against the deliberately dichotomized gender roles inculcated and codified by the *Code Napoléon* for its own ideological ends. *SAL* demonstrates *ancien régime* absolutist principles, male power, and authority which will find their continuum, not abolition, in France after 1789. The divinely appointed king in league with a divinely appointed papacy was not in fact eradicated by the bloodbath of the Revolution or the setting-up of elected government based on the Rights of Man in its aftermath. As Carthaginian allegory for post-revolutionary France (Green, 1982), *SAL* thus strikes at those discrepancies of ideology and practice in the regime of the 'republican' despot, Hamilcar. He and the other 'great men' in the novel are not uncivilized Carthaginians of a bygone era, but as 'civilized' in their barbarities as Flaubert's political contemporaries. Flaubert's analysis of State power through male and female principles in *SAL* therefore develops his social critique of *MB* with a fundamental twist: macro- and micro-cosmic orders are the *locus* of enquiry, with Culture and Nature not so much set at odds with one another, but put together as male power, force, and violence against the larger backdrop of the forces of the cosmos itself— cataclysm, chaos, and the birthing of new empires.

The constant critical approach to *SAL* is to read the various levels of the text as binary opposites or antitheses, as almost fixed patterns in a semi-archaic universe on the brink of change.[1] My reading offers instead a study of the polarities of male position to show that they are often points on the same continuum. The further advantage of this approach is that female character and feminine elements remain discrete and unmerged with male characters and male characteristics as secondary and negatively comparative. Polarities between men and masculinities will prove to be not necessarily in linear relation (hierarchy), but rather emerge also as circular, as in the image of the serpent biting its tail. In an intriguing note, Griffin (1988: 361 n. 23) highlights the uroboros as symbol in his reading of the novel:

In Carthaginian mythology, originary hermaphroditic form of the uroboros reappears in the relation between the masculine morning star and the feminine evening star, both incarnations of the planet Venus. Androgyny in a deity is a primitive characteristic: so too are virginity

---

[1]   See e.g. Frier-Wantiez (1979: 1) and McKenna (1988: 312). Brady (1977, 316) quotes other previous critics who focus on the binary oppositions. Starr (1985: 41) states that '*SAL* in fact puts real pressure on the barbary/civilization dichotomy' but does not expand this. C. Lowe (1974: 87) does use the word 'polarités', but states that they 'restent au niveau d'articulation du stade du miroir'. Leal (1973) studies antithesis as key structuring principal in the novel. See also Hilliard (1993) for a developed psychoanalytic reading of binary patriarchy in *SAL*, and Leenhardt (1992) for a Jungian reading. Schehr's reading is sophisticated, but none the less 'binary' (1989: 332): 'Alterity—the dream world, the Orient—is considered to be the Crypt into which is cast what differs from the self of identity, conceived either objectively or as the transcendental subject of knowledge. Thus the realm of alterity is by and large the repository of desire; it is a world of the dark side . . . Flaubert sets out to determine alterity for itself, and not as it relates to the realm of identity. Clearly, he situates the text as a spatio-temporal point removed from the epistemes that define alterity in terms of difference from, negation of, and relation to identity.'

and fertility combined in goddesses, fertility and castration in gods. Masculine traits of the female coexist with the male's feminine traits; eunuchs are male prostitutes and priests . . . In *Salammbô* however, gender transposition marks separation, not proximity to divine will.

While the novel questions at all junctures the male–female polarity through Tanit–Moloch and Salammbô–Mâtho, and I have discussed elsewhere the ambiguous sexualities of Tanit and Schahabarim (Orr, 1995–6), polarization of maleness further avoids the conflation of ambiguous sexuality with hermaphroditism or androgyny, both of which, in the nineteenth-century mind, were often asexual categories.[2] By focusing instead on polarities, *SAL* is thus a novel of extremes which prove to have peculiar similarities when regarded analogically. The world of Carthage therefore operates on the same civilization scale (imperialism) and according to the same gender-divisions (patriarchy) as Flaubert's France, the latter inheriting from the Roman empire which overturns the pseudo-victory of the Carthaginians over the invading 'Barbarians' (including Gauls) at the end of the novel. The pre-Christian, pagan, exotic setting of Carthage does not, then, provide an orientalist point of view as the Other of the West, so that the latter may reaffirm its superior identity.[3] An understanding of this landscape of extremes as polarities of the Same not only provides a reading of *SAL* that unsettles previous *idées reçues* based on the so-called binary or orientalist oppositions in the text. More importantly, this novel

---

[2] Laforge (1985) reads *SAL* as the myth of the hermaphrodite. Heilbrun (1982) offers a cogent study of androgyny and in particular remarks 'Stendhal, Balzac and Flaubert, while they are aware of the sexual disorientation in the times of which they write . . . never conceive of the culturation of "sexual" attributes. . . . not even Flaubert can imagine that "feminine" impulses might hold any promise for the future of mankind' (86). Brady (1977: 317) is one of few critics to have argued that the snake in the novel is both a male and female symbol.

[3] See Mullen Hohl (1995) for a critique of exoticism. For the orientalist and orientalism debate, see Saïd (1978) and Constable (1996) for a critique of the application of Saïd to *SAL*. Against orientalism, see variously Karoui (1974) for a modern Tunisian perspective, or Gaillard (in Toro, 1987: 46), 'Le détour inattendu par Carthage va avoir pour principal effet de désembourgeoiser la vision flaubertienne de l'histoire, de la désempoisser de son bourgeoisme, c'est-à-dire de la dégager d'une certaine idée de sa rationalité et de sa finalité' or Leenhardt (1992: 52), 'comme l'avait noté Maxime du Camp . . ., Flaubert n'est pas à la recherche d'un Orient où fuir dans l'exotique. La volonté de situer son roman à Carthage relève bien plutôt de la recherche d'un terrain propice où développer, comme *in vitro* une vision radicalisée des lois de son propre monde.'

challenges notions of cultural superiority and civilization itself within the heritage of occidentalism: empires, monarchies, and democracies. The same brutalities, violence, warmongering and homicidal tendencies which undergird the social structures in Carthage and between Carthage and her neighbours remain essentially unchanged in patriarchal nation-states like Flaubert's France. The basic principle is power: who has it and how it is maintained. Although it appears that a totally different value-system is in operation—droit de Seigneur, religious and social rites of purification through human sacrifice, placation of the gods, a judicial system situated in an oligarchy masquerading as a theocracy—the reign of terror in the aftermath of the Revolution and its subsequent mini-revolutions replicate such atrocities. Names and styles change, but the fundamental patterns of domination and control do not.

The first part of the chapter examines polarity as similarity by looking at the principle of hierarchy itself. Three faces of this male authority structure will be examined: the cosmic-divine of the god, Moloch; the human ruler-figurehead, Hamilcar; and the slave, Spendius, seemingly on the 'other side' politically and socially. The king, the supreme commander, the high priest, the warrior, the intrepid slave are all inflationary versions of 'ordinary' masculinity and configurations of male power. Masculine inflation, according to Wyly (1989), is a defence mechanism against the fear of the feminine and hence offers an explanation for the body politic of the ubiquity of patriarchal values in western culture. Having this power, however, involves a careful silencing of opposition, or challenge and reinforcement of position through allies who may therefore also become rivals. This is where *SAL* is a blueprint of the strategies and diplomacy required in hierarchy, particularly between first and second ranks, because competition is the mechanism and dynamic of its power structures.

The processes of stratification by rank is in fact similar to ways in which animals organize themselves in packs or herds. It is no accident that all the secondary male figures are likened to such animals. Narr'Havas, described as a leopard, the elephantine hippopotamus-like Hannon, and the snake-like Schahabarim, all demonstrate the second-rank extensions of, and dependency on, primary rank and power, with the authority and potential to move up or down in the pack. All three exhibit in various ways their (overmasculine) modes of survival and delineation from the top, among whose traits are supreme cruelty, complete selfishness, sadism, and the bullying of those in a weaker position. These find wider corporate expression as warmongering, xenophobia, misogyny, and misanthropy. And the two contexts which permit male–male forces their most intense and spectacular manifestation in *SAL* are ritualized slaughter—in the immolation of Carthage's children and the 'ethnic cleansing' through Mâtho's sacrifice—and wars. The second part of the chapter will close with the Mercenaries and Barbares as commentators on contestation of rank as international male conflict. These two destructive fora of Promethean male rage not only project outward to invaders and named enemies with internecine implications: they also hide intensely interiorized defence mechanisms against the powers of (pro)creative horror. Cannibalism of children and violation of the feminine are the exteriorized symptoms of other kinds of male sicknesses, psychic and physical.

The final part of the chapter investigates the point of juncture of male polarizations as personified in Mâtho, the male enemy/self-same, the most virilized/de-virilized male character in *SAL*. Mâtho is the embodiment of the paradox of hierarchy. As victim and supreme sacrifice, he is top and bottom, same and other, hero and villain, foreign rival and brother in one. As impossible solution, he demonstrates the violences of patriarchy against itself. In this regard, the highly figurative ending is worth another look. *SAL*'s complex rhetoric of the phallic raises the issue of Flaubert's narrative politics in this novel, the naming and concealing in a web of words of 'an explicitly masculine power that castrates or exterminates' (Starr, 1985: 49). Is the pleasure of the text then primarily the writer's 'pleasure of mastery', a writing of revenge?

The fictional world of *SAL* is not merely an allegory of Moloch (as Wallen, 1989–90: 243 claims), nor allegorized history of post-revolutionary France as Curry (1997: 105) indicates: '[i]ndeed Flaubert's great achievement is precisely his avoidance of the archeological and historical as a genre of the novel ... its refusal to perpetuate the traditional historical novel's simplistic view of the past as "knowable" in some absolute sense'. In its pseudo-epic form and *Verfremdungs-effekten*, it is contingently related to both allegory and the double sense of the French word 'histoire' by dint of patriarchal core genre concepts. '[Flaubert's] version is less a fictionalised reconstruction of a historical period than an exploration of the base and violent impulses inherent in man and which, although normally held in check, must break out in certain circum-stances' (Green, 1982: 57). *SAL* shares with allegory a belief in universal significance behind the visible, and with nineteenth-century history and the historical novel, a chronicle of great men and leaders. Where it differs is in its borders with history and fiction—the epic (Jay, 1972), or in Busst's term (1990), pseudo-epic dimensions. In that the epic author expresses 'the accepted unconscious metaphysic of his age' (ibid. 70), and that the epic is an enlargement within national bounds of individual superlative qualities, then the epic *à la* Flaubert is an experi-mental form of the very inflationary masculinities this chapter examines in its themes, characters, and rhetorical tropes. Epics allow for the involvement of cosmic and supernatural forces; the pseudo-mythic dimension permits of essences and universals as orders of meaning. One such is the 'pre-civilized' principle of male power, 'virtu' as physical force and prowess, lauded in evolutionary models of civilizations and in anthropology and found even in Beauvoir (1949). All the main patriarchs and male protagonists in *SAL* demonstrate and embody this 'tradi-tional' masculine attribute in battle (or in Schahabarim's case in ritualized conflict), with its factors, as Castelain-Meunier (1988: 74) elucidates, of risk, courage, self-affirmation in the pecking-order. Brawn and physical supremacy are frequently combined with mental superiority. In each of the leaders, class and inher-ited order (of Moloch), compound the notion of 'greatness'. Interestingly, sexual potency and paternity, which are often thought of as expressions of virile masculinity, are singularly unimportant on both the human and cosmic levels of this novel. Real men make war not love. The one player who usurps power by affiliation is the bastard slave, Spendius. These two labels of exclusion and inferiority, however, engage him in tactics of masculine domination in a new key (including the building of siege engines). Dussardier in *ES* will be thoroughly *engagé* for similar reasons, but for fraternity, as the next chapter will demonstrate. One-time successful trader of prostitutes, with a linguistic prowess equalled and surpassed only by Hamilcar and Salammbô, Spendius' strong self-identity and survival mentality will add a pre-Darwinian spin on the group of 'endowed' patriarchs and princes in the novel. Spendius, as we will see, represents the slave-to-master force of the rising form of patriarchy (Rome) which will usurp Carthage as master order of birth and privilege.

Contrary to critical wisdom, the transcendental signifier of the city of Carthage is not the so-called goddess Tanit, or even Eschmoûn (Mullen Hohl, 1995), but Moloch. Gilmore (1990: 166–7) offers an explanation: 'Male rites and cults occur most commonly in patriarchal societies where the sexes are strongly segregated and ranked. These rites often lend a certain mystique to men that makes them "superior" to women, or they enhance male unity, which in turn can bolster this sense of superiority.' We will discover that in *ES* the men-only clubs fulfil the same function. Overt descriptions of the horrors of this god are delayed until the final fifth of the novel. Beginning with the chapter devoted to Moloch, there ensue the holocaust of Carthage's children, the mass slaughter of the Barbares in the Défilé de la Hache, the revenge of the crowds on Mâtho—so that the impact on the reader of this cult of cruelty is first concealed, later to be revealed in its full horrible glory. The axe is a particularly potent weapon in *SAL,* perhaps reminding a French readership of the 'civilized' engine of death, *madame la Guillotine.* It is a leitmotif of the final fifth of the book. In 'Moloch', Mâtho is aware of a penetrating look of hate upon him—it is Schahabarim on the ramparts of Carthage—and hurls his axe in its direction. The sacrifical implement the priest uses is part axe-knife, part spatula, and the dead-end valley of carnage ('Défilé de la Hache') magnifies the political and religious dimensions of mass homicide. The apocalyptic finale then has even more hideous implications regarding the unchallenged nature of Moloch's rule because his double antagonists, Mâtho and Salammbô, have been eradicated. Moloch has a particularly ironic place in the bestiary of Flaubert's novels. The god of the tribe of Baals and Mithras, he is often depicted with the horns of the bull; in the Bible he is the god who immolates children (an abhorrence in the eyes of God); and his shadow is 'bull-like passion, raw desire and power: sadistic bull-dozing violence, demonic bullying' (Brinton Perera in Lauter and Schreier Rupprecht 1985: 168). Flaubert's Carthage represents Moloch as the cosmogony of Bovaryism.

Moloch is the god of extreme response from his adherents (none of whom seem to be women), of domination, destruction, exploitation, oppression, immolation, rape, pillage, mass slaughter. The overemphasis on dominion, physical power, and overpowering in the cosmological dimension, replicated in the earthly and allogeneous contexts, has two corollaries. First, the opposite pole of values is to be eschewed at all costs—that is, castration, feebleness, effeminacy. Second, stereotype 'supermen' figures are essential to guard a channelled Ideal so that inferiors are kept in controlled submission. Violence (like the wanton cruelty of the crowd to Mâtho) in its institutionalized religious and secular forms is less a positive form of revolt to change the old order, than a reactionary bid to conserve the current one from attack. As Balandier explains, '[l]a violence qui est devenue une force instituée n'est plus employée à fonder, mais à conserver: alors il s'agit de ce que l'on pourrait appeler une violence de fonctionnement, une violence de maintien. Ajoutons que [cette conservation] est principalement celle du rite pour les moyens symboliques, et celle du droit pour ce qui est des normes, des règles, des lois' (in Maffesoli and Bruston, 1979: 13). Even the architecture of Carthage replicates this negative conservative aspect of fortification against invaders, as DeJean (1984: 335–9) convincingly elucidates. Power and dominion are maintained by policing any deviations from the norms, whether these are religious rites or social rules. So for example, while Schahabarim may not be a high priest of Moloch, and Hamilcar may not be exempt from the sacrifice of sons to the flames, both 'cheat' by substitutions of other males to cover their own variance and deviance from collective religious or social manhood because they know how to borrow Moloch to justify their own ends. As highest order of authority, no one therefore dares challenge them. They also justify their exterminatory actions to mirror the homicidal and internecine faces this cult and god keep hidden behind the cloak of the goddess Tanit, whom Carthage associates with itself. Thus the allegedly female Tanit channels the real sadism of Moloch as god of fire, blood, and war into more benign energies of eroticism (orgies, feasts) and mysticism (the zaïmph). The cult of Moloch is a defence mechanism of the most sophisticated kind, wherein only the real initiates can manipulate and flout the rules of horror. Their corporate way of doing this is to daemonize the male outsider as enemy-other. Engaging him in battle categorizes him as opposition, oppositionally different and foreign, so as to smokescreen the inner destructive forces of Moloch-Carthage: 'Tous étaient faibles près de Moloch-le-dévorateur. L'existence, la chair même des *hommes* lui appartenaient' (*SAL*, 332, my emphasis); 'il n'y avait pas de douleur trop considérable pour le Dieu, puisqu'il se délectait dans les plus horribles . . . Il fallait donc l'assouvir complètement' (ibid. 333). The violent and bestial appetites of the Mercenaries at the opening orgiastic feast of the novel or Hannon's bulimic gluttony are as nothing compared to the extreme ingestion of ovened, homegrown, child flesh, baked in a holocaust-like oven in the Baal-machine of Moloch, specially constructed for the consumption of such hyperbolic quantities. The ballistic engines of war destroy by spewing out the destructive missile, whereupon death takes its natural course. The Moloch-machine operated with Hamilcar and Schahabarim in attendance goes beyond death in nature and its laws of mechanics and physics, to the horrors of culture. Levi-Strauss's terms, the raw and the cooked, as anthropological metaphors for the primitive and the civilized respectively, gloss, in ironic contradistinction here, the message at the heart of Flaubert's novel: the extreme 'cooked' is so uncivilized that it cannot be in any part natural:

Les bras d'airain allaient plus vite. Ils ne s'arrêtaient plus. Chaque fois que l'on y posait un enfant, les prêtres de Moloch étendaient la main sur lui, pour le charger des crimes du peuple, en vociférant: 'Ce ne sont pas des hommes, mais des bœufs!' et la multitude à l'entour répétait 'Des bœufs! des bœufs!' . . .

Cependant l'appétit du Dieu ne s'apaisait pas. Il en voulait toujours. Afin de lui en fournir davantage, on les empila sur ses mains avec une grosse chaîne par-dessus, qui les retenait. . . . Cela dura longtemps, indéfiniment jusqu'au soir. . . . Le bûcher, sans flammes à présent, faisait une pyramide de charbons jusqu'à ses genoux; complètement rouge comme un géant tout couvert de sang, il semblait, avec sa tête, qui se renversait, chanceler sous le poids de son ivresse. (*SAL*, 349–50)

Moloch, grotesque parallel-wearer of a chain like that of Salammbô, monstrous provocateur of 'chancellements' surpassing those Salammbô experiences in Mâtho's tent, translates Tanit-mediated Eros in the earlier part of *SAL* into unmediated Ares. This scene is the 'hors d'œuvre' in the culinary and transcendent senses to the meal the Carthaginians will make of the Barbares in the final battle which is the epitome of defilement of the masculine in the Défilé de la Hache. The Mercenaries' orgy of destruction of the Barca fish at the beginning of *SAL*, their forced cannibalism, mass suicide or abetted euthanasia, their resorting to homosexual acts in the face of inevitable death in the Défilé de la Hache, become extreme, but still human, responses to the limits of life, an impasse not of their own making, but nature's combined with the fanaticisms of true inhumanity. 'The civilisation of Carthage is an institutionalized barbarism' (Levin quoted in Kennard, 1978: 57). Everywhere, by the mirror of parallel lesser degree, the 'Barbares' criticize the truly barbaric practices of the Carthaginians, who are anaesthetized to cruelty when they sacrifice their very children to the flames; in the final words of the chapter dedicated to Moloch, 'Ce grand bruit et cette grande lumière avaient attiré les Barbares au pied des murs; se cramponnant pour mieux voir sur les débris de l'hélépole, ils regardaient, béants d'horreur.' Explicitly and implicitly, the negative destructive forces of inhumanity are on display and can be summed up as Moloch-masculinity. *SAL* has everything here of allegory as secular prophecy: the construction of the ovens of Auschwitz finds very similarly motivated forces of defensive patriarchal power to express man's inhumanity to man.

The superlative power of Moloch finds its human equivalent in Hamilcar. As the supreme male of the novel, his status is endorsed by analogy as he stands 'en manteau rouge *comme* les prêtres de Moloch, se tenant *auprès* du Baal, debout *devant l'orteil de son pied droit.*' (*SAL*, 348, my emphasis). Hamilcar, however, demonstrates clearly that he is 'above' religious mumbo-jumbo. To paraphrase Bem (1980: 24), Hamilcar's unpunished sacrilege and religious masquerade match all his fraudulent double-deals and negotiations. Leenhardt (1992: 61) also puts Hamilcar firmly on the side of politics not religion as 'l'homme de l'échange' *par excellence*. His phallic stance and appropriation of position as biggest toe of the hierarchy, however, illustrate his primary allegiance to the cult of Man, to 'la sainte virilité' (Reynaud, 1981) and of himself, for 'l'intégration et l'identification à une hiérarchie est le principe de base des relations entre hommes dans le patriarchat' (ibid. 142). The apotheosis of power in *SAL*, Hamilcar represents Man, as king, emperor, supreme ruler, commander-in-chief. He can therefore only name himself tautologously, for each superlative title is the self-cancelling magnifier of the others: 'Et moi, Hamilcar Barca, Suffète-de-la-mer, Chef des Riches et Dominateur du peuple, devant Moloch-à-tête-de-taureau, je jure' (*SAL*, 160). This supreme oath, in the face of the accusation of his daughter's 'fall', is taken by extension with many natural, but all-consuming, liminal and fiery forces—deserts, meteors, volcanos—and erupts almost exactly in the middle of the novel. As with Moloch, Hamilcar's power and embodied presence are suppressed until the second half of *SAL*. However, his importance would seem the greater as he is in pivotal-power position; his eponymous chapter is at the centre of the novel and thus is its structuring fulcrum. Blood-brother with the fire of Moloch, Hamilcar has, however, further natural powers which come because of his supremacy equally over the sea. He is chief of a highly successful maritime civilization, his name doubly synonymous with it by the echo with its first syllable: HamilCAR BarCA/CARthage. As its chief admiral, there is a further tautology. The word 'amiral' entered French in the thirteenth century and comes from the Arabic, 'âmir' (like his name's first syllable), and means simply, 'chief'. He will later bring water to the besieged Carthage once the aqueduct has been destroyed, and it is this supremacy over water and knowledge of its vital force for power that makes Hamilcar almost omnipotent in his humanity, as symbolized by his ascent to the highest tower in Carthage and his purview of his empire, land and sea.

As figurehead and figuration of the Masculine as Great Man, Hamilcar's indomitable position as symbol of earthly power itself is established by the quasi-religious mystery he creates around himself by his frequent physical absence. His hold and control, knowledge and leadership, are none the less all-present by default. The opening and closing sentences of the novel encapsulate his overarching position by the place of his name as synonym and extension for everything of Carthage: 'C'était à Mégara, faubourg de Carthage, dans les jardins d'Hamilcar'; 'Ainsi mourut la fille d'Hamilcar pour avoir touché au manteau de Tanit'. Everywhere the possessive collocates with him and his rule, for example, 'le visage d'Hamilcar', 'les cuisines d'Hamilcar', 'le palais d'Hamilcar'. Patriarch potentate of his nation-state, he is also one of the novel's very few family heads, a lineage Salammbô proclaims before the Mercenaries. His untouchable, godlike, position outside the real affairs of men is, however, matched by the distance he keeps between his daughter and son. In fact, it is the real, secret power-game of hiding his personal intentions *vis-à-vis* his children for the continuation of his own empire that reveals the fundamental insecurities of patriarchy *à la* Hamilcar/Moloch. Children are pawns, not humans, and hence can be sacrificed at will on the individual or national scales:

> Son père n'avait pas voulu qu'elle entrât dans le collège des prêtresses, ni même qu'on lui fît rien connaître de la Tanit populaire. Il la réservait pour quelque alliance pouvant servir sa politique.   (*SAL*, 61)
>
> Elle lui était survenue après la mort de plusieurs enfants mâles. D'ailleurs, la naissance des filles passait pour une calamité dans les religions du Soleil. Les Dieux, plus tard, lui avaient envoyé un fils; mais il gardait quelque chose de son espoir trahi et comme l'ébranlement de la malédiction qu'il avait prononcée contre elle.   (*SAL*, 164)

The double standard he operates with Salammbô, hiding politics in religious justification, reveals his typical male rage and shame about his inability to produce sons, his misogynistic devaluations of the feminine, his use of Salammbô as symbol for the people of Carthage as he effectively keeps her imprisoned in his palace. His belatedly begotten son, Hannibal, is also imprisoned for political safe-keeping, but kept in the dark too about his real lineage by the slave Iddibal (who functions like Schahabarim for Salammbô, disguised in 'female' garb as a cover for their patriarchal loyalties, *SAL*, 144). In Flaubert's hallmarked style of detail, Hannibal's bloodline eventually comes out 'naturally' in his fearless prowess as warrior in the making. 'Junior' version of his father's Moloch slaying-machine, 'Il invente des pièges pour les bêtes farouches. L'autre lune . . . il a surpris un aigle . . . et à mesure qu'elle agonisait ses rires redoublaient, éclatants et superbes comme des chocs d'épées' (*SAL*, 144–5). Julien is not the only bloodthirsty boy hunter in Flaubert's fiction. The later secret exchange of another slave boy for Hannibal in the sacrifice to Moloch is but a further exchange of pawns in Hamilcar's hands, a trickster's sleight of hand because of superior power and knowledge.

On both the private and public fronts, Hamilcar operates according to the important principle that knowledge is power. But he illustrates (beyond Foucault) that such knowedge relies most on the withholding of it from other people. To this end, his intellectual weaponry includes threat, mystery, surprise but dazzlingly intense appearances, clever silence, having jokers always in his pack, and ensuring the cards are stacked against his opponents. He manifests himself and these traits when he first appears at dawn, which represents the point of rising from the sea of his planetary equivalent, the sun, to surprise the look-out and bedazzle: 'on aperçut auprès du pilote un homme debout, tête nue. . . . Il portait autour des flancs des lames de fer qui reluisaient; un manteau rouge s'attachant à ses épaules laissait voir ses bras; deux perles très longues pendaient à ses oreilles, et il baissait sur sa poitrine sa barbe noire, touffue' (*SAL*, 139). The castratory, sunray-like knives, the beard extension of male potency, combine with the jewels from the other part of his symbolic empire of power, the deeps of the sea. Standing, he resists stand-offs from other potential leaders in order to assert his supremacist position, most clearly seen on display at council meetings (also held in secret) in Moloch's temple.

Tous étaient savants dans les disciplines religieuses, experts en stratagèmes, impitoyables et riches. Ils avaient l'air fatigué par de longs soucis. Leurs yeux pleins de flammes regardaient avec défiance, et l'habitude des voyages et du mensonge, du trafic et du commandement, donnait à toute leur personne un aspect de ruse et de violence, une sorte de brutalité discrète et convulsive. D'ailleurs, l'influence du Dieu les assombrissait. (*SAL*, 148)

Hamilcar is the most high male, the superlative of these patriarchs gathered *en bloc* because of his superior guile, his control of ritual and rhetoric which is every bit as bloody as the battle tactics he also excels in. Redrawing and maintaining power requires calculated risk and the ability to call the other's bluff or expose his weakness. The above blueprint of the characteristics of ruling patriarchy demonstrates the negative, toughly competitive, and remorselessly ruthless masculinity this entails. Hamilcar has to 'better' this by being even more evil: hyperbolic in his terrible ingenuity, mephistophelean and machiavellian in the assessment of any chink, present or future, in the other's armour. Note the snake-like cicatrice between his brows made visible when he tears off his emerald crown and hurls it so that it smashes on the stone slabs (*SAL*, 159). The secret of his success is contained in his brutally simple manifesto: 'il faut être plus ingénieux ou plus terrible! Si l'Afrique entière rejette votre joug, c'est que vous ne savez pas, maîtres débiles, l'attacher à ses épaules' (*SAL*, 154). Both imperviousness to pity and extreme double-dealing are Hamilcar's hallmarks, from his refusal to pay the Mercenaries, his checking-up on all his officials, and the monopolies he foresees as useful, to his later plans, such as being the sole owner of all the grain in Carthage. Hamilcar thus proves unassailable on campaigns away because he has subjugated powers at home. Supreme duper, he is quick to spot and punish any treachery he comes across, with the zeal of an Inquisitor on a single or mass scale to make an example of any who might try such tactics again.

This reign of terror is the other side of the same coin of his military tactics, a combination of the terrible beauty of big war-machines, double-phalanged mathematical field formations, and the stealth, ambush, and guile of guerilla warfare quintessentially reliant on the absence of his men so as to sow fear, suspicion, anxiety, and rumour in the enemy and weaken them psychologically. The Macar ambush at night even shocks Spendius in its brilliance, and is the prelude to the terrible and simple ambush in the Défilé de la Hache, the expression on a large scale of Hamilcar's ruthless exchange of his slave's son for his own: human life, except his own, is expendable. What wins Hamilcar the war against the Mercenaries is not sheer force or might, but his military intelligence, his reform of his army to ensure their machine-like obedience and precision, his alliance with a rival to ensure reinforcements not only in terms of men but in Punic allegiance so that the strike from a potential enemy within is turned to concerted attack on the enemy without.

Such a reign of terror of course strikes chords with the aftermath of the French Revolution. In that Hamilcar synthesizes and magnifies the ruthless power of a Sun King, a Robespierre, a Napoleon I, it is not the colour of politics which counts. Flaubert has painted in Hamilcar not a fictional reconstruction of the actual leader, but the portrait of the politics of potentates from time immemorial. This figure questions what the human cost to civilization such leadership entails as empires rise and ultimately fall because their excesses and excessive limits overstretch natural capacities. In all his stances, Hamilcar represents the Phallus not as transcendental, but transcending signifier.

The master–slave basis for power in *SAL* paradoxically ensures the survival of the fittest in all ranks, and serves the principle of competition inherent in such hierarchies of the masculine. With nothing whatever to lose and everything to gain, the thrusting, wily Spendius, while at the bottom of the ladder, is frequently seen in high places, like the top of aqueducts. While rank, wealth, and physique may clearly classify them at opposite extremes of the chain of command or the masculine, Spendius is strangely similar to Hamilcar. The other inherent qualities of successful patriarchal power as listed above for the Anciens are all abundantly present in this thoroughly masculine Roman and are signalled not least by the Latin, '-ius', ending of his name. There may be an intentional pun as well. 'Spondere' means 'to swear allegiance to', which fits Spendius' faithful and fickle double nature. Disdainful, unscrupulous, adept liar, trafficker, active user of every situation for his own ends, trickster, Spendius compensates for his puny form with natural courage and quick thinking, quick-talking, arrogance not unlike that of Hamilcar.[4] The only strategic male character of *SAL* not to have a chapter dedicated to him, he none the less circulates and shuttles throughout the novel between its two

---

[4] For a detailed analysis of 'traduction' and treacherous exchanges in *SAL*, see Cozea (1990). The trickster is a well-known figure in alchemy and myth. See e.g. Makarius (in Maffesoli and Bruston, 1979: 125–6). He discusses the trickster as 'un être sacré' and this is 'pourquoi sa vie est un tissu de violations, d'interdits, pourquoi il est aussi le héros culturel, l'inventeur des outils, le donateur du feu, le transformateur de la nature. Et pourquoi l'excès, l'obscénité, la cruauté font partie de son personnage'. Spendius clearly fulfils all these functions on the side of Moloch (Culture) against Nature (Tanit) and also as a pseudo-Hermes figure, messenger of the new gods, and of the Roman empire.

oppositional leaders, Mâtho and Hamilcar. If the latter is of the lineage of rulers, Spendius has no legal heritage as the illegitimate son of a prostitute and the 'fils d'un rhéteur grec'. Being a 'nothing' in social terms, bastard and slave, he has nothing to lose except his life. This gives him total freedom to affiliate himself with any group or person who will bring him social advance. Much of his motivation is revenge: his hatred of the Légion Sacrée causes him to incite the Mercenaries to defile their sacred cups; his captivity and lacerations in the ergastule will lead him to kill others without pity in order to maintain his freedom. (His master, Mâtho, will of course, outdo Spendius' tortured and bleeding body in the sacrifical tortures which crown his career at the end of the novel, thus completing an inversion of the master–slave relation on a symbolic plane.) His previous position prior to the story proper as slave-trader in women for prostitution maps his path out of his own slavery, for he will have a similar plan to placate the Mercenary leaders and save his own skin by asking the Carthaginian Grand Council to repay with their virgins of high birth (*SAL*, 76). His hatred of women is altogether apparent in this and in his contempt for Mâtho's fascination with Salammbô. For Spendius, anything 'feminine', like love, is utterly to be despised.

Spendius has a clear idea of what is virile, however, and consequently what is non-virile. Antisocial, but homosocial for his own purposes, he uses all the lessons of life to advance his plans. Vautrin-like, he wheedles and commands Mâtho into action ('A Carthage!'), into the quest of the Holy Veil (the zaïmph), but as an act of political sabotage, rape, and pillage, though not to 'get the girl' (which is Mâtho's quest). Spendius' repeated calls to action are always calls to destructive acts, to violence, often overreactive, sacrilegious, and inflationary because they are so hyper-virile and compensatory of the manhood he has not been born to, but which he lives vicariously through Mâtho, the warrior who constantly wants to slip out of his role: 'Laisse aller ta colère comme un char qui s'emporte . . . Crie, blasphème, ravage et tue. La douleur s'apaise avec du sang, et puisque tu ne peux assouvir ton amour, gorge ta haine; elle te soutiendra!' (*SAL*, 70) While Bizer (1995: 987) rightly stresses the significant use of invective in *SAL*:

'Conformément aux haines et aux craintes terribles qui animent la plupart des personnages principaux, le roman est rempli d'invectives, d'anathèmes et de malédictions', in this speech we learn more of Moloch- and Hamilcar-like motives in Spendius. It mirrors both the vocabulary of the immolation of the children ('assouvir', 'gorge') and the 'dominus' position of Hamilcar, especially in his angry reaction to the slight to his daughter's honour. We shall see Hannon react very similarly as compensation for his impotence. Antagonistic force is clearly the only method whereby one conquers, either another man, an army, or a nation. Spendius uses the same antonymical and inimical vocabulary to incite Mâtho to steal the veil: 'Mais Tanit est ton ennemie . . . elle te persécute, et tu meurs de sa colère. Tu t'en vengeras. Elle t'obéira. Tu deviendras presque immortel et invincible' (*SAL*, 91). Spendius' root of hatred against the female as potentially all-engulfing and his overt misogyny include defiance and penetration of the Female in symbolic form—the city of Carthage and the goddess Tanit in his 'mission' to take her veil. Rivalry coupled with hatred forms the heady brew of negative energy which enables him to individuate himself, as seen most clearly in his single-handed sabotage of the aqueduct and in his demonic inventiveness at making penetrative siege-engines capable of destroying his real enemy, Carthage, with a force far beyond his physical being. We shall see a development of this negative power and invective in consideration of the curse and the prophetic in *H*.

Spendius also has many of Homais's traits. Social climber, toadying, self-promoting, vociferous, desirous of the luxuries and acceptance of ranks above him, able to manipulate the rhetorics of false praise, he too has a criminal past, the double of his profession. 'Transfuge' from the Roman army and therefore a traitor, his treacheries, trickeries, and yet peculiar fidelity to Mâtho are not conflicting but integral facets of his operation. Speaker of Greek (inherited from his 'rhéteur' father), Ligurian, and Punic (through various services), Spendius is the translator ('traducteur') across groupings of the mercenary army and traducer of Hannon's words about their non-payment. He is a leader through words at all junctures, whether this is taking over command of Mâtho's inertia, or taking initiatives when he has the linguistic upper hand, or literally taking over ('trans-mission'), as he leads Mâtho across the aqueduct on the mission into the heart of Carthage. Spendius takes this prominent channel of communications, then sabotages it later. This double-dealing with media is therefore constant in his character. Immoral and amoral, nothing matters except his end in sight, for nothing and no one are sacred. His boastful mouth makes up for any lack in his physical stature, and like Hamilcar, he has the guile of the serpent: 'Je peux, comme une vipère me couler entre les murs' (*SAL*, 20). Invidious and insidious, Spendius' hallmark is infiltration, the mark of the 'parvenu' of the same brand as Homais. Literally and metaphorically he will slip between blocks where a large physique would be detrimental. In the Défilé de la Hache, he unscrupulously hides physically from the other Mercenaries as cannibalism becomes necessary, and then hides his selfish survivalist discovery with words. Having found a plant to eat, he tells all the others it is poisonous. He always knows instinctively how to gauge pecking-orders to save his own skin, and the only point where he is rendered powerless and speechless is the parley with Hamilcar after the Défilé de la Hache. He is forced to acknowledge Hamilcar's ultimate and complete linguistic superiority, perhaps himself in mirror image, so that he is unable to kill him. This recognition has the force of a quasi-religious experience, so overwhelming is it: 'Lui! fit Spendius; et il répéta plusieurs fois: Lui! lui! comme si la chose eût été impossible et Hamilcar quelqu'un d'immortel. . . . Spendius tomba évanoui sur la natte' (*SAL*, 372). Hamilcar's presence and sparing use of words strike him so deeply that he can only repeat, babble, and stammer where normally his loquaciousness and linguistic dexterity carry him through.

Competition cannot be anything but supreme individualism and selfishness, refusal of community and family. In Spendius' experience, one is either conqueror or conquered, master or slave. His last verbal denunciation to save his, and only by implication the Mercenaries', skin lays blame on Hannon whom he knows to be Hamilcar's enemy. Verbal catalyst of the final elephant attack and *coup de grâce* of the Punic Wars, Spendius cannot buy grace for himself from one even more ruthless and verbally adept than he. His punishment is crucifixion with Zarxas and Autharite in a black parody of the thief alongside

Christ. Spendius is thus eradicated from the novel, and its empirical order, because slaves cannot yet conquer masters, and Mâtho's greater destiny has still to come. However, true to character, he leaves the novel as he enters it, talking: 'Te rappelles-tu les lions sur la route de Sicca?' (*SAL*, 387). His comment not only implies his pseudo-victory by comparison with the crucified lions (animal symbol of rulers, not slaves). The world of real barbarism is the Carthaginian one, and Spendius, as Roman prefiguration of a civilization to come, heralds in the ultimate demise of Carthage and all Hamilcar's victorious machinations. Indeed, the polarized terms, victory–defeat, life–death are demonstrated to be the same continuum from two vantage-points. Hamilcar and Spendius represent the motivating and interchangeable forces of patriarchy, with everything to gain or lose for success and survival. Polarized and hierarchized patriarchy is a body with a Janus head: an imperial face of rights, rites, and privileges to maintain, a democratic face of rights and privileges to grasp, as the next chapter on *ES* investigates.

Such hyper-virile constructions of masculinity as Moloch, Hamilcar, and Spendius are not all-conquering. *SAL* is too carefully constructed a cross-section and vivisection of hyperbolized masculinity, grounded in warrior-prowess physique and intelligence, to omit figures embodying the negative aspects and import of 'la sainte virilité': weaknesses and illnesses, failures, impotence and sickness, marginality. The Barbares and Mercenaries demonstrate how these truncations, mutilations, and castrations are written on the male body *en masse*, just as the second-rank leaders, Hannon, Schahabarim, Narr'Havas, are all stigmatized in different ways. As extensions of the spiritual or earthly rulers, they bear the physical stigmata of patriarchy's corporeal and corporate problems.

Schahabarim is, with Narr'Havas, a vaunting winner-loser, particularly at the close of the novel. In the second rank of men with Hannon, feminizing elements are more apparent and almost more virulently policed. All three are intermediaries between higher authority and those under them. All three resist congress with women except as symbolic channels to further enhancement of their own superior male power. The High Priest of Tanit enjoys considerable authority as the first syllable of his name implies; 'shah' comes from the Persian for 'king'.

However, the repetitive, almost self-mocking, 'ha-ba' of the remainder of his name extends his derisory masculinity—he is a eunuch—and flags up his chief character-trait, derision of (hetero)sexuality particularly when it is embodied in superb male form such as Mâtho's. As High Priest of Tanit, a position gained by long initiation, and guardian of Hamilcar's daughter as extension of the all-important Tanit cult to the people of Carthage, Schahabarim is fully aware of the problematic sexual theogony and form of this god(dess). As I have outlined in response to Forrest-Thomson's heterosexual reading (1972: 796) of the following quotation from *SAL* (Orr, 1995–6), there is a strongly coded homoerotic validation of superior love: 'Elle inspire et gouverne les amours des hommes . . . les Baals hermaphrodites ne se dévoilent que pour nous seuls, hommes par l'esprit, femmes par la faiblesse' (*SAL*, 64). Mirroring Hamilcar, Schahabarim relies on secret knowledge and rhetorical economy to keep the full truth hidden for his own ends, which are alliances with other powers, with a woman chosen to be the sacrifice in the deal. Salammbô will go to retrieve the veil and lose both herself and Mâtho to the rising cult of Moloch by which Schahabarim, too, will gain ascendency as 'veiled man' (Orr, 1997). Like Spendius, he stakes all to climb by affiliation into male ranks, but via a religious route of authorities. There is nothing quaintly exotic, fantastic, or unvirile about the description of his lengthy training. Like Phanuel in *H*, his search for wisdom and the essences includes travel, ritual deeds of bravery, and initiations throughout the regions and religions of the known world, hiding post-Copernican science in a pseudo-alchemical orientalism:

Personne à Carthage n'était savant comme lui. Dans sa jeunesse, il avait étudié au college des Mogbeds, à Borsippa, près Babylone; puis visité Samothrace, Pessinunte, Ephèse, la Thessalie, la Judée, les temples des Nabathéens . . . et, des cataractes jusqu'à la mer, parcouru à pied les bords du Nil. La face couverte d'un voile, et en secouant des flambeaux, il avait jeté un coq noir sur un feu de sandaraque, devant le portail du Sphinx, le Père-de-la-Terreur. Il était descendu dans les cavernes de Proserpine; . . . avec des armilles placés dans le portique d'Alexandrie, il avait observé les équinoxes . . . si bien que maintenant grandissait dans sa pensée une religion particulière, sans formule distincte . . . toute pleine de vertiges et d'ardeurs. Il ne croyait plus la

terre faite comme une pomme de pin; il la croyait ronde . . . De la position du soleil au-dessus de la lune, il concluait à la prédominance de
Baal, dont l'astre lui-même n'est que le reflet et la figure; d'ailleurs,
tout ce qu'il voyait des choses terrestres le forçait à reconnaître pour
suprême le principe mâle exterminateur.   (*SAL*, 236–7)

Revenge on Tanit for his physical castration and position of
impotence *vis-à-vis* the properly male divine order is first
rechannelled through Salammbô's overtly female and vestal
virgin body, sacrificed to the power of earthly male dominion.
Released of vestigial 'femininity', Schahabarim has then to pass
into the all-male religion of Moloch. The problem is that his
emasculation debars him from Moloch's orders: 'imberbe', he is
automatically excluded by the bearded priests of Moloch. This
further humiliation of his manhood, in spite of the fact that he
has committed apostasy in Moloch's temple, calls for his double
revenge which mirrors the pattern of the stars. Tanit's hermaphrodite inferiority has been proven when Salammbô has returned
with the sacred veil, deflowered, and yet Carthage remains
besieged because of Mâtho's indubitable spiritual maleness.
Although the female of the moon is conquered, the male of the
moon, Mâtho, lives. As female Tanit-conqueror through union
with Salammbô, Mâtho embodies the symbolic male face of
Tanit, and Schahabarim needs to rid himself of all moon
vestiges to allow the sun full force. The perfect sacrifice is the
treacherous heart which loved a woman and was inspired and
governed by Tanit. By rooting this out, Schahabarim's own religious change of heart, in this sacrificial act of the fanatical
convert, can be made visible to all Moloch's priesthood. Hence
the cloak really covering Tanit's veil, the source of light lighting
up its colours, is Moloch—which Salammbô has indeed
touched. Salammbô therefore has to die in the face of a male-
only ritual where vaunting homicidal Moloch patriarchy wins
out over anything of mediating Tanit—heterosexuality, union,
eventual paternity. Schahabarim in the end makes worship of
the (destructive) male principle of civilization and barbarism
overt and supreme over the male making of love or war.

   If Schahabarim becomes the negative human religious extension of 'Moloch-le-homicide', emasculated worshipper of the
Phallus, Hannon is the negative extension of Carthage's political force for extermination. His name shares its first syllable

with its ruler, Hamilcar, but the second underlines the negative side of this shared power-base. Hannon is an 'Ancien' politically and in years, often designated as 'le vieux Suffète'. Former establisher of colonies for Carthage and still a commander of its armies, Hannon is both historically sourced (See Renaudin, 1979–80, and Bizer, 1995) and fictionally drawn, most notably in the descriptions of his physical person. Past his prime, slow, old, and sick physically, he often arrives too late. His body and character are the negative of the patriarchal myth and image of great warrior leaders, for ever young, handsome, virile, with superlative brain and brawn. Like an overripe fruit, Hannon's physical form and despotic power are on the verge of decay, so that he becomes richly the embodiment of the unhealthy underbelly of virile belligerence and domination forged in pain and 'rancune'.

Blood is the quintessential symbolic male stuff of power in *SAL*. 'Malsain', Hannon is the negation of Hamilcar's republic of the 'mâle sain' and uses the fresh 'sang' of hostages as one of many cures to assuage his skin complaints (*SAL*, 135). An old veteran, his illness is constantly overlooked by the Anciens because Hannon's blue blood, wealth, and lineage preserve him where his impotence of various kinds would not. His experience and his elephants are invaluable but they are bought at a price: the negative consequences of waning power. Hannon is a thoroughly fascinating study of why illnesses and their compensatory masculinities are permitted and excused in world leaders and thus why old despots are propped up by imperialist or authoritarian regimes.[5] Hence, at times of threat to national security, internal conflicts and rivalries are patched up to be harnessed against external forces. The egos of seasoned and solid leaders past their prime are flattered, especially rich and useful ones, whom, as expendable assets, the nation can use as resources until they run out.

---

[5] Sick world leaders clinging to power are no better exemplified currently than in Syria's Hafez-el-Assad, Saudi Arabia's Fahd ibn Abd al-Aziz, Iraq's Saddam Hussein and Libya's Gaddafi. The Orient is of course no different from the Occident, the point Flaubert is making in *SAL*. Take Pope John Paul II or Russia's Boris Yeltsin, who has managed to outlast in power America's Ronald Reagan and France's François Mitterrand. For a fascinating examination of sick despots, see Pierre Accoce, 'Ces Malades qui gouvernent le Monde', *L'Express* (23–9 July 1998). I need not point out that all these regimes are patriarchal.

Hannon embodies in abundance this extreme solidity (as positive and negative) that has its uses in times of volatile national crisis. To conscript forces from his enemies the Anciens, yet preserve his own power and authority, Hamilcar uses Hannon as a buffer: 'A lui seul il se chargeait de la guerre, du gouvernement et des finances; et afin de prévenir les accusations, il demanda comme examinateur de ses comptes le suffète Hannon' (*SAL*, 189–90). Accountant and bureaucrat par excellence, solid and ponderous in method and speech as well as in body, his style is rightly described by Bizer (1995: 978) as 'gras', 'style de la torpeur, de la lenteur et de la lourdeur'. Hamilcar would seem to allow double standards when it serves State interests, for he refuses to recruit the Suffète's lookalikes, soldiers from among the sedentary, or those 'qui avaient le ventre trop gros' (*SAL*, 189). Hannon's is of course positively enormous, a true underbelly or several. Hippopotamus-like, because of his illness, venality and self-indulgence, Hannon's body speaks of inflationary excess and corporeal self-aggrandizement, and everything he does he does to hyperbolic degree. This is part of the negative state of his solid, immobile, powerlessness (he has to be carried everywhere in a litter or on an elephant), powerfully magnified by his investment in big projects (which often never move anywhere). His chief accountant's and head bureaucrat's mind has, like two sides of a coin, positives and negatives in equal measure:

C'était un homme dévot, rusé impitoyable aux gens d'Afrique, un vrai Carthaginois. Ses revenus égalaient ceux des Barca. Personne n'avait une telle expérience dans les choses de l'administration.

Il décréta l'enrôlement de tous les citoyens valides, il plaça des catapultes sur les tours, il exigea des provisions d'armes exorbitantes, il ordonna même la construction de quatorze galères dont on n'avait pas besoin; et il voulut que tout fût enregistré, soigneusement écrit. Il se faisait transporter à l'arsenal, au phare, dans le trésor des temples . . . Dans son palais . . . pour se préparer à la bataille, il hurlait, d'une voix terrible, des manœuvres de la guerre.

Tout le monde, par excès de terreur, devenait brave. . . . Utique avait déjà réclamé plusieurs fois les secours de Carthage. Mais Hannon ne voulait point partir tant que le dernier écrou manquait aux machines de la guerre. Il perdit trois lunes à équiper les cent douze éléphants . . . Hannon fit refondre les plaques d'airain dont on garnissait leur poitrail, dorer leurs défences. (*SAL*, 119–21)

Weight is all to him—authority, wealth, the force of 120 elephants, the massive siege engines as Moloch extension—but it leads to ponderous, inflexible thinking, stubborn adherence to authority and tradition (the elephants may only appear in national dress). When swift immediate reponse is required, Hannon always chooses (the bureaucratic) summation which will inevitably take longer and hence in many cases be impractical and irrelevant: the one screw missing (as cited above) is one extreme of this tendency; the other is 'des mesures atroces et impracticables, comme de promettre une forte somme pour chaque tête de Barbare' (*SAL*, 71). Hannon's implacability before the plight of the unpaid Mercenaries at the beginning of the novel is typical of his tram-line thinking and mentality. His speech is wrapped in uselessly ponderous, self-important, and florid prose which omits not one single statistic of State expenditure (*SAL*, 44, 47). Its weight of irrelevance, boredom, and incomprehensibility is one of the catalysts to the Punic Wars and it is Spendius' quick-thinking (mis)translation which wins the day. Hannon's intolerance and intransigence, however, in typically juggernaut proportions, do achieve victory in certain circumstances. While his legion guards on their '*gros* chevaux' (with battle-trappings on their heads resembling a rhinoceros horn), his '*lourde* infanterie', his cohort of grotesquely over-spiky merchants 'comme des *porcs-épics*, étaient *hérissés* de dards', his overcumbersome engines which include 'onagres' (wild asses and catapults) and 'scorpions' (*SAL*, 127, my emphasis), all contribute to an unwieldy army which the Barbares easily pick off as sitting ducks. Hannon wins this day only by his sheer physical presence harnessed with the force and weight of his elephants. These trample under foot all who are in the way. Elephant Man *par excellence* conquers this time because he plays the brawn game to its maximum potential. The writing is, however, on the wall. Sheer weight will not win out against more flexible strategies and tactics. It will be his toppling over-weight which will inevitably bring his end, his death quickened when he is crucified because his huge, decaying, body only adds to the forces of its own self-destruction.

Symbolically, the many 'underbellies' of protruding skin and flesh Hannon possesses—'Des bandelettes, comme autour d'une momie, s'enroulaient à ses jambes, et la chair passait entre les linges croisés. Son ventre débordait sur la jaquette écarlate qui lui couvrait les cuisses; les plis de son cou retombaient jusqu'à sa poitrine comme des fanons de bœuf' (*SAL*, 44–5)—are the physical manifestations of the inflationary masculinities that are the hidden face of the order of Moloch. The deformities, extensions, monstrous growths the bloated simulacrum of an oriental body where fat is a sign of wealth, all speak of degeneration, the ugly side of male strength and physique, potency, and power. Yet even his hideousness still has its place in the male hierarchy as extension of the dominant violence; as scavenger—his nose is 'crochu comme le bec de vautour'—he leaves no bone unpicked. He is a destroyer as juggernaut and as pure vengeance. The places where he knew defeat, he eradicates—not just other flesh like his co-male counterparts of Moloch masculinity, but also the very earth, nature, in a scorched-earth policy which is the destruction of an impotent and dying man:

Les habitants et les Barbares étaient morts, cachés ou enfuis. Alors sa colère se déchargea sur la campagne. Il brûla les ruines des ruines, il ne laissa pas un seul arbre, pas un brin d'herbe . . . il donnait à ses soldats les femmes à violer avant leur égorgement; les plus belles étaient jetées dans sa litière—car son atroce maladie l'enflammait de désirs impétueux; il les assouvissait avec toute la fureur d'un homme désespéré. (*SAL*, 381)

Yet again we see the repeated 'assouvissements' of destructive, uncontrolled and unfettered masculinity with a misogyny and misanthropy that matches Hamilcar's, Spendius', Schahabarim's, but against nature in all senses of the term. Hannon is Excess and Orgy personified, excess defined by Bataille (1957: 47) as 'la violence l'emporte sur la raison' and that '[l]'origine de l'orgie, de la guerre et du sacrifice est la même: elle tient à l'existence d'interdits qui s'opposent à la liberté de la violence meurtrière ou de la violence sexuelle'.

The paradox is however that Hannon's body is obeying nature's course. In fact, it 'feminizes' him because, in order to cover the overinflationary 'health' of massive appetites of all kinds, the violently reactive behaviours of his skin demand covers and camouflage, a veil and make-up (*SAL*, 152). Physical descriptions of Hannon's body are more extensive than those of any of the other male protagonists in *SAL*, and from the outset his body is strangely parallel in a negative form not only to Moloch's, but also to Tanit's in size and in the rolls of fat and buddha-like inertia. Hannon's Carthaginian body with Tanit's moon symbols on his boots and on his breast(s) are the grotesque male form of Salammbô's equally veiled body and demonstrate the ambiguities of his body's defence mechanisms at war in his frame. This oozes fluids in alarmingly quasi-female ways; his mood-swings and weight-gain are 'menopausal' manifestations in male guise. Creature of the water, baths, and unguent treatments to relieve his complaints, Hannon is the human-animal version of the hippopotamus or elephant using mud for the same purposes. As metaphorical 'monstre marin', the last description of him, this overweening and overblown figure of both Moloch and Tanit in human male guise embodies the monstrous and decadent forms of masculinity; his illness is a metaphor for the decay of a nation on the brink of extinction like the race of the dinosaurs.

While money buys Hannon respect, power, and potency which cover over his failing physical masculinity, not even all the wealth of empire can save his broken skin with the Barbares. Hannon to the end bargains with his wealth to escape, but cannot avoid death itself. The Barbares' choice of Carthage's own most inhuman method, crucifixion, is especially fitting for this 'vrai Cathaginois'. Cantankerous male rage, like the angry cankers on his skin, meld together inflammation and violently reactive anger as the inner and outer manifestations of the doomed sick body patriarchal (Le Mâle); for his 'mal' is uncurable, out of control, and ultimately self-exterminating. Cabanes (1991: 210) names this disease as leprosy, as does Mullen Hohl (1995). My own interpretation of the cures that are recommended by his doctor—baths and tinctures—is that Hannon's disease is syphilis in its tertiary stages. Male overinflation personified, hypertrophy of organs and metaphors, Hannon is the lesson Hamilcar fails fully to recognize as he has difficulty recognizing the old Suffète's remains. Even all-vaunting masculinity has limits: of empire and mortality.

If Hannon, l'Ancien, epitomizes the monstrous and grotesque face of patriarchy, Narr'Havas represents its new, young, animal, blood. Thrust by his father into Carthage and Hamilcar's court from the peripheral margins of his territory to the centre of empire and to secure alliances (political and personal), Narr'Havas embodies second-degree masculinity in age, status, and stature; he is 'un jeune chef numide' of warrior force, but pales beside Mâtho's 'taille colosse'. Narr'Havas is a compound character in name and nature. Sharing the 'Ha' syllable with Carthaginian leadership and male power, his name is a pivotal term with 'nard' (oriental perfume) and 'hâve' (thin, pale, emaciated—like Schahabarim in his fasts) and these feminizing terms thus conjoin him to the ranks of the priest and Hannon. Indeed, his slightness and thinness, even girlishness, are emphasized not only in his adornments ('des courroies . . . serraient ses bras minces' (*SAL*, 112)), but in his figure in Salammbô's negatively comparative eyes at the end of the novel. In mufti, not warrior garb, wearing a long robe strikingly reminiscent of her own or Schahabarim's, '[c]e jeune homme à voix douce et à taille féminine captivait des yeux par la grâce de sa personne et lui semblait être comme une sœur aînée que les Baals envoyaient pour la protéger' (*SAL*, 380). The irony is that while Narr'Havas successfully fulfils his father's brief for him and 'gets the girl', he wins her only by default, as second best, and in fact never possesses her.

Narr'Havas's 'enivrement d'orgueil' as he seizes Salammbô's waist at the wedding, of which his father-in-law not he himself, has been the broker, sums up this character. His egotistical *amour propre* and ostentation find their fullest expression against this borrowed backdrop of masculine spectacle, pomp, and circumstance, in which Narr'Havas can now shine alone. His jealousy of Mâtho from the outset over Salammbô may have less in fact to do with sexual rivalry than with his pride because, after six months, his own beautiful person has not been noticed by her, whereas she notices Mâtho (who has the quintessential handsome male body) immediately. His pride at the end therefore is for himself, that he and Salammbô are the supreme, 'beautiful people'.

Narr'Havas constantly seeks out situations for glory. Thus his composite and contradictory character is treacherous for its glittering superficiality. He attaches himself to whichever side is the winner of the moment and will show him off to best advantage. From the outset, his marginality and independence, and proclivity to disappear for long stretches to take glory at a later calculated moment, would seem to indicate a Hamilcar in the making. His own ego, however, the youthful selfishness which is fickle in friendships (although he swears blood-brother allegiance with Mâtho, he betrays him, and ultimately 'nets' him as if he were an animal not an equal) and political allegiances, is a quintessential trait of his competitive desire to be the best. Torn between the need for, and the abhorrence of, male company, his audience, and competition, Narr'Havas provides a telling insight into the conflicting demands on maturing masculinity within the warrior framework. Much of his body- language speaks of the emphasis on the exterior aesthetics of the warrior, not innate attributes, making him even a potential artist-figure on the margins of society. He is particularly aware of his clothing as effect: 'ceinture était hérissée de dards, qu'elle faisait une bosse dans son large manteau, noué à ses tempes par un lacet de cuir . . . et l'on n'apercevait que les flammes de ses deux yeux fixes . . . et assis sur les talons . . . il la [Salammbô] considérait en écartant ses narines comme un léopard qui est accroupi dans les bambous' (*SAL*, 17–18). A camouflaged hunter who does not change his spots throughout the novel, Narr'Havas remains the solitary and most showy predatory big cat. A cloak-and-dagger operator (like Schahabarim who brings forth his sacrifical dagger-spatula from under the cloak of Moloch which is not quite his to wear), his claws come out to seize prey that others have long pursued. However, he does not realize that his liking for a place on the margins from which he can pounce, unthwarted, is an isolationist tactic which patriarchy will not suffer, except decoratively, alongside its more central concerns. Real power is displayed by pack predators such as lions according to open rules, not backstabbing, just as Narr'Havas's early attempt on Mâtho is thwarted by the company of the watchful understanding of his equally perfidious and fickle double, Spendius. Thus, entrepreneurial perfidy, from princes or slaves, is demonstratively second rank in the high stakes of the life-or-death power struggle at the heart of corporate patriarchy. The showy, individualizing leopard spots, derivative patterns of dress, and short-cut methods of achieving glory do not hoodwink Hamilcar, who knows marginal and superficial masculinity when he sees it.

Little critical attention has been paid to the 'Barbares' except negatively or in comparison with the Carthaginians. Bernard (1996: 114) for example sees them as 'cohues en furie ou les troupeaux abrutis'. The Barbares and Mercenaries none the less demonstrate their group individualities and corporate differences from the Carthaginians by degree. Bodies with critical mass—physically (for example *SAL*, 199–200) and metaphorically (they comment on the barbaric crucifixion and immolation practices)—they operate according to common purpose; they all understand and rise to the word 'frappe!' (*SAL*, 83). Separate entities, however, by race and tongue, they guard their particularizing customs, such as striking camp, and thus overcome potentially conflicting male interest because army unity serves their higher interests. In an analogy of nation-building, Flaubert uses this mixed international block of otherness of warrior masculinity to critique and confound 'united' Carthaginianism. The ethnic 'superiority' of the Carthaginians is implicitly undermined by the need to resort to racist or classist labels, such as the seemingly synonymous 'Mercenaires' or 'Barbares'. Men like, yet not like, their enemies are either semi-civilized when in Carthaginian employ, but inferior; or uncivilized hordes when they become Barbare enemies, but then equals in battle. The initial confusions readers may experience in discerning which side they are on at any time in the novel stem from this mutablity of status and the higher-level interchangeabilities of all the fighting men in *SAL*. There is in fact no radical difference between Carthaginian blood and other kinds, especially as cannon-fodder. In the Défilé de la Hache, mutilated male flesh is indistinguishable racially. Victories or defeats comprise the quantity not quality of shed blood and the power of one side to be more bloodthirsty (internecine) than the other. Dominant Carthaginian masculinity and Empire in *SAL* thus reveals its essential founding premiss: self-definition by blood. Not only does this explain the hierarchizations within its walls and between male and female. Racial purity is to be guarded from threats outside which could breach its sanguinary (self-) defences. This is most manifest when the Mercenaries, even though of many ethnic origins, are inside at the 'festin' and might mix their 'foreign' blood with the Carthaginians via their women. This 'métissage', not eradication in war, is the ultimate destructive threat to Carthage's racial purity, identity, and survival. By casting them outside their walls to become free-agent outsider 'Barbares'/the Enemy in the ensuing novel, the Carthaginians can then separate out male blood into unmixable kinds, making revaluation of superiority once more possible in the male–male terms of war. Thus, Carthage's polarization of civilized and barbaric in the enemy mirror constantly reflects back excessive similarity, especially with regard to massacred and mutilated flesh. These foreigners (the root meaning of 'barbare') are civilized when compared with the cruel, pitiless, inhuman (the pejorative meanings of 'barbare') acts of the Carthaginians who enact man's inhumanity to man. It is culture which creates difference, through xenophobia and homophobia. Carthage's practice of human sacrifice shows itself to be the unnatural transgression of cannibalism, just as consensual homosexual love, *in extremis*, is natural when compared to Hannon's perverted heterosexual couplings with non-consenting beautiful girls. The Barbares' choric reiteration in diverse tongues throughout, therefore, is that it is the other as 'almost-the-same', in second place moving up, which most threatens the hierarchy of power as the supremacy of empire. At its zenith (the hyperbolization of power itself) at the close of the novel, the ultimate reversal of Carthage's fortunes and decline are ensured.

Where the Mercenaries and Barbares challenge civilization's dichotomies *en masse,* Mâtho does so as supreme individual. Other, he can be sacrificed. Same, he provides the perfect surrogate. Prime, his perfection makes of him a synecdoche of pure barbarism. Hamilcar's arrogance eschews the gods but assumes his own hyperbolic stance of excellence above all men. By scapegoating his/the Enemy, and thus daemonizing/divinizing him, Hamilcar does not realize that in fact he is putting Mâtho in a category beyond his own as superlative, the epitome. Mâtho embodies a strange totality of male nature within Culture, the paradox of civilized man yet ostracized as its opposite. He has nothing to do with Carthage's doxas of 'civilization' yet everything to do with the thwarted apotheosis which, as ideal male part, he might forge with Salammbô, perfect female, in a symbolic and embodied match. Altogether male—'un Libyen de taille colossale', a fearsome warrior—there is nothing effeminate in Mâtho, yet he is happy in the so-called female positions of submission (religious and sexual) because his masculinity is not a defence against the feminine. The opening descriptions of him reclining at the 'festin' at Salammbô's feet underpin the Nature–Culture unity in his flesh and being. 'Il n'avait gardé que sa jaquette militaire, dont les lames d'airain déchiraient la pourpre du lit . . . Un collier à lune d'argent s'embarrassait dans les poils de sa poitrine' (*SAL*, 18). The silver moon-shaped torque, his mystical nature as well as his virility ('poils') make him a Tanit-like figure in human male guise even though s/he is the god(dess) of Carthage, his enemy. His bravery, courage, and superlative battle-skills throughout the novel are unquestioned, but he is not moved by the inflationary destructive forces of hatred (and homophobia) as are the best of the Carthaginians. Revenge certainly motivates all the warriors of *SAL* and one might argue that Mâtho's hatred and vengeance against Salammbô puts him on the same footing as the other misogynistic males discussed above. However, Mâtho's love of Salammbô lifts him onto a different plane and is part of his integration of, and struggle with, the archetypal feminine and the understanding of Eros in Thanatos. The 'petite mort' in his tent with Salammbô rends the veil of his understanding as he accepts the principle of loss for gain, thus preparing him for the final obscenity of the concluding sacrifice. It is here that his apotheosis as man—sexual, spiritual, symbolic—lifts him to the point of the Hero. This 'fin des fins', almost defying definition, describes the paradox of patriarchy itself. The sole possible salvific alternative to Hamilcar's version of patriarchy, Mâtho's Tanit- and Salammbô-inspired unifying masculinity, has to be eradicated so that patriarchy can maintain its power to divide and rule. Schahabarim's ritualized offering of the heart of Man (symbol of life and the sacred) exchanges his own surrogate emasculated Tanit manhood for Mâtho's virilized version. This intentional devirilization–revirilization for Moloch ('Civilization') through sacrifice of Mâtho is also Flaubert's, the offending male organ which can love is symbolically pierced on the nib of his pen.

Mâtho is never concerned with power because he is unaware of his own. A complete natural (*coincidentia*)—brave, heroic, and attractive by default not affect—Mâtho shows up by similarity and different reaction (*oppositorum*) the arrogant and counterfeit heroics of Narr'Havas, Hamilcar, Schahabarim, and the scheming power-gaming of Hannon and Spendius. Because his bravery is effortless, he is therefore open to others and moved by them as they cross his path, regardless of their 'status' on the male hierarchy. His ease and ability to follow Spendius, as well as to lead an army, are indicative of leadership unthreatened in its authority which Mâtho always takes up when circumstances demand. Being second hardly concerns him because he is innately first-order, the stuff heroes are made of.

Compared with the detailed descriptions of the other male protagonists, Flaubert's bionote of Mâtho is singular in *SAL* because it is a conflation of pure clichés from any epic hero's curriculum vitae:

Il était né dans le golfe des Syrtes. Son père l'avait conduit en pèlerinage au temple d'Ammon. Puis il avait chassé les éléphants dans les forêts des Garamantes. Ensuite, il s'était engagé au service de Carthage. On l'avait nommé tétrarque à la prise de Drépanum. La République lui devait quatre chevaux, vingt-trois médines de froment et la solde de l'hiver. Il craignait les Dieux et souhaitait mourir dans sa patrie.   (*SAL*, 32)

In equal measures are active and passive response, leader and led, giver and taker. Unlike the other defensive, calculating, male protagonists, Mâtho (like Charles) is altogether content with whatever fate deals him and thus freed to be in life's adventure. Supremely the adventurer, the free-spirit alternative of the warrior—he also embodies the old meaning of 'aventurier' as 'soldat volontaire, mercenaire, corsaire, pirate' (*Petit Robert*)— Mâtho is unafraid of danger, risk, or death. And as with all heroes of the 'roman de cape et d'épée', there is the due measure of love interest with the prettiest girl, interleaved with daring feats and rescues, incursions into enemy territory and castles (the fortifications of Carthage). Mâtho replicates the positive life-force and energy of the genre, its endorsement of the future, and the cathartic purposes of its dénouement of victorious outcomes and vanquished villains. The twist Flaubert brings to *SAL* is to combine adventure and mission with the ideological historical novel and to write the story of a quest into manhood framed by patriarchy's bid to extinguish all that this adventure stands for.

Mâtho thus shares the same role and ending as the unlikely Charles in a different context. As mediator between male Nature and Culture, he is patriarchy's quintessential scapegoat. 'In Jungian terms, scapegoating is a form of denying the shadow of both man and God' (Perera, 1986: 9). While for Hilliard (1993) Mâtho rejects patriarchy, but as Freudian, pre-Oedipal, instinctive child, it seems clear, rather, that he does so by embodying adult male emotional response to the drives of 'virtu', love, and death. Moreover, as Romeo figure (Green, 1989: 170), he incarnates all that is reaction to overweening hypermasculinity and its deviant elevation of power over relationship. Where Charles represented this reaction within domestic *coniunctio*, the couple as male and female principles, the cosmic, cosmological dimensions of *SAL* allow the *coincidentia oppositorum* or myth of totality to find expression in Mâtho. Prefiguring Antoine at the end of *TSA*, Mâtho is 'mat-ière', and the fire which burns Salammbô in his tent. In an intriguing exploration of the primordial elements, Eliade (1962: 111) states that '[l]e feu "naît" des ténèbres ou de la matière opaque comme d'une matrice chthonienne, et il rampe comme un serpent . . . Autrement dit, il est présenté comme un Ouroboros, image à la fois de la conjonction des extrêmes et de la totalité primordiale.' Mâtho offers a fictional representation of this creative force. His name further speaks of this union of opposites, winner and loser, in the game to the death of patriarchal conflict. 'Mat' means death; '(xiiᵉ; arabe *mât* «mort») Se dit, aux Échecs, du roi qui est mis en échec et ne peut plus quitter sa place sans être pris' (*Petit Robert*). The etymology of 'mat', 'echec', is the modification of the old arabic *eschac* 'arabopersan *shâh*, dans l'express. *shâh mat* «le roi est mort» ' (ibid.). The ending of *SAL* in Mâtho is therefore a double checkmate in the game of empire, to Schahabarim (religion) and Hamilcar (imperialism). Both have to remove him from the chess board to maintain their own positions.

The hyper-male epic of 'Moloch-le-Homicide' unleashed by Hamilar mid-point in the novel becomes a new tale of Prometheus, the fire he wrested from the gods spreading with gathering momentum as a catalogue of carnage, massacre, homicidal destruction, immolation. The denouement seems to vaunt the nineteenth-century spirit of success and scientific

progress with its technologically beautiful methods of mechanizing or ritualizing death by taking it into male hands and leaving nothing to Fate. *SAL* almost outdoes the form of the
paradigmatic novel itself in its unrelenting causes and effects,
and control in tying up all the ends. The representations of the
masculine uncovered above, while three different categories in
this patriarchy, none the less endorse the overall significance of
the male principle over the female. Indeed, *SAL* reveals all three
as also figures of rhetoric undergirding the peculiarly remote
and excessive style of *SAL*. The primary characters are transpo-
sitions of inflation as hyperbole (Moloch, Hamilcar, Spendius),
while its related trope, *pars pro toto* that is extension (not as
Reichler, 1985, interprets it in *SAL* as fetish within a Freudian
frame of reference), covers the second-rank characters,
Schahabarim, Hannon, Narr'Havas; this then bears direct relation to the third figure, synecdoche (incorporation or encapsu-
lation), Mâtho. *SAL*'s complex rhetoric of the phallic, as
'phallotext' (Schor, 1985: 28), is a stylized, orchestrated, and
hierarchized *summa* summed up perhaps in the novel's very
closing words, '*le manteau* de Tanit' (my emphasis). Is this
metaphorical cloak a figurative phallic signifier in *SAL*,
subsuming its prior and exchangeable metonymic variant '*le
zaïmph*' as symbolic foreskin (as I have previously elucidated,
Orr, 1995–6)? If so, then figuration, disfiguration, and transfig-
uration of the masculine (my three categories of male characters
in this chapter) are all equally and essentially *Le* Verbe made
fictional flesh. Flaubert, their creator, would then seem entirely
complicitous with this male power structure, male style, and
hyper-male form of novel in epic proportions.[6]

But there is a coda. Hamilcar's defeat of Mâtho is a hollow
pseudo-victory, not merely because the historical conquest of

---

[6] Starr (1985: 48) presents a male critic's endorsement that 'the pleasure
Flaubert takes in writing is first and foremost a pleasure of mastery'. Many women
critics, e.g. Tondeur (1989), castigate Flaubert for his censorship of fluid, 'female',
style both in Louise Colet and in himself. Schor (1985: p. xii) is overtly feminist in
reminding readers of the essential parody or '*patriody*' of any woman's speech
because it is always already patriarchal. With reference to *SAL*, Bem (1980: 31)
concludes that 'le langage est toujours ce dieu dévorateur que l'Artiste approvi-
sionne de sa chair', while L. Lowe (1986: 57) highlights that Flaubert's 'mastery of
the "femme/machine" of the oriental woman . . . founds the male authorial voice'.

Carthage by Rome lies imminently just beyond the end of the novel. Within it, Salammbô's willed death, her 'heroine-ism' after Mâtho's, closes the novel and is her *coincidia oppositorum*. Picking up from her active conquest of Mâtho to retrieve the veil from his tent, and the *coniunctio* of their physical union of opposites under the cloak of the zaïmph, her timing of her 'suicide' (*coincidentia*) robs Narr'Havas and her father (*oppositorum*) of her earthly body in the marriage brokerage of patriarchy. It also elevates her mystic union with Mâtho in his tent to a sacred marriage in death and offers at the same time an alternative pseudo-sacramental ending to a tale to undermine the deterministic power of 'Moloch the sacrilegious'.

'Ainsi mourut la fille d'Hamilcar pour avoir touché au manteau de Tanit' has been interpreted literally to mean that Salammbô's death is punishment for sacrilege against the goddess and her loss of virginity at Mâtho's hands, a necessary sacrifice of Woman to male principles. What has not been appreciated is the irony that the very last word of this novel of male power is 'Tanit' and that this is the symbolic end to the story beyond its point of closure, the 'return of the repressed'. The penultimate sentence, 'Elle retomba, la tête en arrière, par-dessus le dossier du trône, — blême, raidie, les lèvres ouvertes, — et ses cheveux dénoués pendaient jusqu'à terre', reverberates with parallel physical details from Salammbô's visit to Mâtho's tent, although there it is Mâtho who is 'blême'. It is the alternative tale of Tanit, unfolding its imagery and circular structure of the tail of the tale, that brings the novel back full circle (the ouroboros) to its beginnings.

Not enough attention has been paid to Salammbô's song during the opening 'festin' of the hero Melkarth, who prefigures Mâtho and sets forth the Saga of Tanit which counterpoints the epic throughout. He repeats her words verbatim later, 'becoming' her by imitating her tone and hand movements. Throughout *SAL*, Mâtho and Salammbô frequently echo and repeat one another in word and deed. The exchange of the 'voile' provides the dynamic of the parallel Tanit tale which does not climax in the episode of the tent, but is driven by higher cosmic forces to bring to fruition their death as couple at the very end of the novel. Leenhardt (1992: 34) has come closest to a mythic, Jungian, reading of *SAL* by acknowledging the double logic of the novel, but as two opposing economies: 'le système traditionnel du don et du religieux' and 'le système moderne politique de l'échange'. I would argue that because both Salammbô and Mâtho have been enveloped in mystical initiations, and in the exchange of the zaïmph, both submit to the most powerful forces of desire, Nature, transcendence, Eros (Tanit), and Thanatos (Moloch). Their different individual quantities are therefore not oppositional, but complement, challenge, and transform the other as in the alchemist's alambic.

The tent, then, is like the ambiguous male–female space of Tanit's temple (Orr, 1995–6) modified into warrior male-Tanit mode: 'avec un mât dressé au milieu' (*SAL*, 258); it is an outer contextualization of Mâtho's inner being. Salammbô penetrates this intimate space as he has her Carthage bedroom, so that passive and active male–female roles are also reversed. The episode in the tent, however, operates a second set of reversals beyond the roles of giver–taker, active–passive agent, to the place where such polarities are taken up into unities, mutual self-giving, and passion. It is Mâtho's transformations in the tent which are as much a figurative breaking of the male chains of patriarchal power and command as Salammbô's ankle-chain, snapped in two by this incident. The outcome of these transformations through the private symbolic realm (love) into the public 'real' happens in the Tanit ending of the novel in death. Both protagonists are centre-stage in their self-immolation to the higher symbolic and mythic order of unity, harmony, and concord. Their paradoxical discovery of exalted manhood or womanhood arises out of consubstantive experience in the natural and transcendence of master–slave hierarchies and dichotomies by sex, class, or race in the earthly or symbolic orders. Mâtho's ease with Spendius or Salammbô 'in control' prefigures his transfigured virility at the hands of Schahabarim (Moloch) to join with Salammbô in their apotheosis under 'le manteau de Tanit'.

In parallel with the 'too-early' wedding in *MB* and the challenge to write the novel of the 'after' of the traditional 'happy-ever-after', *SAL* ups the stakes of the cosmic-symbolic dimensions of the romance or epic by positioning union at the beginning of the all-important conflagrations of the final third of the novel. The knotting of opposite and opposing threads in

Salammbô and Mâtho creates a complementary and circular narrative of myth and of the eternal return troped onto the (Moloch) story of progress, victory and success, hierarchy, rivalry and hatred. Salammbô is not, then, the token woman, an appendix to the main story demeaned by Giscon as (divine) prostitute or bride-pawn in the politics of triumphalist masculinity. She is fictional embodiment of the partner of Man truly lacking in the real history of Carthage, whom Flaubert had to invent to offset all the powers of horror of patriarchy. As catalyst of, and in conjunction with, Mâtho's unselfing to power, both protagonists voice and enact the Saga of Carthage as alternative story which, in one sentence, undermines all of the orders, commands, dictats, and official rhetorics of the ruling patriarchs and their record of the 'facts'.

The ending of *SAL* is then doubly apocalyptic. Overtly concluding a story of the cataclysmic force of events, it paints the internecine power struggles operating at all levels of hierarchy—cosmology, politics, religion, the army, class, and gender—to close on Carthage, State as Patriarchy, at its most hyperbolic state of affairs: it is at its zenith of power yet at war, overtly with barbarian others for international supremacy, but mainly with itself. There is no future place for the sacralized body (male or female) except through death by profanation of the sacred by the Moloch world of history and empire, with its antagonistic and disfiguring logic of opposition to anything which speaks of inner quest, unity, and love. Moloch-Carthage will win the day, but not the one thereafter.

The last sentence crystallizes the second, mythic, force of apocalypse, to voice the blessings or the curses, or to warn of impending disaster. The Saga of Tanit is foreclosed in the terse coda remythification of 'significance'. Its moral import for the novel is the interpretative challenge of its cryptic message read as 'the repository of fragmentary and desacralized remnants of sacred myth' (Brooks, 1976: 5). As punctum of the macrocosmic story of Man on the cusp between one 'civilization' and the next, it challenges the iterative histories of patriarchies themselves by invoking 'melodramatic imagination', which, for Brooks, requires 'both document and vision, and it is centrally concerned with the extrapolation from one to the other' (ibid. 9). Flaubert's attention to the details of the history of Carthage and his fictional creation of the eponymous heroine do combine history and fabulation to create modern myth. 'Myth frees the narrative from its Carthaginian context and illuminates the universal, unchanging nature of the fundamental human traits of love, hate, cruelty, greed, jealousy and fear' (Green, 1982: 117). In this powerful novel of male hierarchies, the unmasculinist hero and heroine, Mâtho and Salammbô, stand out so powerfully that, like Emma and Charles, they must ultimately be eradicated for their iconoclasm, their refusal to worship patriarchy's sacred cows. Readers must decide whether Flaubert can then be on their side. What he has certainly done in *SAL* is create an ending which is above all a 'déesse ex machina'.

3

L'Éducation sentimentale

IF *Salammbô* revealed the cosmic, imperial, patrician, workings of hierarchy and patriarchy, with the homophobic and homicidal power-politics which ensure such sovereignties, cloaking in Carthage the history of France, *ES* is overt about its historical and political context. With the gods, monarchs, and the polarized inequalities of the master–slave hierarchy destroyed in the Revolution of 1789, the equalizing space of the middle ground is the focus of this novel. The driving forces of democracy, the aims inherent in its slogan 'Liberté, Égalité, Fraternité' of increased status, autonomy, and freedom for the enfranchised individual, are the major concerns of post-revolutionary France and the central plot of *ES*.[1] This is arguably Flaubert's most homosocial novel. While it shares with *MB* and *BP* overt investigation of French social structures and the relationship between the individual and society, *ES* looks at the individual as social unit whereas *MB* and *BP* focus on domestic units, either married masculinity and fatherhood, or the selfsame of guardian paternities respectively. Sharing with *SAL* in Flaubert's *œuvre* the greatest number of men, *ES* has comitantly more women, and an increased concentration on the architecture of group dynamics, the city. Civilization as urbanization, or the State as *polis* of various group interrelationships, however, do not bring with them greater homophilia (understood both as the opposite of homophobia and as the *mise-en-scène* of the homophile). *ES* will reveal the logical

---

[1] Flaubert as historian of 1848 and whether *ES* is a 'historical novel' or a *Bildungsroman* have been critics' most frequently covered topics. For the former, see e.g. Vidalenc (1969); Agulhon (1981); Crouzet (1981*a*); Falconer (1991). For the latter, see Redfield (1996) or Doyle (1991).

consequences that hide under the revolutionary banner, 'Liberté, Egalité, Fraternité'. Far from being a static novel centring on the inertia of Frédéric, the thematic dynamics of *ES* stem from the problematic tensions, dissensions, and overt rivalries of male groups and individuals. *ES* is therefore the diptych novel to *SAL*, documenting enormous upheaval and politico-social change. The difference is that the configuration of male power has now become concentrated in the middle ground of democracy, where the small man has more to gain and therefore more to lose than his soldier counterpart in *SAL*. And in *ES*, the man in the street is no nameless one among many, but 'Monsieur Untel', with his own enfranchised position to insert into a shifting power-nexus as France lurches from republic to empire to republic. The stabilizing force, the ever-growing artisanal middle class had, however, also to provide its own governors, the public men of politics, banking, and industry. The double standard created by the Same of class but the Different of status thus returns hierarchy to democracy. *ES* thus partners *SAL* as a study of the configurations of patriarchy but in middle-class guise. The internecine battle with the 'Barbares' in *SAL* is now not polarized by race, but condensed on the one side of civilization and progress (see Fig. 1, p. 20). Whether this battle manifests itself as revolutionary action or peacetime competition between men in the public domain, or over women, it only endorses patriarchy itself. Misogyny becomes institutionalized and legalized in the *Code Napoléon*, to push women further into unvalorized space, for every 'civilization' requires its 'other'.

ES is the novel of the 'homme public': men are mostly on the streets throughout, in demonstrations, on barricades, or as idle flâneurs as Ferguson (1994: ch. 3) has noted, highlighting particularly the concept of dispossession this entails. Throughout *ES* the message is that the impersonal is political; the male crowd is a physical mass, a political force for change, but like Frédéric, its refracting individualizing mirror, it is in disarray, moving, with no clear direction because there is no blueprint to read as guide. This visible circulation of male power matches the economic circulation and traffickings in status, position, women, services, goods. Entrepreneurialism lies at the heart of this masculine economy of social advancement through 'affaires' (public business and extra-marital). 'L'homme public' has also to make a name for himself. Arnoux does his own self-advertisement (as Homais in *MB*) through his press empire, *L'Art Industriel*. Dambreuse operates his through networks of the club or salon. It is Frédéric's difficulty with this problem of how to make a name for himself that will be the focus of the first part of this chapter. Why, in a world of such enormous opportunity, and when Frédéric has huge personal advantages on his side, should this be the case? Frédéric's 'liberté' and égalité' therefore crystallize and focalize the knotty question of the legacy of the individual in democracy, and the process of individualization it necessitates.

The second part of the chapter returns Frédéric's negotiation of the politics of the subject to its wider political context. There has been much excellent critical analysis of the political accuracy of Flaubert's representation, through his secondary male protagonists, of the ideological spectrum of the Revolution of 1848 and its aftermath, which I will not revisit here.[2] What has not been discussed is the politics of 'fraternité', the all-important third term of the equation of republicanism. Because the metropolis centralized the corporate nature of work, politics, business, and male leisure, brotherhoods of different kinds emerge at this time in French history in the form of guilds, clubs, masonic lodges, business houses, and cafés. This novel of the brotherhood of man will, however, demonstrate particularly ironic reverberations with *SAL*. Man's inhumanity to man in the Punic Wars is the older version of republican fraternity and fratricide. The industrial economy of *ES* will demonstrate that it is in the same trade as Carthage.

The final part of the chapter then takes up the major themes — inheritance and history, the self and his brother — into the generic conundrum of *ES* as H(h)istoire-*Bildungsroman*. To what extent is Flaubert experimenting with 'brother' genres to the novel, or with the mix of the freedom, representational co-validity, and sibling likeness in all three? Is this a *Bildungsroman* of corporate (r)evolution of male subjectivity, the portrait of youth in its

---

[2] See Biasi (1989) and Grandpré (1991). On the subject of 'égalité' in *ES*, see Crouzet (1989*b*). On both 'liberté et égalité' see Dethloff (1989).

generation? Does the narrative point of view in *ES* add to this debate, indeed replicate the voice of debate?

For all Frédéric's seeming directionlessness, drifting, and political disinterest, his centrality in this novel is paramount; he is the subject as independent spirit, moving or static amid many different groups of the new men of his age. Because they judge him largely by (their own) criteria of public masculinity as achievement, success, or power, critics read him as passive or frustratingly inert. Frédéric is, however, one of Flaubert's key catalyst-narrators; Antoine in *TSA* is another (see Orr, 1998*b*)—oblique critics of their times, they are almost *démodé*, strangely uninvolved in events revolving around them. Like the scientific control of an experiment against which the test-tube reactions may be gauged, Frédéric is central to an enquiry into legal, political, personal, and sociological factors of the new republican masculinity of industrialization, entrepreneurialism, and meritocracy. Like Mâtho, he is the outsider–insider figure of contrast by his very similarities. Through Frédéric, Flaubert gets at the roots of the double value-system which is the legacy of post-revolutionary France.

The first value-system Frédéric embodies is the law of primo-geniture, the blood-test of citizenship after the Revolution. Only (and therefore first-born) son of a dead father, inheritor of his childless uncle's estate, Frédéric channels the legal and financial aspects of legacy as outlined in the *Code Civil* (Book III), which gives detailed instruction for patrilinear inheritance. The legalities surrounding the uncle's will and Frédéric's position as next male in line comply with Book III to the letter. The *Code* itself was the new model for the bourgeois State to legitimate itself against old absolutist power and control of property. Inheritance and property law under the *Code* has been demonstrably democratized—juridical headship is in the hands of State or family fathers—but without revision of the fundamental pre-revolutionary principle of lineage, itself previously epitomized by the divine right of kings. As Conroy (1985: ch. 4) argues, the old values of family connections and money still play a large part in France's social structures. This chapter will show how essential they are for the securities a young man can furnish to creditors, and for finding a suitable position, as well as a place in the marriage market. Family legacies in fact provide much of the plot in *ES* and play the role of Fortune's intervention in its strictly financial sense.[3] Cutting across class—the aristocrat Cisy inherits an enormous fortune from his grandmother (*ES*, 196), the petit-bourgeois Deslauriers inherits a paltry sum from his mother (*ES*, 62)—they also show the double standards of class. Frédéric's unconscious words to Deslauriers concerning his belated literary position in the lineage of passion, 'Je suis de la race des déshérités' (*ES*, 23), cloak his actual class advantages, while the politically aspiring and socially disadvantaged Sénécal commits himself to abolishing inheritances altogether because he will never have one, but yet demands political-purity credentials of Frédéric, in order to 'disinherit' him politically in his battle for candidature. Inheritances also cut into class and gender territory in the form of dowries, a means of advancement for women and through them for men. Both the grand bourgeois Dambreuse and his steward, le Père Roque, put money on their daughters. By leaving everything in an earlier will to the (illegitimate) Cécile, not to Madame Dambreuse as she has speculated, she and consequently Frédéric are cut out of inheritance, while the wily Martinon, who has previously married Cécile, will inherit the money. Roque wants to make of his only daughter Louise a 'countess' (*ES*, 348), in order to secure an alliance with the Moreau line because of his fascination with aristocratic blood lineage and to retaliate against Madame Moreau's snobbery. Deslauriers, not Frédéric, will marry Louise, but he fails to get her money before she runs off with a singer.

The consequences of Frédéric's inheritance (private filiation) launch him into the second value-system, public legitimacy of citizenship through financial and entrepreneurial affiliation. As Mauran (1996: 81) observes, 'le grand paradoxe de la filiation paternelle réside dans le fait qu'elle ne peut être qu'adoptif'. The heartland of male paternal fear is the potential illegitimacy of

---

[3] Some critical work has been done on fortunes (Olds, 1997) or inheritance in *ES*. Okita (1996: 100) focuses on the 'usage d'une fortune héritée' and rights and defence of private property in *ES* based on a comparative reading with the intertext of Prudhon's *Qu'est-ce que la propriété ou recherches sur le principe du droit et du gouvernement?* My approach is new and brings out the central importance of the *Code Napoléon* as legal intertext over many aspects of the novel, not least the career choice of law not only for Frédéric but for several of the secondary characters.

the child and hence that he might be a cuckold. The *Code Napoléon* is immensely interesting as a legitimization of paternity through a complex system of (male) witnesses to births. The Republic too is 'adoptif', an affiliation of male power to replace monarchist 'divine right'. At the end of the novel Frédéric and Deslauriers debate both sides of the issue with characteristic inconclusiveness: 'C'est peut-être le défaut de ligne droite, dit Frédéric.—Pour toi, cela se peut. Moi, au contraire, j'ai péché par excès de rectitude, sans tenir compte de mille choses secondaires, plus fortes que tout. J'avais trop de logique, et toi de sentiment' (*ES*, 609–10). As dilettante beneficiary of fortunes not of his making in an age of active careerism, his peculiar immunities to the goal-driven competitiveness of his age mark out Frédéric as singular. They also mark him out as a target for others' gain. Meritocracy, with its parvenus representatives Arnoux and Deslauriers, has no scruples when it comes to taking advantage of, and squandering, the rich pickings of fallen aristocracy. Frédéric has the unlucky fortune to be a *young* man of independent means, a greenhorn with knowledge only of provincial life. While this differentiates him from the mean, this meritocracy of the city across all its middle-class spectrum, it makes him magnetically attractive to impecunious, and mean, men. Like Charles and Emma's wedding, like Mâtho and Salammbô's union, the inheritance comes to Frédéric too early according to the legacy of fictional paradigms. It arrives at the crucial point where he might have made a choice of career and found through work 'existential' direction and meaning. A hindrance rather than a reward, it gives him the freedomless freedom to live, travel, socialize, but in a derivative way compared to the truly wealthy of a bygone age. Frédéric's social legitimacy turns out to be a strange deformation of two conflicting and complementary philosophies of individualism. He has neither enough private means to be a poet or gentleman of leisure, nor too little money to need to capitalize his personal assets and enter professional or business life. So while his brand of post-Romantic individualism contrasts with the negative ruthlessness of the self-made man, it leaves him high and dry as a secular solitary speculating about love in the desert of this cityscape.

    This single state is also an important indicator of the other laws operating in the middle-class social jungle, and another marker of the double standards under patriarchy, pre- and post-Revolution, of sexuality. Designated as being of unmarried status, the *célibataire* (m.) is not a celibate, but, on the contrary, is expected to enjoy the freedoms of sowing wild oats prior to later advantageous marriage to the *célibataire* (f.) a virgin bride who will guarantee that all-important legitimacy and continuation of his line and name. Such a practice of having of one's cake and eating it clearly links the *jeune homme* (as garçon/célibataire) and the older married philanderer/adulterer as represented by Arnoux. Paradoxically, however, social stigma rests on the young man as improperly part of the club of enfranchized and legitimized manhood/fatherhood until the marriage barrier has been crossed. Frédéric is in fact under the age limit (27 for men, 15 for women) to marry without paternal consent under the *Code Napoléon*. The *Code* also implicitly protects married men's 'rights' to commit adultery (the penalty for wives caught *in flagrante* results in divorce, whereas the wife can only divorce her husband if a concubine is brought into the household). The *Code* stipulates complex proceedings for the registration of legitimate children but there is nothing to codify the position of any other children born of his adulteries. The *Code* merely blocks them from benefiting from the inheritance. Even daughters, if legitimate, take precedence over any number of illegitimate sons. As husband-in-waiting, then, the bachelor with money (as Borie, 1976 underscores) is the target of parents with eligible daughters (Père Roque for example). He is also therefore de-personalized, either as a bank balance or as one insignificant specimen among many of free-floating male sexuality, active but without the direction which legalized commitment in the public domain requires. The most reprehensible and least palatable part of Frédéric's story demonstrates the hypocrisies and double stigma of free-floating *célibataire* sexuality. On Rosanette's news that she is pregnant by Frédéric, his reaction is one of suffocation, both internal and external: 'Il alla ouvrir la fenêtre, fit quelques pas de long en large, puis s'affaissa dans un fauteuil. Cet événement était une calamité, qui d'abord ajournait leur rupture, et puis bouleversait tous ses projets. L'idée d'être père, d'ailleurs, lui paraissait grotesque, inadmissible. Mais pourquoi? Si, au lieu de la Maréchale . . .?' (*ES*, 516).

In fact, Frédéric could be the fictional model for Segal (1990: 42):

> pregnancy can reactivate all the terrors and pleasures of men's early relations to their mothers ... The intense emotions aroused in men watching childbirth and handling infants take them back to the emotionality, generalized sensuality and tenderness of childhood so utterly tabooed in most areas of adult masculinity. Fatherhood can thus threaten men's perception of themselves as adults, arousing jealousy and anxieties of inadequacy, leaving them feeling tired, confused, vulnerable, insecure and rejected.

There is no male equivalent of the term 'fille-mère', but Frédéric comes close to embodying the 'garçon-père' in the experience here of the sense of 'ruin' to his 'reputation'. His repugnance at monstrous paternity refers to illegitimate offspring, for his fantasy about bearing a daughter to Madame Arnoux, which follows from this passage, has the starry-eyed glow of pride because the legitimacy question is shifted: the mother is a married woman. His physical repugnance is then demonstrated in his refusal to pick up his child when he visits the midwife, whose business hides ironically behind 'une petite porte bâtarde' with all her qualifications on it *except* 'accouchement' (*ES*, 553). Flaubert does not spare the full ironies of this episode. Frédéric's callousness has caused him to forget the imminent arrival of his child because he has been caught in a further hypocrisy of obligation over whether to marry Madame Dambreuse (and her money) when her sick husband dies. Rosanette is deliriously happy about her son and having produced a mini-version of Frédéric, whereas he is in the middle of a different 'existence double' (*ES*, 555), not only because he spends nights with Rosanette and afternoons with Madame Dambreuse, but also because the double fictions he invents for both women are doubled by the double perspective (fantasy and reality) he has *vis-à-vis* his son: 'Puis ses yeux retombaient sur son fils. Il se le figurait jeune homme, il en ferait son compagnon; mais ce serait peut-être un sot, un malheureux à coup sûr. L'illégalité de sa naissance l'opprimerait toujours; mieux aurait valu pour lui de ne pas naître' (*ES*, 556). Dussardier, the only secondary character in *ES* who is a 'bâtard', is indeed killed off, at the hands of the legalistically fascist Sénécal. When the child dies, Rosanette has a painting done of the baby and arranges for the little corpse to be embalmed. However, the child becomes doubly unrecognizable as it would have been doubly unrecognized by the law: the painting makes him 'hideuse, presque dérisoire'; as 'still life', the child is 'méconnaissable' (*ES*, 583). In a terrible and eerie prefiguration, Rosanette makes of her child a stuffed creature and *reposoir*, as will Félicité in *CS* with her male 'child', Loulou the parrot. All the adjectives used sum up the pejorative social implications of bastardy, and demonstrate the full horror of patriarchy's paranoia about, and daemonization of, illegitimacy. Through the baby's death, Frédéric will be allowed to escape the consequences of having fathered a child out of wedlock. This negative double of himself as 'un jeune homme de sa génération' (*génération* in the procreative and historical senses) prefigures *BP,* the second experiment of 'birthing' children but without women. Through Frédéric's false *génération* in this key episode in his 'éducation sentimentale', Flaubert focalizes the hypocrisies and double standards of extra-marital male sexual activity but *prior* to marriage and subsequent paternity. Such male sexual freedoms and irresponsiblities actually prove to be the licence for a double-mindedness that imprisons the subject in deceptions and double lives, which in turn prevent the *célibataire* leaving this dubious state and status. This Don Juanism in bachelor guise, however, is not condemned. While Flaubert may reveal the hypocrisies at work in France's endorsement of marriage as definition of good citizenship, his own control of plot none the less replicates the authority, valorization, and prioritization of male sexuality under patriarchy. The use of sick children as hinges in the plot of *ES* would seem only to endorse the message that the irresponsibility of bachelor freedom which produces a baby is of a different order to Marie Arnoux's unfulfilled 'adultery' when the rendezvous (in the love-nest Frédéric immediately uses for Rosanette) is unrealized because her legitimate son falls sick. A woman's potential to cuckold men is of such magnitude that delimitation of it requires the Law and an authorial *deus ex machina*.

The great expectations for this single 'jeune homme de sa génération' intersect in the particular liberties Frédéric encapsulates. The aspects of his circumstances over which he has had no choice—his birth, class, *célibataire* status, inheritance—provide a confusion of equally viable possibilities. The ways Frédéric deals with these and decision-making generally are best illustrated by his application of his 'éducation sentimentale' to real relationships. Frédéric, as *jeune homme*, is a 'bachelier' in both its modern meanings. The beginning of the novel coincides with his successful completion of the baccalaureate to begin study of law whereupon, after three years, he would become a 'bachelier'. However, Frédéric also represents the derivative heritage of the old Gallois and Latin sense of the term: 'Sous la féodalité, Jeune gentilhomme qui aspirait à devenir chevalier.—Par ext. *Vx.* Jeune homme' (*Petit Robert*). The *OED* provides further detail: 'A young knight who followed the banner of another; a novice in arms'. A second later meaning is 'A junior member, or "yeoman", of a tradeguild, or City Company' (ibid.). While Smith (1984: ch. 3) sees *ES* as 'an allegory of love' and reads Frédéric as Byronic, an imitation of Musset, I would argue that thanks to his reading of the Romantics, behind whom lies a certain medieval troubadour tradition, Frédéric is bedazzled by Marie Arnoux, not so much as a Brigitte, but rather as the derivative form of the 'Lady' in Courtly tradition. Jacques Arnoux is then the derivative 'Lord' whose banner Frédéric all too quickly follows in business and pleasure. Frédéric's initial fantasies about Marie Arnoux, which seem to match the contemporary cliché image for young men of social and romantic advancement, are a further means by which Flaubert can represent the strong undertow of nostalgia, reactionary monarchist-feudal politics, and patronage systems which run concurrently and parallel with new republicanisms. I will return to this double politics shortly. Frédéric is less an anti-hero than the protagonist in an anti-quest. There are no dragons to slay or crusades to embark upon. All that is left is an image of the Lady in his heart at key moments of decision-making to 'inspire' him. Close reading reveals how Flaubert imbricates several representative kinds of women from medieval romance and the romance tradition updated to the nineteenth century. On almost every occasion when Frédéric is required to make a choice between one course of action or another, and/or between one woman and another, the image of the woman in a different strand of political and romantic inclinations pops into his head.

Consequently he does nothing, and misses everything because he tries to keep all his options open with Marie, Rosanette, Madame Dambreuse, and sometimes Louise, at the same time. The most ironic counterpoint example is his presence at the beginning of the insurrection of 22 February 1848, date of his rendezvous 'manqué' with Marie Arnoux and history. At Fontainebleau with Rosanette he misses the workers' insurrection of 22–5 June in the double anachronism of history and 'idyllic' love.[4]

As liege-lord, Arnoux is also an anti-model, not least concerning codes of allegiance and honour for which one fights duels. In *ES* the duel Frédéric fights with Cisy is a double caricature both as satirical drawing in *le Flambard* (*ES*, 341) and as arcane and anachronistic legacy from the much older medieval tradition. As Nye (1993: 133–4) outlines:

France was the society par excellence of the civil duel. . . . France differed from all other Western European nations in not making the duel the object of special legislation. A bit of apocrypha that circulated amongst partisans of abolition during the nineteenth century had it that the framers of the Napoleonic Code did not wish to honor the duel by naming it . . . Though efforts were made at regular intervals— 1819, 1829, 1848, 1851, 1877, 1883, 1888, 1892, 1895, 1921—to abolish or regulate duelling through legislation, in each case abolitions suffered overwhelming defeat.

Frédéric defends Arnoux's 'honour' to a drunk Cisy who turns into a sissy when the event actually takes place, only to be interrupted by Arnoux's arrival to 'rescue' Frédéric. This farce version of the imitation in the *incipit* of Frédéric as young knight and Arnoux as liege-lord demonstrates Flaubert's graft of history and fiction onto older historical and fictional worlds.

---

[4] A number of important critical studies have focused on Frédéric's women. Among these, Tabaki-Iona (1989: 40) sees Madame Arnoux as 'mater dolorosa, protectrice de l'ordre, modèle de la femme idéale, aimée d'un amour impossible' and a parallel ideal to the 1848 revolution. 'Rosanette substituée à Madame Arnoux serait le symbole de l'idéal trahi . . . L'avènement de la République correspond à la trahison de Madame Arnoux par Frédéric, au passage de la femme unique aux aventures nombreuses. Le passage de la République aux républiques se traduit par une mise en marge de l'idéalisation qui cède la place à la dégradation' (ibid. 39). For a fuller discussion of Marie Arnoux and history see Adam (1989: 35). For an excellent overview of Rosanette's monarchisms see Burton, (1996). For a discussion of the Fontainebleau episode as idyll see Masson (1993*a*).

Frédéric therefore demonstrates ubiquitous 'bachelier' tendencies framed in the particular context of nineteenth-century
France. Indeed, Frédéric inherits them directly from his father,
who was killed in a duel, as Frédéric tells us in the lead-up to
his own. The pointlessness of duelling is seen in the psychological preparations on both sides. 'C'est un reste de barbarie!'
Frédéric's duelling is, however, the closest he gets to political
engagement, for he is of course at Fontainebleau with Rosanette
when the main events of the 1848 Revolution are taking place.
Frédéric is therefore a rather ordinary young man but becomes
extraordinary by default because his passive pursuit of 'love'
takes precedence over politics and the public face of the cult of
individualism. By contrast, all the other male protagonists
actively seek enfranchizement and 'égalité'—of name, reputation, public position—thus relegating their 'éducation sentimentale' to minor corners of wider social concern. To answer in part
the questions posed at the outset of this chapter, concerning
Frédéric's difficulty with the problem of how to make a name
for himself, it is Frédéric's derivative expression of bachelor-
hood *per se* which consigns him, in spite of his many advantages, to banality. It is only by returning to the root forms of this
term that Frédéric finds some sense of comparative differentiation from the past. And it is only in looking back in conversa-
tion with Deslauriers, in the anticlimactic final chapter of the
novel, that Frédéric achieves retrospective chief-protagonist
status.

The relationship with Deslauriers points up Frédéric's lack of
the interpersonal relationships and friendships one has with
siblings, and brothers in particular. Flaubert's novels are littered
with single male children, Frédéric joining the company of
Charles (*MB*), Mâtho (*SAL*), Antoine (*TSA*), Julien (*LSJ*),
Bouvard, and Pécuchet (*BP*). With this 'big brother' and school
mate, loyalties and rivalries figure equally when 'frère' becomes
'faux frère', as Biasi (1995*b*: 70) notes in relation to
Deslauriers's overriding desire for social advancement. The jealousies, wounded ego, and competition between 'brothers' map
back onto the wider configurations of a male society which
demands that individuality be carved out of invisibility. *ES*, as
D. A. Williams (1987: 180) has pointed out, is 'concerned not
simply with the complex psychology of relations between the

sexes, but also with the shifting pattern of intimacy and estrangement ... which characterizes relations between friends'. This view is amply echoed by Borie (1995), who similarly studies male desire as primarily friendship rather than necessarily love or sexuality. While Sckommodau (1971) views the Frédéric-Deslauriers couple as a bisexuality, a kind of androgyne totality of a self and other, he none the less remains coy on the subject of the homoerotic facets of their relationship. I have treated these in some detail and also investigated the other 'big brother' relationship Frédéric has with Jacques Arnoux (Orr, 1992). I want to develop this sexual/homoerotic facet within the main subject of this chapter, 'fraternité', to reveal something of the new ethos of the 'homme privé' emerging alongside the democratization of public male power in Frédéric's generation.

ES prefigures the utopia–dystopia brother-state of Les Chavignolles in *BP* in its focus on a male couple experiencing the social and political change of 1848. However, *ES* looks more closely at the taboo areas of male friendships of various kinds and the intimate male fears, phobias, and strong feelings often verging on the homoerotic or homosexual between young men. Flaubert is graphic about male–male bloodshed, war, and violence (as evident in *SAL*), but always hides male sexual performance in nuance, innuendo, ambiguity. Public male power exteriorizes private potency and 'successful' sexuality most obviously through children, legitimizing fathering abilities even if the child is illegitimate. Less obviously, but everywhere apparent between the lines in *ES*, is overcompensation for all shades of impotence and 'non-successful' sexual activity. Slama (1971: 31) offers a rare discussion of impotence in *ES*, literal and metaphorical. 'Impuissant' was a term which was used at the time as a euphemism by mothers with daughters to marry, before the word 'homosexual' entered French. 'The nineteenth century invents the homosexual as an individual with a life. The very words "homosexuality" and "homosexual," coined in 1869 by a Hungarian writer, Benkert, signal the individual behind the action, as did the earlier nineteenth-century word "uranist" ' (Schehr, 1995*b*: 3). Voiced through male bravado, mistress-swapping, seducing and/or marrying one's best friend's girl, or talking about sex through mockery, which in Hussonet's case is transposed into the ribald caricature of Frédéric's duel saturated in *homosexual* innuendos, 'impotence' hid under many cloaks. Quintessentially important is the shoring-up of any perceived lack of masculinity (weakness and effeminacy might be interpreted as homosexual), such as might arise from being made a laughing stock or a cuckold, or the target of a marriage-obsessed woman or mother for her daughter, even though the whole marriage market-place had to be negotiated for homosocial credibility. In their intimate moments, Frédéric and Deslauriers discuss relationships endlessly, with men and women. In so doing they are negotiating that fine line between vulnerability and need for male support, encouragement, or verification in the other of 'normality', wherever on the hetero-homosexual scale this finds its expression. Talking about another man's sexual relationships is one way of advancing the knotty subject of a sexual relationship between the speakers. 'Sexual self-confidence is seen as one of the yardsticks of masculinity' (Weeks, 1989: 190). Weeks goes on to stress that 'performance anxiety is a leading cause of secondary impotence. At the same time the over-emphasis on sexual success by men is clearly an indicator of a "relative gender fragility". Masculinity or the male identity is achieved by the constant process of warding off threats to it. It is precariously achieved by the rejection of femininity and of homosexuality.' This is why the ending of the novel, its anticlimactic and flaccid repetition of a mutually disappointing experience at the brothel, is crucial as moderation in a male–male key of Frédéric's non-consummation of his idealized love with Madame Arnoux in the previous chapter. The fear of incest, of failing desire, will appear again in Hérode's waning potency in *H*. Problematic sexual expression, whether it is Arnoux's philandering to bolster the financial disaster and public face of his masculinity, or Frédéric's unfocused desire between male and female partners, or Sénécal's outright rejection of sexual intercourse and truck with women, or the homoerotic homophobo-philia between Dussardier and Frédéric, all speak implicit volumes about the politics of performance which is the mechanizing world of reproduction of objects but not children. Frédéric, then, is a 'jeune homme de sa génération' caught in the bonds and freedoms of sexual expression, engendering, and progeniture as well as the bonds of 'amitié' with all its many attaching strings. 'Sibling' rivalries, jealousies, fratricides, competitiveness, and vaunting individualism give the lie to the ideology of 'fraternité' in both the private and public spheres. On the surface of this novel, what is left are shallow friendships, the gamut of male–male 'partnerships' (right-hand man to arch-enemy, love-friend to foe) to replicate the relationship of this Revolution of 1848 to its big brother of 1789. The deeper layers of *ES* suggest homosocial relationships which are altogether homosexual, the coining of this term coinciding exactly with the date of its publication.

From Frédéric's singular representation of his epoch, let us now turn to its corporate face, the group of satellite male characters orbiting round him. Advance is determined everywhere in *ES* by the laws of *homo*social climbing. Unlike Rastignac and other Balzacian heroes who advance via moneyed women, this route is constantly thwarted for men in *ES*. Unlike the clearly demarcated ladder of hierarchy in *SAL*, this novel of male–male interrelationships works through overlapping networks of individuals, or by interlocking triangular relationships (Orr, 1992). The individuals remain free to join other or several groups. This liberty and equality of male rights is of course underwritten by the principles of the First Republic. The issue at stake in the events of 1848 spanned by *ES* is the extension of the vote to include the full brotherhood of man in France, and not just a certain moneyed electorate. Political election to leadership positions in politics is mirrored as a process by the other forms of elective affinities in *ES*—those inclusions or exclusions, advances or blocks in professional and social groups effected by patronage with its post-1789 democratic face. While the empowering of men collectively throughout the *res publica* put pressure on former hierarchical male orders of privilege, exclusivity, exclusion, *ES* demonstrates how and where this pressure reasserts itself. Nowhere is this clearer than in its exploration of the public and private faces of the 'fraternité' that the Revolution was to create from liberty and equality. It will be my contention that the events of 1848 are on the margins of Frédéric's consciousness because this replicates paradoxically their relative unimportance to collective purpose more generally. 'Like the 1848 events, the time of Moreau leads nowhere: but unlike those events, the novel has compositional integrity which is ironically based upon sterility, celibacy and eccentricity' (Saïd, 1975: 148). The history of the Second Empire in *ES* has been described by Biasi (1989: 105) as an 'ellipse impressionnante'. The cult of selfishness is the real impetus behind any euphoric or idealistic moments of 'fraternité' which collective or humanitarian action at the barricades may bring. Flaubert, in *SAL*, has already unglamorized war as collective male endeavour for higher principles by dramatizing its violence, cruelty, inhumanity. In *ES* he banalizes corporate activism to fit the democratic key of its context. Public fraternity is nowhere more trenchantly demythologized than in the episode of the 'Club de l'Intelligence'. As D. A. Williams (1987: 180) notes, the whole political cross-section of Frédéric's generation is represented. What has not been noticed is that it is a privileged moment in *ES* because they are all in the one place. Intergenerational fraternities, notably the salon, are the second space Flaubert explores. These semi-public homosocial worlds necessarily demarcate insiders and outsiders and are far from being centres of camaraderie. The final locale which I want to focus on highlights the 'family' implication of public fraternity, to give the lie to bonds of 'amour du prochain'. Dambreuse's funeral is the public–private manifestation of unfraternity and the ethos of the age: charity begins at home but money determines that one is not one's brother's keeper.

The motto of *Les Trois Mousquetaires*, 'Tous pour un, un pour tous' (Alexandre Dumas Père, not Fils) of mutual assistance, disinterest, and altruism as clarion-call to the emerging new men in *ES* of universal suffrage, is nowhere more ironic than in the 'Club de l'Intelligence'. This is the new-look democratic *locus* of the temple of Moloch in *SAL* and centre of political Bovaryism through its ritual of the calf's head. This 'signifies the decapitated head of Charles I of England, and, antonomastically, the abolition of monarchic rule. The calf's head is consequently synecdochic of democracy' (Madureira, 1996: 70; see also Oliver, 1988–9). It is not the revolutionary events on the streets in *ES* but the milieu of this Club, one among many to have sprung up, that Flaubert depicts as the heart of the 'Revolution' of 1848. Designed to unite the like-minded as 'confrères', this Club in fact produces 'l'éclatement du cénacle' (Pliskin, 1994: 99), with Sénécal as its Iago. This critic sees the main differences between the male protagonists based on class, whereas Raitt (1982: 161) discusses Flaubert's characterization by various factors including 'métier'. Mitterand (1984: 68) focuses on the socio-linguistics of the different political monologues: 'Pas de projet commun, ni de loi commune, ni de langue commune', but comes up with the same result, that 'L'intercompréhension et l'intercommunication se bloquent, les personnalités se heurtent, les dogmatismes s'entre-choquent, les rôles se théâtralisent jusqu'a l'outrance. . . . C'est la Tour de Babel' (ibid. 67). Disunity and ostracism stem from similarities of creed, but doctrinaire need for purism will be the bone of contention and lead to the ultimate republican fratricide: Sénécal's murder of Dussardier.

Universal suffrage is the main issue of the Club's agenda on the night when Frédéric is invited by Dussardier, and crystallizes the process of election *per se*. However, Flaubert is careful to frame the events of the fateful evening in a *mise en abyme* operating by a dynamic of 'pistons'. Dambreuse, abetted by Martinon, ensures their new republicanism (they spout Proudhon) by suggesting that Frédéric stand in the elections:

—Et peut-être aussi, ajouta le banquier en souriant, grâce un peu à mon influence.
Frédéric objecta . . . Rien de plus facile, en se faisant recommander aux patriotes de l'Aube par un club de la capitale . . .
—Apportez-moi cela; je sais ce qui convient dans la localité. Et vous pourriez, je vous répète, rendre de grands services au pays, à nous tous, à moi-même.
   Par des temps pareils, on devrait s'entr'aider, et, si Frédéric avait besoin de quelque chose, lui, ou ses amis   (*ES*, 427)

The cloaked 'ultra' viewpoint is meshed with Deslaurier's liberalism. Frédéric consults his absent friend and receives his 'exhortations violentes'. Delmar the actor and he join forces to reconnoitre the various clubs and launch their respective careers. This is Flaubert's opportunity to imbricate comment on the terrible reality of their so-called differences: 'partout, les locataires maudissaient les propriétaires, la blouse s'en prenait à l'habit, et les riches conspiraient contre les pauvres' (*ES*, 432). It is Dussardier who brings them to the 'Club de l'Intelligence' along with Pellerin, Hussonnet, Regimbart, Compain (note the irony of the name) and the 'patriote de Barcelone'. Cisy the 'légitimiste' is of course absent, but present by default as he also tried to enter a club (*ES*, 316).

The company is completed by Sénécal, president of the Club and demagogue. What ensues is his censorship of Frédéric's credentials to 'belong' by criteria which not only replicate the generalities of rich versus poor above, but endorse the actual superiority of 'la blouse'. Sénécal is not only a 'répétiteur de maths' but a repetition of ideological positions from 1789, with rigid adherence to the chosen formulaic line because he has no lateral mobility of thought or act: 'et comme chaque personne se réglait alors sur un modèle, l'un copiant Saint-Just, l'autre Danton, l'autre Marat, lui, il tâchait de ressembler à Blanqui, lequel imitait Robespierre' (*ES*, 434). As Vidalenc (1969: 18) remarks, there is interestingly no attack on Barbès in *ES*, 'un des dirigeants les plus en vue, des clubs, le rival de Blanqui dans l'opinion d'extrême gauche, mais un homme bien moins dogmatique, plus libéral'. In fact Barbès is the diametric opposite to Sénécal, whose 'aspecte rigide', his eventual function as defender and 'agent de police', his abhorrence of women, make him the 'frère jumeau' of Binet in *MB*—mechanistic, repetitive, and ultimately solipsistic. This machine to cut down opposition makes Sénécal a guillotine. In the Club, he first cuts out with words the parameters of endeavour for 'citoyens purs' for this new workers' state. His 'policies' only repeat his own lack of social standing and privilege, so he makes of no privilege the new privilege, of no inheritance a manifesto for social services: 'On établirait un fonds social pour les travailleurs.' Sénécal is frequently unemployed (and unemployable) so he then cuts out Frédéric, moneyed but unemployed, altogether and sends him packing, 'majestueusement' (*ES*, 442). The irony of this adverb should of course not be lost, given the political colours of Sénécal. This first act of symbolic fratricide will be replicated later when he uses his sabre literally to cut down Dussardier. In the mayhem of this partisan anti-brotherhood, the unfinished speeches from many quarters equally cut into one another, including socialism's 'haine de l'intelligence' and art (discussed in detail by Ogura, 1994). The most ironic is the stichomythia of double departure, Frédéric's silenced speech and the Spaniard's untranslated and prophetic 'oraison funèbre de la liberté' (Mitterand, 1984: 73), which Frédéric then embodies by being evicted. Sénécal thus demonstrates that election and republicanism can only take place by exclusion, by new rules for exclusivity, that 'fraternité' is only for those who come from the same ideological and impecunious heritage. His anti-social and anti-homosocial behaviour is a hallmark throughout *ES*: 'Sénécal s'exclue lui-même de la société' (Grandpré, 1991: 629). His desire to have the last word, to guillotine proceedings, is an act of terrorism to free speech and democracy. Biasi (1989: 121) states that 'Il est de la race de ceux qui veulent avec acharnement arrêter le cours de l'histoire, en avoir raison, bref, conclure.' Flaubert's abhorrence of the act of concluding puts in a nutshell the antipathy this character embodies. It is also driven by hate, jealousy, rivalry, antagonism, prejudice, and his own belief that the world owes him a higher, if not the highest, position in the political and public world of the *polis* and hence the political. This meshes with Seidler's recent re-evaluation of socialist traditions (1991: chs. 1 and 4) and the foundations of a politics which either considers itself a higher form of consciousness, or which can only think oppositionally.

Although Dussardier introduces Frédéric and hence the narrative action to the 'Club de l'Intelligence', he is invisible and inaudible in the seething mass of shouting and posturing pseudo-'hommes politiques'. Critics such as Paulson (1992: 108–9) and Biasi (1995*b*: 78) have often presented him as Sénécal's foil, and thus overidealize Dussardier's 'goodness', 'l'homme du cœur pur' (Aurégan, 1989: 66). In an earlier essay, Biasi (1989: 119) sees him almost as embodiment of 'liberté, égalité, fraternité' in his 'croyance naive, mais exemplaire dans les valeurs de la vie, de la liberté, de la justice et de la fraternité . . . Il croit profondément à la perfectibilité de l'homme et du progrès. Il parle d'égalité sans jamais envier la situation des amis qui sont plus fortunés que lui. . . . Bref, Flaubert a construit avec Dussardier une figure entièrement positive.' What has not been properly recognized is that he embodies the spirit of inclusion, *confrérie*, the union of outcasts. As a bastard, his unvoiced hope for legitimacy finds its outlet in republican action that has nothing to do with passive heredity. In this he mirrors the status of the Revolution of 1848 as a bastard form of the politics of 1789, and it is the challenge to the very fraternity of universal suffrage that Dussardier stands as martyr. While naïve victim at the outset (for example his view of 'Le Pouvoir' (*ES*, 333)), he later understands the catch-22 of the notion of 'notre République' (*ES*, 571), that it is not a collective with one mind, heart, voice, but a collection of the self-interested selling out for personal gain. He arrives at this conclusion from personal experience, for the context of this speech is his desire to cease being an accomplice with La Vatnaz, and so he begs Frédéric to take his money. La Vatnaz, he realized, while she was altruistically nursing him after his wound on the barricades, had other interests at stake—marriage. In his longest speech of all in the novel, 'écartant ses bras comme dans une grande détresse', he realizes that 'Les ouvriers ne valent pas mieux que les bourgeois . . . Des misérables traitent Barbès d'aristocrate!' (ibid.) and that he is not exempt: 'Moi, je n'ai jamais fait de mal; et pourtant, c'est comme un poids qui me pèse sur l'estomac. J'en deviendrai fou, si ça continue. J'ai envie de me faire tuer' (*ES*, 572). This death-wish is realized in the eventual murder by his republican brother's hand, and replicates the gesture of his despair, but with Christ-like implications: 'Il tomba sur le dos, les bras en croix' (*ES*, 599). This 'suicide', self-sacrificing martyrdom to a higher purist cause (Feyler, 1991 likens Dussardier here to Barbès), is the logical outcome of the republican politics that Dussardier tries to negotiate, a kind of open confraternity with no bars on birth or bank balances, set against the impossible odds of entrepreneurial reality. Throughout, Dussardier's actions always speak louder than words and in this he forms the visible contrast to all the other characters, but perhaps most to Frédéric; although Denommé (1990) may have a point when he compares Dussardier's idealism as a parallel to Frédéric's love for Madame Arnoux. Participant in all the major events of 1848 from the student protests to the barricades where he is wounded, Dussardier, however, sheds his own blood as the seal of republicanism in action. Yet his generosity to Christ-like extremes has a double edge: done to make a point, it is also supremely pointless. Having been Frédéric's seconder at the duel, having given him his money, having given his life, his end is and is not justified by its means. Like Mâtho and Charles Bovary, the singular unhero can only find heroism in death, which removes him from the reality that would force him out of existence anyway. By comparison to the selfishness of the other 'comrades', Dussardier stands out, but as derivative, momentary, and ambiguous hero by the contingencies not causalities of events. Unlike Charles and Mâtho, however, he fails to have his finale in the closing pages of the novel. Out of sight, he is completely out of the minds of the *compte rendu* Deslauriers and Frédéric make of their peers. As in the case of Rosanette's child, illegitimacy is in the end punished by the censures of the plot of the novelist. The gap he leaves has no positive ideological import, but it does underscore the almost impossible odds for the establishment of a fraternity of equals within the root structures of democratic politics and a law which excludes illegitimacy. His generosity and connection to the political in the feminine (represented by Mademoiselle Vatnaz's equally disappointed feminism), are further markers of his potential as an alternative model of masculinity which would join brothers with sisters. The gap he creates, however, problematizes causal, dialectical, Marxist interpretations of the progress of history and opens various textual silences, aporias, and hiatuses in the tales others are left to tell.

If the 'Club de l'Intelligence' offers a space for the emerging voice/vote of the new generation and its hierarchy of the loudest overruling (excluding) the others, the salon offers an equivalent club of male power by private (exclusive) network. Here, the old hierarchies of influence, based on age, rank, and status, are maintained by wealth. The dinners and salons display this to the less fortunate both in financial terms and in a *savoir faire/savoir vivre* which younger men cannot imitate, not even the aristocratic Cisy. An elaborate code of contacts (like the elaborate dinners) ensures exclusivity of membership, pecking-order, and system of favours, all the while protecting the interests of the centre of power. Arnoux's dinners and the chambers of his *L'Art Industriel* provide the locale *par excellence* for the important mix of male business and culture in all its post-1789 ebullience. However, Dambreuse is even more adept in the game of chameleon adaptations to ensure one's own because he embodies the old-world values and privileges in new form by simply dropping his 'particule'. His dinner and funeral, surprisingly ignored in critical debate, mark two ritualizations of an elaborate *confrérie* which operates most powerfully not by opening up to mass membership, but, on the contrary, by selection of the few. Powerful symbolizations of history (as Cajueiro-Roggero, 1981 remarks regarding the dinner), events *chez* Dambreuse are pivotal social commentaries of the same order as the marriage feast in *MB* and the 'festins' in *SAL* and *H*. Revolt happens not just on the barricades but is as bloody between the 'grand' and the 'petit' bourgeois in the opulence of their receptions.

Dambreuse embodies the double standard throughout *ES*, politically, financially, socially, and personally. Monarchist caught between the July Monarchy and the Second Empire, he replicates on the right what Sénécal and other younger-generation republicans represent on the left: politics on both sides duplicate the events of the monarchy of Louis XVI and the Revolution of 1789. The prosperity of France under the Bourbons enabled Dambreuse to double his industrial and financial base so that when 1848 overturns the July Monarchy, his money allows him a standing alongside the new rich such as Arnoux. His double life, already evident in the simple rearrangement of his name, is refracted in his 'niece', Cécile, and the double-dealing operated on her behalf. His duplicity over the double will disinherit Madame Dambreuse, but gives legacy and legitimacy to this natural daughter.

Every aspect of the Hôtel Dambreuse, moreover, reflects the double image of empire and wealth, double-dealing and hypocrisy. On Frédéric's first visit in part one of *ES* he notes its 'deux portes cochères', a 'double escalier', 'deux candélabres de bronze' (a metal which is itself an alloy), and in Dambreuse's office, 'deux coffres-forts'. Like Lheureux in his double nature (Orr, 1999*a*), Dambreuse's face replicates the combined contradiction of hot–cold, health–sickness, his youthfully thin body given away by his gnarled hands (*ES*, 28). Benet (1993: 19) rightly describes him as 'l'homme des masques et des retournements de vestes', but without seeing quite how double are also Dambreuse's salon and house. Frédéric's second visit is for the dinner and business arrangement, and for adding a liaison with Madame Dambreuse to the two he has already with Madame Arnoux and Rosanette. It also takes place in the second chapter of the second part of the novel. On the second occasion in the office, Frédéric records the pair of portraits of Général Foy and Louis-Philippe hanging on either side of the reflective mirror and the two monstrous 'coffres'. In the salon itself, a copy of that of Louis XV, many of the women are seated in wing-chairs in two rows. The men form a homogeneous single mass—grey-headed, periwigged, balding—but belong either to politics or business (*ES*, 224–5). In superb double irony, not only is everything doubled in the mirrors, but the groaning sideboard in the dining-room is described both as like 'un maître-autel de cathédrale' and as 'une exposition d'orfèvrerie' (*ES*, 225). Business and pleasure, money-making and card-playing go hand-in-hand in this environment, which is the Paris equivalent of the La Vaubyessard Ball in *MB*, with its class differences and snobberies, yet strange reflection in higher key of the banalities of Emma's real world (Orr, 1996). The gathering, however, separates the 'intimes' from the others, the (ugly) 'niece' from the unnamed beauties, and will prefigure in almost every crucial detail—music, flowers, speech-making, gossip, best clothes—the negative 'festin' of Dambreuse's 'obsèques'. Dambreuse's chest-pains are enquired after here by the man who becomes his son-in-law, Martinon. Like diptych double mirrors, these will magnify into Dambreuse's 'hémoptysie', and subsequent death, which leads in turn to the grandiose, almost State funeral in the Madeleine church, an ironic monument to the famous sexual sinner, and to the revelation about Dambreuse's real 'amour du prochain'.

MB's mix of sacred and profane, boudoirs and churches, suppurating corpse and grotesque funeral with triplicate coffins, have all evoked critical comment, but little attention has been paid to 'le motif de "l'enterrement parisien chic" ' (Biasi, 1990: 93), the mix of the grotesque, the grandiose, and the grandiloquent in *ES*. The funeral is an all-male affair, a privileged ritual of male grief and respect, a public celebration of masculine values. At the Père Lachaise cemetery the speech-making and gathering of public worthies makes this the Parisian version of the Comices in *MB*. Dambreuse's true colours are fully on display: his escutcheon (in triplicate) has the motto '*Par toutes voies*' to sum up his chameleon politics. The service inside the church has its master of ceremonies, who does more of the officiating than the priests; the flowers, candelabra, music, paintings inside the church underscore the Funeral as a secular social gathering. The funeral cortège of Dambreuse the double-dealer has everything in further multiples of two: the hearse is drawn by four black horses; twelve funeral carriages follow; at the graveside there are six funeral orations which double as political propaganda.

Everything about Dambreuse is on a grand scale and his burial plot in the Père Lachaise is in the vicinity of the double monument of 'Manuel et Benjamin Constant' (*ES*, 549). Surpassing even the description of the scene inside the Madeleine is that of the cemetery itself, and the ironic parallels set up between the style of the tombs and funerary monuments and Dambreuse's salon furnishings. Some are 'espèces de boudoirs funèbres avec des fauteuils rustiques et des pliants'; the tombs have 'chandeliers, des vases des fleurs ... des statuettes de plâtre' (*ES*, 548). There is in fact little shift in context between Dambreuse's July Monarchy business dealings and those of the present ('le bonhomme Dambreuse avait été un des *potdevinistes* les plus distingués du dernier règne' (*ES*, 549–50)), or between the ceremony and the world of business to which his bourgeois mourners proceed afterwards. The public graveyard, the salon, and the *res publica* are all facets of the same homosocial world of male *affaires*. It is also not without irony that Dambreuse, as later Dussardier on the opposite political side, is seen as socialism's 'mort victime' (*ES*, 549). Thus male 'clubs' on the political right and left demonstrate equally, and in equally selective if different keys, the diverse, ritualized, and transient bonds between 'equals'. As public networks of allegiances, hero-worship, enmity, affinities of interest, shift and change in this competitive arena, so too do the unstable politics of this generation.

If Frédéric has been the focalizer of questions of birth, sex, gender, and political persuasion in the *genus* 'republican', the novel he inhabits questions further its generic heritage and revolution. Critical debate has raged concerning the categorization of *ES*. Is it about education, or sentiment? As an 'histoire d'un jeune homme', is it a story or a historical novel or a *Bildungsroman*? Is it a parody of such genres as the historical novel and the *Bildungsroman*—an 'Unbildungsroman'?[5] One

---

[5] For critical response to the first of these questions about the genre of *ES*, see Biasi (1995*a*) who discusses both terms of the title, the connotations of 'sentimen-

way to answer these generic questions is to consider them in the context of 1848 as epoch of derivations. I have explored the personal and political manifestations of derivation throughout this chapter through Frédéric and company. A major part of this 'confrérie' has also been actively connected to the role of art, as collectors (Dambreuse), dealers (Arnoux), writer-journalists (Hussonet), painters (Pellerin), actors (Delmar), or potential artist figures (Frédéric). I now want to open *ES* to scrutiny as an aesthetic encounter with, and journey into, 'La République des Lettres'. Once more, it is through Frédéric that Flaubert further focalizes questions about the world of art as path to individuality and originality, and whether these are possible within democracy and the industrial revolution. My argument will state a case for *ES* as the novel of male artifical miscegenation. No matter how clever the mix, the reproductions, it only reveals the very masculine bias at its multiple roots. Redfield puts it this way: 'the novel may at least be said to demonstrate the inextricability of aesthetic history, phallocentrism and commodification, and to suggest that only the contingency of artifice, *facticius*, determines this tradition's erection of the maternal phallus as a figure of its fears and desires' (1996: 186).

The world of art in *ES* is this resoundingly male universe where women are decorative objects epitomized in Rosanette's portrait (discussed more fully by Gothot-Mersch, 1996), or metonymic symbols of exchange. Madame Arnoux's famous 'coffret' is an oft-cited example (See Baker, 1990, and M. Jameson, 1990–1.). For Bourdieu, 'L'éducation sentimentale de Frédéric est l'apprentissage progressif de l'incompatibilité entre les deux univers, entre l'art et l'argent, l'amour pur et l'amour mercenaire' (1992: 43). Earlier he commented on Arnoux as 'le

tality' by 1835 and hence the parody of the 'sentimentale' in *ES*. Martin-Berthet (1993) develops the notion of apprenticeship in love from the two terms before opening the discussion to the *Bildungsroman* implications of such a training. To the second question, Campion (1991) sees *ES* as a parody of the historical novel, an imbrication of individual destinies into history. Biasi (1995*a*: 48) sees it as quasi-autobiographical. Many critics, e.g. Martin-Berthet (1993: 120), link it to the double portrait of the artist which is the first *ES*. The term 'Unbildungsroman' is Redfield's (1996: 172). See also Madureira (1996: 66): 'For Flaubert . . . parody seems to have represented the century's definitive genre . . . If 1848 is a parody of 1789, the latter . . . is thus not the original but a copy of medieval jacqueries, and 1848 is downgraded, as a result, to the status of a simulacrum twice removed.'

double jeu permanent entre l'art et l'argent ... Cet être double
... cumule à son profit, au moins pour un temps, les avantages
des deux logiques antithétiques, celle de l'art désintéressé, qui ne
connaît de profits que symboliques, et celle du commerce' (ibid.
26). Critics (Gothot-Mersch, 1996 and Shillony, 1982 among
others) read Pellerin as the representation of the artist-in-crisis,
torn between aesthetic principles and ideals and the need to earn
a living, finding in portraiture a way of resolving his dilemma
before eventually turning to photography. The artistic centre of
operations in *ES* is Arnoux, owner of the ironically named *L'Art
Industriel* with its publications, offices, 'official' artists, and
hangers-on like Frédéric and Regimbart. Bem, rather inge-
niously, points out the numerous name-puns of 'DelMAR',
'RegimbART', and 'L'ARnoux' with art. 'L'Arnoux, c'est l'art et
nous' (1986: 108–9). 'Peintre raté' from the outset, Arnoux's
downwards spiral of 'artistic' endeavour for business ends takes
him through manufacture of 'faïences' to mass-production of
religious objects. Shillony remarks that 'L'objet religieux
fabriqué en masse révèle ... la crise de valeurs qui caractérise
l'art moderne, la décadence de l'inspiration authentique et la
rupture avec le passé' (1982: 44). Eventually Arnoux quite
simply becomes a 'raté'. Hussonet's art-critic writing is also
devalued. He will buy *L'Art Industriel*, but turns it into a
tabloid paper before becoming a kind of Rupert Murdoch figure
of the Second Empire, stultifying journalism in populist gossip.
And Frédéric will become neither an artist nor a writer in the
vein of Walter Scott.

   Journalism, photography, mass-reproduction of objects—all
resoundingly depict the copy and get to the heart once more of
1848 as revolution. However, the frame of these forms of copy
in the non-quest of the non-portrait of a non-artist as a young
man are what make *ES* paradoxically original. It is deeply
concerned with finding a figuration of the unfigurable, the secular version of the unrepresentable God as 'the I am that I am',
through the word as multi-genre. While the novel in many ways
already fulfils this secularizing form of the parable, the history
of the chosen people, Flaubert takes it back to its Romance
roots (Frédéric's role as 'bachelier', Pellerin as a secularized
pilgrim) to prevent it spiralling down into a mere anti-model of
either the historical novel or the anti-*Bildungsroman*. *ES* is

therefore a demonstration of artistic originality in the Renaissance sense of the copy as against the modern kind of mechanistic reproduction. It seeks to graft onto the old genus and heritage of the epic its nineteenth-century realist novel form. In this it cannot but replicate the overtly masculine concerns of war and history, trial and goal-oriented endeavours, high (heroic) ideals. I want to return briefly to the contents of *ES* to show that the reactionary nature of this move, the nostalgic harking-back to pre-revolutionary epochs, does permit the individualization of certain male characters as against the clone-like reproductions of others.

While I noted the Louis XV furnishings of Dambreuse's *Hôtel* and the semi-State trappings of his funeral, his taste is nowhere in question, nor is his own particular brand of cleverly adapting monarchism. He collects originals, not copies, and so can 'collect' wealth in this industrial world in the same way. Through his salon, he can replicate old orders of patronage. His death signals the passing of inheritance out of the 'family' through the female and illegitimate line. Symbolically, it depicts in suitable ritual, splendour, and decoration the end of an aristocratic line and of the art connoisseur who patronized the specialist dealer. He cannot be replicated because his generation is naturally dying out. At most he will end up as his name suggests as a piece of amber, fossilized in time.

The person who arranges his funeral is the other individual, Frédéric. Of the same mould but different stamp, he looks back constantly and his tastes and inclinations match Dambreuse's not least in his trip to Fontainebleau while the main events of 1848 are raging. Stepping into a bygone historical and artistic epoch, Frédéric's empathy with and understanding of his surroundings, particularly the art around him, ironically fall only on untuned ears—Rosanette's. The same kind of nostalgia for a prior 'golden' age is delicately ironized in the famous ending of the novel, as if he were discoursing with Deslauriers on his early chivalresque campaigns.

Frédéric's other male contemporaries stand on the repetition side of the copy, even Dussardier. Some, such as Pellerin, Hussonet, Deslauriers, start with higher aims, but sell out to successful money-making, not creativity. Others, such as Sénécal and Regimbart, can only disappear because they have been simulacra and parasites anyway on ideologies of power, not higher values such as art. Arnoux is their older brother. Supremely the debtor in *ES* to both art and industry, he can pay back neither from his bluff but empty self. He is the counter-representative of fine art and the Old Masters because he trades through *L'Art Industriel* in earthenware not porcelain, and in fake paintings and copies. The debt he owes to baroque art is converted into cheap plagiarism and bad artistic taste and heralds in the era of kitsch in all its cheap, nasty, and vainglorious heterogeneity. Except for Duchet (1969: 176) and more recently Frølich (1997: 51–83), kitsch in *ES* has been very little discussed. Arnoux is perhaps Kitsch Man personified as copy of the new art (l'art nouveau—'L'Arnoux-veau') with that all-important bovine 'bêtise' so antipathetic to Flaubert built in. So, while an Arnoux would deal in 'un aimable bric-à-brac, d'une variété sans fin où l'élégance côtoie le mauvais goût, le rare le cliché et l'art la pacotille' (Rincé 1990: 33) or collage forms of artifical miscegenation, Flaubert's *ES* is sufficiently singular to hold even its counterfeit double within its high-art version of the same aesthetic of the copy. Frédéric, the artist *manqué*, is none the less anti-kitsch, a kind of original creation by default. Iterable his pseudo-artistic expression may be, but his dandyism has at least a motivation towards a higher aesthetic.[6]

Flaubert's control as artist is everywhere apparent in the bid in *ES* to elevate banality to some form of ideal. In this is a degree of education for the reader. The *Bildungsroman* with its *dépassé* sentimentality and anachronistic protagonist is the ideal vehicle. The grafting of his own art into a noble tradition of great masters only endorses the superior masculinity which muscular writing brings to the 'bachelier' form *par excellence*, the *Bildungsroman*. '[T]he ascension to the exalted status of

---

[6] The dandy as figure is discussed by Kelen (1994) to differentiate male aesthete from artist. She defines dandyism as the 'recherche de la singularité la beauté, mais faire de sa vie une œuvre d'art' (257). Among the dandy's traits are a horror of banality, vulgarity; the desire to be unique; intellectal distinctiveness; non-conformism; idealized love; and 'un romantique froid, supérieur'. Kempf (1977: 67) discusses Flaubert in the company of Baudelaire as 'un dandy, peut-être pas, mais sûrement son cousin'. Cohen sees the anti-hero in dandy terms as someone who was 'tortured about aggression, was artistic, and was more concerned about integrity than valour. He believed in being true to himself, which meant defying established values' (1990: 32).

manhood under the tutelage of knowledgeable elders, with the fear of failure always lurking in the background'. . . . 'literature of masculine *Bildungsroman*' (Gilmore, 1990: 19). The *Bildungs-roman* form also allows the first/third-person voice a ubiquitous authority. Flaubert's stylistic innovations in *ES*, most notably the technique of impersonality, are well documented (D. A. Williams, 1987). I want to conjoin this 'objective', insider–outsider, viewpoint with my argument for *ES* as a formal miscegenation of male genres. The history, the historical novel, the *Künstlerroman*, the realist novel *à la* Balzac complete with omniscient author, all rely on the universalizing narration from the 'on' perspective. History and aesthetics in the nineteenth century could only be narrated and constructed by the male voice of authority, erudition, reason, and judgement thanks to the legacy of Enlightenment philosophy and politics. The 'impersonality' of *ES* relies both on the force of authority of these pseudo-scientific genres and their literary brothers, and on modes of self-perception within the same contexts of history and art in their making and unmaking. These modes are similarly visible in new degrees in *ES*: the use of ellipsis, ambiguity, semantic aporias, and the novel's cruel romantic irony which leaves no position unchallenged. Ramazani (1993) names romantic irony as the nihilistic voice of the absurd, whether this is of revolution, aesthetics, individualism. This non-partisan irony none the less also allows the ironist the ultimate voice of power. In *ES* therefore, Flaubert makes out of history and fiction and the 'parvenu genre of the novel' (Conroy, 1985: 29 quoting Fletcher, 1980), a sublimely 'art for art's sake' fiction of its anti-models. *ES* can therefore not itself be copied, except perhaps through oblique descendancy in fictions of degeneration and decadence which must always then ultimately acknowledge their literary fraternity with Frédéric Moreau as literary 'big brother'.

4

La Tentation de Saint Antoine

The heightening of hyperbole, the polarized conflict, the menace and suspense of the representations may be made necessary by the effort to perceive and image the spiritual in a world voided of its traditional sacred, where the body of the ethical has become a sort of *deus absconditus* which must be sought for, postulated, brought into man's existence through the play of the spiritualist imagination.

(Brooks, 1976: 11)

WHEREAS discussion of Flaubert's earlier novels has focused on configurations of the masculine as social structures within hierarchy and patriarchy—the couple and marriage in *MB*, the hierarchizations of leadership and imperialist power in *SAL*, the splits in democracy caused by the contradictory forces of fraternity and equality in *ES*—*TSA* explores the male self and the structures of the Cartesian mind, as Bem (1979) argues. The central questions of the *cogito*, whether they concern subjectivity or what is knowable, come from the standpoint of rational scepticism, but in Descartes's case, with the ultimate aim to prove the existence of God. In and behind *TSA* lies the dual intertext of both *Discours de la Méthode* and *Méditations*, not so much as two books among many in this work's famous 'bibliothèque' (Foucault: 1971), but as successors of ideological mindsets already in existence in the context of their eminent third-century precursors. The detailed study of Cartesian intertexts in *TSA* lies outside this chapter. The focus here is their function as proleptic palimpsest to provide the invisible, but no less present, median term of reference. Thus, where Rome and its empire were the hidden but no less pivotal terms in *SAL*, Descartes and his legacy on the Enlightenment and positivist

France are the watershed separating the pre-modern from the modern worlds. *TSA* points forwards, while *BP*, its diptych twin, looks back, to Descartes. Both texts investigate Montaigne's 'Que sais-je?' but in very different ideological frames; *TSA* is a semi-autobiographical or ideobiographical enquiry and essay, whereas *BP* is the ironic fictional version of a potted self-help series (encyclopaedia or compendium) on every topic known to man. Thus the two works together mark the shift from metaphysical speculation on *gnosis*, what is knowable, or *Savoir* as transcendental term in *TSA*, to the empiricist logic of scientific method or *savoir* as empirical *voir* in *BP* (and not only between of *TSA1* and *TSA3* as Séginger, 1988: 84 argues). However, while *savoir* is a primary verb in *TSA* and generates dialogue with other forms of the gnostic, all the modal verbs, *pouvoir, vouloir, devoir, falloir*, in fact converge around it to arrive at the site of aesthetic and ethical judgement of a given culture, *valoir*. Ultimately, the problem Antoine faces is not simply to know, to desire, to be able to obey or acknowledge Truth. It is the validation of his discernments by the search for ultimate Authority in these matters in the maelstrom of conflicting truths which will be his own subjective validation. One might formulate this as 'Qu'Il vaille, donc, je suis.' The democratization of such values on the 'other side' of Descartes will in *BP* reappear as merit, or the self-validating merito-mediocracy of the double *pupitre*.

In accord with the pattern outlined in the previous chapters, the male hero chosen to express this *valoir* would have been unplaced in any nineteenth-century scale of values of male success, role models, or social icons. 'In a world in which the couple remains the social ideal, failure to make a relationship is a stigma. . . . For a man, il suggests failure or pathology. The male hermit is no longer a saint but someone who needs a social worker' (Cohen, 1990: 153). Flaubert has not only chosen to remodel a saint, but an inert, cerebral, and largely unknown one, diametrically opposed to 'muscular Christians' such as Saint George or Saint Francis, who are overtly involved with justice or a crusade for values of right and truth. This chapter investigates how Flaubert's Antoine none the less speaks directly to the spirit of the age of positivism and science in a secular nineteenth-century France with no obvious connections with third-century Egypt. Such deliberate anachronism will draw out 'hero' aptitudes but in the quintessentially Egyptian frame of his persona. This then opens up the other crucial speculation of the work that Flaubert revised three times: which is *the* temptation to which the title refers? In order to answer these questions, this chapter will examine the text from three perspectives which have largely remained undiscussed in the secondary literature. The first is due reflection on the multiform importance of the original Antony of Egypt, Father of Monasticism, not least as situated in the material Egypt of his day rather than as understood through later artistic representations such as those of Brueghel, with which Flaubert was also familiar. The second optic revolves round the debate about the heresies in the all-important fourth and middle section of this text. Critics have argued over them as the erudite, pro- or anti-religious hub of this work and its saint, and hence evaluated its episodic and abstruse accumulation of syncretic or intertextual ideas.[1] Equally important, I will argue, is the frame of this section, parts three and five, where Hilarion and the ideas he embodies are centre-stage and will be the key to unlock discussion about what the *real Tentation* might be, the subject of the third debate of the chapter. Where Reff (1974: 126) as one critic among others cites the Queen of Sheba, Ammonaria, and the flesh as the essential temptation against which the Antonian mind, spirit, and soul all struggle to the bitter end, an Egyptian- and Hilarion-eye view may offer a rather different response.

Although deeply influenced by Renan, Creuzer, and Matter

---

[1] See Guillemin (1963) for a pro-religious interpretation. For anti-religious or non-religious analyses, see e.g. Seznec (1945*a*: 207 and 1945*b*, 314–15), and Donato (1993). Less positively see Nancy (1994: 105); 'La *Tentation* est un texte singulier en ce qu'il tient tout entier dans sa fin, mais que son corps, son développement, n'est rien qu'un bourrage d'images et d'informations, de poncifs de langage hiératique ou ésotérique, sans rien qui touche à l'écriture . . . Il n'est bon qu'à faire toucher du doigt la bêtise d'un certain fantasme romantique.' For readings of the intertextual dimensions in *TSA*, see Foucault (1971) or more specifically Rétat (1990) for a discussion of Renan's relativism on *TSA* and the central role of criticism to explore various intellectual or spiritual states. Of particular pertinence here is Renan's *Avenir des sciences* and its author's attempt to 'recréer en lui, par la réflexion, les états spontanés, instinctifs de l'inspiré, du martyre, du prophète'. See Séginger (1997: ch. 3) which relies heavily on Bowman (1986: 16–36) as one of the fullest accounts to date of the influence of the works of Creuzer and Matter *inter alia* which Flaubert used as background to *TSA*.

as nineteenth-century sources for the comparative religious background of *TSA*, Flaubert's reading knowledge of Greek philosophy, Neoplatonism, Gnosticism, and the Vedas challenges their occidental, post-Christian cultural assumptions and superior value-judgements. Similarly, his personal account of Egypt in *Le Voyage en Orient* offers a surprisingly oriental view (as Moussa, 1996, and Orr, 1998*a* argue), while his thorough-going critique of Western Christendom in *TSA*, through his imitation of the original, and unorthodox, third-century Antony of Egypt as propounded by Athanasius in his *Vita Antonii*, makes of this text a fictionalized ecclesiastical history (Orr, 2000). Rather than rehearse these complex Church-history facets of *TSA* again, I want to draw out the wider material parallels with nineteenth-century France, and those ideological (politico-philosophical) reverberations which demonstrate the mind–body split in its corporate dimensions. Personification of this dichotomy in Antoine is matched by a similar characterization of stances through named 'people' in *TSA*: Urtexts of dialectical materialism, Marx and Hegel thus find their ancient Alexandrian forms.

Flaubert's reconstruction in *TSA* of the history of Alexandria in the third century at the time of Antony is surprisingly well drawn, one might even claim redundant, in a work which is supposed to be all reflections and cerebral visions. Alexandria of the period was a cultural, religious, and philosophical melting-pot, as well as the *locus* of political, economic, and ecclesiastical power in the Middle and Far East (Orr, 2000). Through its central position as a Roman port, it concentrated cultural, artistic, educational, and financial interests. An economic, intellectual, and religious centre of the civilized world, its great wealth, power, and luxury were in the hands of the few. This led to heavy taxation of the poor, and Alexandria acted as a magnet to unskilled agrarian workers because of food shortages in the country.

In the manner of the Carthage of *Salammbô* which Anne Green (1982) so convincingly uncovered, the historical and social problems of Alexandria in the third century foreshadow those experienced by France in the 1840s. The cholera epidemic, the bread shortages, high taxes, increasing urbanization, a Paris with a large, unskilled workforce, reverberate with Antony's Alexandria at every point:

[T]he second half of the third century witnessed a growing economic and social crisis in Egypt, not to end until the late fourth century. The Roman exploitation of Egypt through heavy taxation and the direction of the economy towards export, coupled with military requisitions and the oppressive system of collective obligations, the liturgies . . . were the reasons behind the desertion of many villages and the widespread escape from land and civic obligations, the *anachoresis*. Rapid inflation, corruption, neglect of irrigation, and the indifference on the part of those responsible were obvious consequences, as well as a movement towards urbanization and the subsequent demotion of the traditional aristocracy.   (Rubenson, 1995: 90)

Haussmann's programme of new buildings and boulevards matches the description of the mushrooming new quarters of Alexandria. The concomitant opulence and availability of luxury goods from every part of the globe for the rich in Paris reflect Alexandrian affluence and decadence. Wealthy outsiders were therefore the gauge of a city's élite and its value as international capital. This I would stress is almost the main, comparative, force of the Queen of Sheba in *TSA*. While critics have seen her as the epitome of sexuality, the incarnation of Antoine's temptations of the flesh, she personifies and externalizes the material and philosophical value-systems of the civilized world.[2] Representing not just its pleasures, the luxury, excess, and value of her jewel-encrusted garments reinforce the hard physical reality of her 'pierreries', which are art and currency of

[2] For Thomas (1990: 42), the term is 'Femmes-écrins, la Salomé de Moreau, la reine de Saba de Flaubert sont livrées au même sort. Elles passent du côté de la marchandise. Prisonnières des joyaux qui les ornent, elles en constituent le support . . . Froid, scintillant, et dur, ravissant spectacle de la nudité oubliée au profit de la mise en évidence des matières précieuses.' For Gothot-Mersch (1986: 40) Sheba is also a 'représentation de la luxure', but she proceeds to reiterate the cliché about her oriental *femme fatale* sexuality as a 'fille de joie . . . obscène et immonde'. Séginger (1997: 370) comments on a well-documented phrase from *TSA* spoken by Sheba, both recasting critical *idées reçues* and hinting towards a more than sexual reading: 'C'est un véritable Big-Bang cosmique que la Reine de Saba veut déclencher après avoir déclaré, "Je ne suis pas une femme, je suis un monde" . . . L'érotisme sacré de la Reine de Saba aurait pu lui dévoiler les mystères des origines.' Recently Nieland has taken up the tack of Sheba's excessive sexuality as potentially bisexual: 'The masculinity of the Queen is complemented by reference to the emasculation of the Saint: . . . "je t'épilerai" ' (1998: 62). Gothot-Mersch (1986: 40) deflects the issue by putting ultimate responsibility in the hands of the author: 'Flaubert écrit en marge "hermaphrodite, un 3e sexe".' See my discussion of Emma's 'masculinity' in Ch. 1 as an analogous way of drawing out Sheba's all-encompassing femininity and womanhood.

the period. However, her Sabaean and oriental wealth, splendour, civilization, and culture, pale as she reaches this neo-Salmonic city in a rewriting of her visit to the biblical Solomon. Not only was he the king who requested wisdom: he was the builder of the Temple and a palace for himself in Jerusalem and so echoes the spiritual and civic theocratic models at issue in Antoine's times. She thus sends back an equivalent oriental standard in reflection to the very Alexandria which boasts its huge mirror into which Antoine also looks: 'Un grand miroir de cuivre, tourné vers la haute mer, reflète les navires qui sont au large' (*TSA*, 24). The second mirroring she represents is the incorporation of an alternative, but no less Egyptian/oriental, religion which the critics have only mentioned within sexual confines. When the Queen of Sheba enters the stage, she is dressed not so much as the 'Whore of Babylon' but as Ishtar, high priestess and sorceress of Babylon, supreme goddess of sexual love, fertility, and war. In her costume she also resembles a high priestess of the (Greek) Eleusinian Mysteries, which merge knowledge with sacred prostitution. In addition, in her queenly function, she is Isis, chief goddess and queen of ancient Egypt. Hence she combines three queen-goddess figures in one to incorporate them as superlative refiguration of material and spiritual woman. Her famous speech—'Je ne suis pas une femme, je suis un monde. Mes vêtements n'ont qu'à tomber, et tu découvriras sur ma personne une succession de mystères' (*TSA*, 36)—can now be interpreted as her self-description within a universal physico-spiritual heritage and her supreme jurisdiction as ruler, diplomat, and politician, Queen of Sheba, 'femme savante'. She is not 'masculine' *per se* but only in so far as such roles and attributes are identified in (western) critics' minds with 'male' powers and prominence, or through their overcompensation for Antoine's 'emasculation', by reducing her female identity to that of a mere sexual icon.

The long initial descriptions of the material setting of Antony and third-century Egypt in *TSA* crystallize the burning debates of the age: matter and ideal or the body–soul question within the context of multiculturalism as centre of empire. It seems that from the outset of *TSA* Flaubert was striving to capture the spiritual dimensions of materialism in an original, Antonian, way so as better to lambast the tendentiousness of the same contradictory forces at work in nineteenth-century France: on the one hand, Catholicism as official 'true' religion in an increasingly secularized state; and, on the other, the (false because 'democratic') optimism of interest in comparative religions, the belief that because mythic patterns recur, with variations, they must all be equally true. By engaging Antony in the power-nexuses of the age in Alexandria, the growing motor for social unrest being the shift of authority from religions to the Academy and the economy, a direct parallel emerges with France's increasing industrialization and proto-Darwinian drive for progress rooted in laicization, positivism, and science. Science as 'new religion' in France parallels the 'new religions' in third-century Alexandria. It was the power of the Catechretical school (strongly influenced by Platonism and Stoicism), a training ground for the nations' intellectuals, that caused the various religious communities (including the wide range of gnostic sects as represented by the so-called heresies) to make a stand and search out strong leaders. Griggs (1990: 79) puts the religious, philosophical, and theological context of Antoine in a nutshell:

The time span from Demetrius to Dionysius in Egyptian Christianity can be characterized as the period when Alexandria begins to emerge as an important centre of the church in the Mediterranean world and when the Alexandrian bishop acquired an authoritative position equalling and sometimes rivalling that of other bishops in the major cities such as Rome, Antioch, and Jerusalem. The primary reason for this development occurring in Alexandria . . . was the imposition into Egypt of ecclesiastically and doctrinally well-defined Christianity in the person and bishopric of Demetrius near the end of the second century. The institution in Alexandria which at that time offered the greatest competition to the office of bishop was the catechretical school, directed in turn by Pantaenus, Clement, Origen, Heraclas, and Dionysius. Under the directorship of the first three men, the school was relatively independent in its operations and activities, and to it were drawn students of virtually every philosophical and religious persuasion, both inside and outside Christianity. The tension between Origen and Demetrius, essentially ecclesiastical in nature, led to the exile of the former and the subsequent binding of the school to close episcopal supervision under Heraclas and his successors.

Athanasius as successor Bishop of Alexandria therefore called upon Antony as champion (*faire valoir*) for the crusade against the influences of Hellenism, Gnosticism, and Manichaeism and for Alexandrian Christianity. His various motives for using Antony as mouthpiece in his *Vita Antonii* for a theology of a consubstantial Christ, and to pit monasticism against overspiritual schools and the Logos theology of Greek-Christian intellectual Alexandria, I have discussed elsewhere (Orr, 2000). Ironically this forces Antony into sectarian leadership when he had himself rejected these roles, indeed had actively fled authorities, both secular and religious, to become a solitary in the first place.

Being Father of Monasticism (in the desert) is one and the same as being exemplar of the Spiritual Father (in the city), for neither allows Antony the position of integrity and withdrawal which ultimately made him so potentially ideal as leader of both. It is precisely the position outside all established doctrine, theology, or philosophy that Antony maintained. He was never ordained, yet his status as theologian was never challenged. He made two important political, theological, and philosophical interventions into Alexandrian debates at two distinct phases of his eremitical career, but withdrew increasingly and geographically from all that the city represented to die alone. 'From his monastery he went to Alexandria in 311 to encourage the confessors during the persecution of Maximinus. He lived by gardening and mat-making; in character he combined severe austerity with an emphasis on discretion and the love of God before all else. . . . In 355 he again went to Alexandria, this time to refute the Arians. Even the philosophers were impressed' (Farmer, 1992: 25). With no small sense of ego, Flaubert's fictionalized ideobiography of Antoine would voice the same impossible solitude and separation of the artist-intellectual from the economic herd and from the intellectual horde in late nineteenth-century France.

From the outset of *TSA*, Flaubert positions Antoine with extraordinary historical accuracy in his second eremitical period, post-Alexandria and the Arian crisis and in the crucial final years of his life.

Anthony was a native of Egypt, was born in *c.*251 in the village of Coma near the Thebaid, and was reared amid considerable wealth by his Christian parents . . . Anthony occupied an abandoned fort at the mountain he found, which is called the 'Outer Mountain', and which is at Pispir, some 50 miles south of Memphis on the east bank of the Nile. Athanasius states that Anthony remained there for twenty years, during which time many began to emulate his style of life as one 'initiated into sacred mysteries and filled with the spirit of God'. He rejected not only the attacks of the devil, but also the temptation to assume the leadership of a monastic organization. Desiring to be alone, Anthony journeyed to Upper Egypt, and there found another mountain, the 'Inner Mountain' to live out his days. This second mountain identified with the modern Deir Anba Antonios near the Red Sea, became the unofficial headquarters for this new movement, in Christianity, and both those who wished to ask the monk for advice and those who wished to follow his example journeyed there. . . . Anthony is credited with the gifts and powers of exorcism, healing, prophecy, and virtually all the prophetic functions traditionally associated with the church, but he was not ordained to any clerical office . . . Anthony's death occurred in 356, and just before his death he asked that the sheepskin garment given to him by Athanasius be returned. The individualism and independence from the world which epitomized his life were thus in evidence in his death. Peter Brown in a recent work notes that the rapid growth of monasticism during the third and fourth centuries can be linked to tensions and crises in human relations, which cause men to seek autarchy through detachment from society. (Griggs, 1990: 103–5)

As mature contemplative, Antoine epitomizes reason, sound mind, experience, and the self-knowledge which is his hallmark. The exhortation to 'know thyself' is the main subject of letters three and four of his famous *Seven Letters*. Because of his spiritual training in *gnosis* in its widest sense, Antoine has thus already suffered temptation from the world, the flesh, and the devil, but almost more crucially he has experienced it as champion of the Church in the form of the earthly temptations of importance, power, and status as a crusader-leader. His hardwon knowledge of integration, not separation of the mind and body, in his involvement in the Alexandrian and monastic worlds none the less leaves him open to the revisitation from all 'the world, the flesh and the devil' in the realm of memory, thought, and imagination. Nancy (1994) is right to stress these as an encyclopaedic catalogue of modes of reflection and enlightenment:

TSA est faite . . . de toutes les variations possibles d'un unique thème de la lumière, de la pénétration dans la lumière et par la lumière . . .: illumination, révélation, éclat, chatoiement, forme, vision, spectacle, images de toutes les espèces, prodiges, halos, reflets, mirages, soleils, étoiles et flambeaux, spectacles, apocalypses, scènes, ciels, prunelles flamboyantes, arcs-en-ciel, phosphorescences et transparences jusqu' à l'idée pure et jusqu'à la face du Christ . . . Le Christ *lux in tenebris* est l'unique sujet de ce livre pareil à un astéroïde tombé, lourd témoin calciné. (107)

However, I would argue that in the life of a saint of Antoine's spiritual stature these themes belong firmly to the other mental realms of faith, belief(s), and meditation. In *TSA* Antoine therefore confronts mental images of other faith and belief systems that challenge his own, together with challenges to his will; to his obedience to notions without empirical evidence; to his power to judge what are contradictory or counterfeit ideas; to his resolve or intention; and to every emotional resource which constitutes the ensemble that is his own integrity. This involves confrontation with spiritual forces such as the demonic, madness, and mental instabilities of all kinds. The disintegration of matter which is his ageing body, the hallucinatory or delirious behind his words, or the outpourings of derangement which could be symptomatic of his despair, are the obverse realities of the plaster-saint image that Flaubert consistently destroys through this figure. I have outlined elsewhere (Orr, 1998*b*) the parallels between the manifestations of the ecstatic and those of deliria related to tertiary syphilis, in order to highlight the body behind the spirit in Antoine.

The other sense of the 'mad' demonstrated by Flaubert's Antoine is the Erasmian Wisdom of Folly. In *TSA*, it is the folly of refusing to join causes, institutions, even theological or spiritual élites, which demarcates Antoine's proto-existential authenticity and refusal of 'mauvaise foi' for the real thing. R. Williams (1990: 94) underscores the properly absurd of such integrated spirituality: 'Antony, the founding father of the monastic movement, is alleged to have said, "A time is coming when men will go mad, and when they see someone who is not mad, they will attack him saying, You are mad, you are not like us" . . . As a statement of the intractible absurdity of monasticism, that cannot be improved upon. The world and the Church are mad when they circumscribe human possibilities of serving God.' I will return in due course to the question of integrity and authenticity as oneness, unity, and singularity. It is precisely because Antony is the supreme contemplative, that he sets to the work of meditation (prayer) and mediation, and thereby opens himself to the spiritual realms which rush in throughout the text. It is not, then, without significance that at the end of each temptation and supremely at the beginning of the new day at the climactic revelation of *TSA*, a repetition of the discipline and will-to-believe of the Antoine of the beginning of the work occur. The final line is the sign of faith and the act of faith: 'Antoine fait le signe de la croix et se remit en prières.' The verb 'se remettre' here signals no passive or complacent response or the more dubious start of a 'trip' where the active emptying of the mind heightens the achievable 'high'. This is the essence of Eastern Orthodox spirituality as distinct from the Catholic or various gnostic positions; instead of rejection of the flesh, there is its integration. Antony of Egypt did not see the body as evil in itself, but, like every other aspect of fallen humanity, in need of transformation in the immanent as well as in the transcendent, as Rubenson (1995: 71) states in a discussion of the original Saint Antony's *First Letter on Repentance*.

It is in his bodily confrontation with other tempter figures that Antoine's ultimate experiential folly and stand for truth are tested, just as it was Christ's in the wilderness. Satan had to flee the consubstantial onslaught of God-infilled humanity which refused to overstep the limits either of its incarnated flesh— turning stones into bread would constitute heavenly miracle— or of earthly power, the refusal to bow down to worship Satan in exchange for empires, or over life itself by asking for angelic interventions. Christ's 'It is written' also brings out the stand of informed wisdom, interpretation and knowledge, and unwavering belief in authority which Antoine also echoes. The tempters who are most easily dismissed are the embodiments of doctrines and creeds, ideas or positions, and all have short-lived parts in *TSA*. More discomfiting are the embodiments who represent human figures. Ammonaria from Antoine's past, rather than Sheba as human superlative in female key, touches a chord but is no real challenge to the mature Antoine. It is rather the embodiment of his former disciple, Hilarion, who is the channel to disbelief because of who he was, is, and will become in Antoine's eyes.

Hilarion has been singularly overlooked in Flaubert criticism, and passing references make of him various things: 'merely an extension of Antoine's own personality' (Sherrington, 1965: 278), or more fancifully, an ironic re-embodiment of Saint-Hilaire's 'interest in the monstrous organism and its growth along the same lines as the "normal" ' (Starr, 1984: 1074). Most frequently he is interpreted as a personification of Science often in satanic guise, or as a textual 'accoucheur' whose function is to bring forth the next barrage of doubts to double and confront Antoine's.[3] In the one article devoted to him, Lilley emphasizes that without Hilarion the text 'resterait un lieu de désorganisation ... Hilarion suggère une méthode d'organisation des thèmes et une interprétation nouvelles des faits et des connaissances' (1981: 21). She further underlines his 'esprit objectif détaché de prises de positions' as machiavellian, amoral, modern in his destruction of ancient myths, and that '[d]e la part d'Hilarion, il n'y a aucune coercion: Saint Antoine est libre de faire son choix et l'opération de ce choix est la tentation même' (ibid. 19). Her conclusion is that 'avec Hilarion, Gustave Flaubert a créé un nouveau mythe: l'archétype de l'homme d'une société vouée à la sécularisation croissante et inévitable' (ibid. 21–2).

Valuable though all these insights are, they do not touch the real issues of Hilarion's role and function in *TSA*. First and foremost, as with Flaubert's meticulous reincarnation of Antoine

---

[3] For Hilarion as science in satanic guise, see Seznec (1949: 14) and Digeon (1946: 40): 'Hilarion est bien l'homme qui se veut supérieurement impartial. Il étudie objectivement et ... scientifiquement "le cas Saint Antoine" la pathologie de l'ascète'. Starr (1984: 1072) considers that 'Flaubert actually wrote the contradictory temptations of science and confusion in the 1874 version of the text', while Hélein-Koss (1991) expands his role as doubter, sceptic, scientist to mocker: 'Dans la version de 1874 ... le rire, véhicule du désir, passe désormais par un relais nouveau; le désir assimilé à la *libido sciendi*, personnifié par Hilarion, ancien disciple d'Antoine, surdoué et gai à faire rire les patriarches. Hilarion, nouveau destinateur du rire et régisseur d'une série d'apparitions issues des lectures bibliques d'Antoine assure le lien entre le *lisible* le *risible* et le *visible [ricanements]*', (69, author's emphasis). In his role primarily as harbinger, see Séginger (1997: 314), 'Hilarion soulignera les différences entre les Évangiles et ses réflexions sur les obscurités du texte sacré préparant l'apparition des Hérésies.'

from the historical Saint Antony of Egypt, his Hilarion reworks the original Egyptian, who was indeed Antony's own disciple.

The *Vita Hilarionis* is a complete *Vita*, which describes the life and character of Hilarion, including his short period as a disciple of Antony's. Jerome's authorship has never been questioned and the date given for its composition is . . . *c*.390. Antony is depicted as the teacher of Hilarion, later to become the father of Palestinian monasticism. The purpose is clearly to provide the Palestinian monasticism with a history, and to trace its origins back to Egypt; Jerome supports his writing by referring to Epiphanius of Salamis, who, he says, had been close to Hilarion and had written a letter to him. The text is clearly dependent on the *Vita Antonii*, and adds little to the Antonian image. It relates how Hilarion, at the age of fifteen, stayed with Antony for two weeks to study his discipline; unable to endure the crowds around him he decided to leave for Palestine and take up the life of a hermit. At the age of 65, after hearing of Antony's death, he is said to have fled fame and crowds in Palestine and returned to Egypt. His goal was the 'inner' monastery of Antony, and arriving there he moved in as his successor. By his prayers he is reported to have procured rain after three years of drought caused by the mourning of the elements due to Antony's death. After some time he moved on to Sicily and finally to Cyprus.   (Rubenson, 1995: 76)

Not only does Flaubert cause Antoine to confront Hilarion in his 'inner monastery' prior to his death, it is the obvious confrontation between spiritual son and spiritual Father (of personal faith as well as Monasticism) that compounds the horror of the central sections of *TSA*. From the very outset of section three (Hilarion's frame with section five to encapsulate the theophilosophical debates in part four), Flaubert leaves us in no doubt as to the fictional authenticity of the character who has the most lines of *TSA* because he has flesh-and-blood as well as ideological significance. 'Enfant', 'petit comme un nain', '[d]es cheveux blancs couvrent sa tête prodigieusement grosse', his first words assert his identity as 'ton ancien disciple Hilarion', which Antoine challenges, knowing that 'Hilarion habite depuis de longues années la Palestine'. Hilarion's head is enormous, almost encephalitic, because his brain will prove to be super-charged at the expense of his body. He represents the intellectual, *savoir* in all its new forms, newness itself being its criterion of value rather than any moral or aesthetic order. 'In the Egypt of the late third century, a country where new leaders and new social structures were in high demand and traditional religion was in decline, new religious movements such as monasticism were not the products of people on the margin of society, but of intellectuals dissatisfied with what tradition had to offer' (Rubenson, 1995: 187). And this *savoir* is firmly in the hands of fallible man. Not only does Hilarion from the outset of *TSA* challenge Athanasius as infallible authority and Bishop of Alexandria, he demonstrates his human weakness in terms of his cruelty and corruption, as well as his spiritual limitations in terms of doctrinal 'purity' at the Nicene Council. Knowingly luring Antoine into a position of questioning and ideological openness beyond 'blind' conviction, his chief role is to import dissatisfaction with, and denunciation of, the old order of religion as ultimate authority in matters of truth. 'Nous n'avons de mérite que par notre soif du Vrai. La Religion seule n'explique pas tout . . . il faut, pour son salut, communiquer avec ses frères . . . et écouter toutes les raisons, ne dédaigner rien ni personne.' While Hilarion then quotes the range of such consultation, including necromancers and poets, it is those powerfully close to home, Denys and Clement of Alexandria, who constitute the authority to read secular, especially Greek texts, alongside the scriptural that Hilarion proposes as offering a 'balanced' (scientific) point of view. Griggs (1990: 100) fills in the contextual background: 'Monasticism, an extreme form of asceticism adopted as a way of life for devotional reasons, is a gift of the Egyptian Church to the Christian world, . . . Near the beginning of the third century Clement distinguished all the heresies against which he wrote according to their tendency toward asceticism or toward licentiousness. He fought both tendencies.' The tempter towards excessive asceticism as overblown cerebral function, Hilarion's 'libertinage' is towards greater separation of mind from body.

In fact, all of part three of *TSA* functions as Hilarion's prologue to encourage and persuade Antoine to hear out the counter-positions to his 'conviction' (the heresies) in part four. It contains the nub of issues which will be raised in the central panel of *TSA* concerning authority and discernment of *the* truth among truths, raised through personal challenge to his former teacher's authority and elucidations on the points of faith and contradictions in Scripture which contest both its ultimate authority and potentially Antoine's own. Hilarion's most compelling arguments against Antoine are simply the reply of youth, modernity, new ideas. Theologically then, Hilarion is no syncretist or negator of the spiritual for the scientific, but fully initiated in Scripture and mystery religions (representatives are unfolded throughout part four), which equate hierarchical degree with superiority, like Masonic degrees. His rhetoric of a chosen brotherhood is important here, not only in the context of monasticism and religious orders, but also for a Masonic reading of *TSA* which lies outside this study. He demonstrates the 'truth' that Frédéric dimly perceives in *ES* that 'fraternité' is not 'égalité' or democracy, but a 'confrérie' of the chosen few who desire to maintain their position as an élite. The cacophony of gnostic voices and positions in part four of *TSA* modulates in religious key the political speechifying of the Club de l'Intelligence discussed in Chapter 3. Hilarion's highly sophisticated and authoritative logic and reason is the philosophical version of this, the Cartesian and Enlightenment spirit. In this, Lombard (1934: 81–2) correctly reads Hilarion as personification of 'la Logique et l'Orgueil et dont la déférence perfide et les hypocrites suggestions font surgir et la tentation de l'orgueil et les arguments de la logique si dangereux pour la foi'. This radically opposes revealed truth which cannot be sought or won, only received by humble, open hearts such as Antoine's in communion with God. Hilarion's speculative version of truth is the intellectual, schooled, trained, academically brilliant, a masterpiece of articulacy and rhetorical delivery. Part three of *TSA* illustrates his mastery through its form: a 'demo-Socratic' dialogue, by which I mean the intertextual reversal of the Socratic teacher–pupil relationship and pedagogical form that not only puts the pupil in the place of the teacher but also justifies this role through the argument of the (democratic) right to free speech. Instead of the use of the question to elicit information or form other ways of thinking, Hilarion's method is assertive and imperative in an allegedly objective, neutral, amoral way. Superior thinking is, period. His final appearance at the end of part five of *TSA* will show how far his guise of empirical method and the rationale of enlightened understanding called science has freed itself from its opposites—myth, prejudice, taboo, ritual, or rote — or is a disguise for more sinister versions of these.

In the same way that Hilarion provides the frame narrative to part four in his onslaught on all Antoine holds dear in parts three and five, he also bridges the ideological barrage against Antoine's faith and the heresies by careful stage management of the order by which the attacks are introduced. Again critics have failed to see the choreography of part four, which opens with Manès and closes with Damis and Apollonius. Both are voices which are tantamount to Hilarion-substitutes or surrogates. These new figures are also quintessentially Alexandrian and of the historical Antony's time. The prophet Mani functions first, as I argued for the Queen of Sheba, as a Persian-oriental value-system to off-balance what will ensue as mainly gnostic, therefore pseudo Judaeo-western-Christian, religious ideas. In *TSA*, he is described as 'beau comme un archange', stylized in his attributes as almost a male version of Sheba. More importantly, however, he personifies the cult named after him, Manichaeism.

[F]rom Persia came the Christian heresy of Manichaios, or Mani as a short form. Mani, born in 216 C.E. near Seleucia-Ctesiphon, the capital of the Persian Empire, was raised in a Babylonian Baptist community. Remarkable spiritual manifestations beginning at age 12, including heavenly visits from his celestial alter-ego, led Mani, at age 24 in 240 C.E., to make his first public appearance as a preacher of a new gospel of hope and salvation. The success of this religious leader, who called himself an Apostle of Jesus Christ, was phenomenal even during his own lifetime. He suffered martyrdom in 276 under Bahram I of Persia, who had him put to death by being flayed alive. Missionaries were sent both to the east and to the west, and Manichaeism became a major threat to Christianity in the Roman Empire during the fourth and fifth centuries. (Griggs, 1990: 94)

An oriental, syncretic, religion of radical dualism to counter Platonism, the core notion of Manichaeism was that light and darkness were in co-equal struggle in the universe. Incorporating elements drawn from Indian religions, Buddhism and Zoroastrianism, as well as Christianity, Manès is the further link-man to herald the eastern religious representatives to come before Antoine in part five. Initially the saint laughs outright at the preposterous claims of Manès, but is quickly lured through him by Hilarion into meeting the realm of gnostic heresies which countenance the devil as creator or as powerful as God in creation.

Various central theological debates emerge through the plethora of Alexandrian cult positions represented in part four of *TSA*. The body–soul, light–darkness debates epitomizing various metaphysics of dualism merge into doctrines of good and evil, creation and the created order, the person of Christ in the Trinity and his consubstantiality or place as Son of God/Son of Man, all doubled by gnostic ideas, including Manichaeism, which might be summed up as religions of Antichrists. The reference to Manès as archangel at the outset, his charisma as Antichrist figure of his times, his confraternity with Hilarion, all point to the more familiar story in Job of Satan falling from the heavens, cast out for his pride but a fallen angel of light none the less. This knowledge of angelic and demonic forces is, however, also grounded in the realities of Antoine's experience in his contemplative life and in his public one: he has already confronted and challenged Arius, which allows him in the flesh in part four to withstand the lure of the return of heresies as pure idea or representation.

The finale of part four focuses on the 'mirror' of Antoine-Hilarion, Apollonius and his disciple, Damis, although the relationship is much more 'classically' that of the Socratic master–pupil hierarchy. Apollonius of Tyane was a neo-Pythagorean philosopher in the tradition of his master. Pythagoras, of the mathematical theorem, was 'as much or more the guru of a religious ashram as the head of a research institute: his school constitutes a sort of order, the Pythagorean Brotherhood' (Flew, 1971: 376). From him come the three laws of planetary motion as well as numerology, and it is this double function that Apollonius develops. Apollonius' moral philosophy was widely regarded, as too was his reputation as a magician. Apollonius wrote a *Life of Pythagoras* as well as a treatise on divination. In Ephesus, his native region, Apollonius was regarded as a god in the temples and was made famous by Philostratus in his *Life of Apollonius*, where he was compared to Christ.

As with the details of Hilarion, Flaubert's reworking of Apollonius is strikingly accurate and he is introduced as a figure 'de haute taille, de figure douce, de maintien grave. Ses cheveux blonds, séparés comme ceux de Christ, descendent régulièrement sur ses épaules' (*TSA*, 95). Damis also recounts that 'Thyane, sa vie natale, a institué en son honneur un temple avec des prêtres' (*TSA*, 111). Apollonius speaks of 'la tradition' (*TSA*, 99), and 'l'art' (*TSA*, 108), which are counterfeits of miracles, healings, and exorcisms, like Pharaoh's magicians' responses to Moses. As the final section builds to its climax, with Antoine's use of the name of Jesus as touchstone of discernment between good and evil, Apollonius' magician face has become increasingly apparent, as has the hierarchical nature of his relationship to his disciple, Damis, who reflects and endorses the power of the master.

Part five of *TSA* then allows for Antoine's reflections and contemplations of the gods of other nations, to release the laugh in their face which brings back the sinister double of representation, Hilarion, whose laugh and form also double the Apollonius–Damis hierarchy of disciple–master relationship but as eremitical equal or, indeed, visible reversal of status or grandeur: 'Un autre rire derrière lui; et Hilarion se présente— habillé en ermite, beaucoup plus grand que tout à l'heure, colossal' (*TSA*, 118). The second onslaught of religious underminings and challenges to Antoine's faith and convictions move from East to West but continues in a different key to pick up the Hindu and Persian faces of Manichaeism or Zoroastrianism. Beginning with Buddha, whom Hilarion constantly compares to a Christ-like figure, Persian and Syrian Chaldean and Babylonian gods follow to demonstrate various aspects of sacred bestiality (see Seznec, 1945*b*: 318), magical attributes, and prophetic counterparts. Finally, Hilarion heralds in the Egytian Isis and the more familiar Greek and Roman pantheon, thus returning the survey of comparative religions to the religious melting-pot of the Alexandria of Antoine's times. To my mind, the fifth part is less of a 'temptation' to Antoine in the figures *per se*. His susceptibility is not to the forms these religions manifest but to Hilarion's constant goading commentary on their counterfeiting significance which, like a dripping tap, is designed to wear away at his belief in the one true God. Throughout every manifestation, Hilarion is there, a presence when each departs, and when finally the last voice and form have disappeared there remains only a 'quelqu'un'; 'Et Hilarion est devant lui,—mais transfiguré, beau comme un archange, lumineux comme un soleil,—et tellement grand que pour le voir [Antoine] se renverse la tête' (*TSA*, 166). The monstrous spiritual child has now revealed his 'true' identity: the universal ruler in defiance of God; 'On m'appelle la Science' (ibid.). Rougemont (1982: 33) describes the devil in terms very similar to those used by Flaubert of Hilarion; 'Le prince de ce monde, de l'incertitude—il a voulu singer Dieu.' 'Science' is in fact identical to 'incertitude'. It is then Antoine who sees the connection between this agnostic and pseudo-objective creature as in the same league as the ultimate master of all that is not God, the devil. 'Le Diable est l'anti-modèle absolu, son essence étant précisément le déguisement, l'usurpation des apparences, le bluff éhonté ou subtil, bref, l'art de faire mentir les formes' (ibid. 16). And as Hilarion heralds in the heresies, so he ushers in his 'master', to enable direct confrontation and dialogue between him and Antoine in part six and with monstrous forms in part seven.

The temptation, then, is not so much the power of fleshly, metaphysical, or scientific challenges to Antoine's faith as critics have claimed.[4] Rather, it is the desire to impart, to be in partnership with a fellow creature, to join, to be in unity with

---

[4] For critical debate on the nature of Antoine's 'tentation', see e.g. Testa (1991–2: 141): 'Saint Antony's "training" could be described as the attempt to become God-Matter in and while bypassing the stage of the (threatening) sexualized identity that calls itself "I" '; or Séginger (1988: 65), 'La métaphysique représente une des tentations les plus dangereuses qu'ait à repousser Saint Antoine: le néoplatonisme offert par Apollonius. . . . Dans *TSA3* la métaphysique est bien désignée comme l'ennemi du sentiment religieux'. For Macherey, (1990: 159) 'toutes les religions ont . . . la même irrationalité, le même fond immémorial de bestialité et de bêtise, la même aspiration impuissante à réconcilier définitivement l'âme et les choses . . . mais à l'opposé d'une perspective progressiste, le pessimisme professé de Flaubert l'a amené à dévoiler . . . l'inanité de l'universelle idolâtrie, incarnée dans le culte insensé des images, première et dernière tentation assiégeant l'esprit humain', and 'Cette thématique de l'échec délivrant un message dont l'orientation fondamentale était celle d'une néontologie: la réalité n'étant finalement qu'une obsession parmi tant d'autres, une "tentation" ' (ibid. 176); Leal (1990: 332): 'In this tension the acceptance and obedience inherent in the tendency to become part of the natural world are set against the temptation of a largely egocentric individualism which seeks a position of authority or ascendancy. Such individualism brings physical, intellectual and spiritual isolation and finally threatens the very sense that the individual has of the reality of himself, and of the world. Saintliness, on the other hand, leads to a loss of the sense of the individual self, to a form of bêtise.'

another of like mind or spirit. Hence the terrible betrayal of Hilarion, the spiritual son, who knows his 'father' so well, yet mocks this knowledge by duplicity and double-agency, as summed up in his negative narcissism, the anti-mirror of Antoine's soul. Nowhere is this better illustrated than in his derisory laugh, and Judas-like reiteration of Antoine's own words at the beginning of part five. Where Frédéric and Deslauriers echo one another at the end of *ES* in mutual affirmation of their double past, Hilarion counterfeits allegiance to Antoine's world-view by mocking and undermining his words and actions in empty imitation as pseudo-agreement:

Et il voit passer à ras de sol des feuilles . . . de vagues représentations d'animaux, puis des espèces de nains hydrophiques . . . Il éclate de rire. . . .
[*Antoine*] Qu'il faut être bête pour adorer cela!
[*Hilarion*] Oh! oui, extrêmement bête! . . .
Antoine et Hilarion s'amusent énormément. Ils se tiennent les côtes à force de rire. . . . A mesure qu'elles se rapprochent du type humain, elles irritent Antoine davantage. . . .
[*Antoine*] Horreur!

(*TSA*, 118–19)

Hilarion is Antoine's greatest temptation because he is like-minded and 'spiritual', a disciple and student of *gnosis*, a potential son and (twin) brother figure to accompany Antoine in his isolation and loneliness at the end of his life and ministry. The effort in upholding his faith is not so much doctrinal as personal. The temptation to become one with Hilarion's world-view, so like his own, yet so diametrically opposite, gives the lie to Hilarion's honey-false persuasion: he is the counterfeit to Antoine's truth or experience which needs no help from *scientia*, nor does it puff up its expertise in mysteries or initiations. Hutin (1970: 6) offers a definition of Gnosticism ('chez les "occultistes" et "théosophes" contemporains') which is tantamount to Hilarion's version of science:

au lieu d'hérétiques pervers ou délirants, nous trouvons des hommes détenteurs d'initiations prestigieuses, invités aux mystères orientaux, possédant des connaissances occultes ignorées du commun des mortels et secrètement transmises à de rares 'maîtres': la gnose, c'est la connaissance totale, incommensurablement supérieure à la foi et à la raison.

Le gnosticisme sera alors rattaché à la sagesse primordiale originelle, source des diverses religions particulières ... La *gnôsis*, apanage des initiés, s'oppose à la vulgaire *pistis* (croyance) des simples fidèles. C'est moins une 'connaissance' proprement dite qu'une *révélation* secrète et mystérieuse   (ibid. 11).

On the other hand, Antoine's position is captured by R. Williams (1990: 77): 'God is not known by *scientia* but by *sapientia*, the contemplative turning towards the object, not the active intellect at work on the object, organizing and analyzing ... And contemplative knowledge can be only the knowledge of love, of desire and delight, the will consenting to the drawing of the divine beauty.' Where Hilarion is duplicitous or double-minded, both a Narcissus figure and a male Echo, wanting a democracy of legion and self-endorsing images to unsettle Antoine's single-mindedness, the latter is single-minded not by steel will but by whole unity with himself and with God in an act of penitence and acceptance of grace. Antoine's reward after all the temptations are over is the image of grace and a new dawn in the last 'stage direction': 'Tout au milieu, et dans le disque même du soleil rayonne la face de Jésus-Christ.' Antoine is permitted to find that he has been made and continues to be in the image of God, having stood against all the false images, idols, and idolatrous 'others' of self which have oppressed him. Not only, then, has Antoine withstood the temptation to join with a political or spiritual crusade in Alexandria, either as a champion of a community outside a theocracy, or of the 'one' true Church under the bishopric of Alexandria. He has also withstood the temptation to join with his double, Hilarion, prodigal religious son with whom he does not enter an 'I–Thou' relationship to substantiate his sense of self. This would itself then be a mockery of Antoine's penitent relationship of 'moi' to Toi–Dieu. My contention is that Flaubert is taking the problem of subject–object much further here than critics have outlined. Séginger (1987: 81) suggests that 'L'hermite expérimente de la même façon que le poète la coupure métaphysique, par une perte de limites ... son expérience ... articule le sacrifice du moi à une avidité boulimique: se perdre ou perdre en soi le monde, il est toujours question d'indifférenciation.' This reconsideration builds on her earlier essay (1984: 5) which contends that '[*TSA*] met en scène une double destruction en interaction du sujet et de l'objet. Le sujet ne parvient pas à se constituer dans une relation objectale qui s'avère impossible. *TSA* s'ouvre sur un monologue qui . . . est un discours à la recherche de son objet: Dieu est absent . . . *TSA* est le texte d'une crise d'un "sujet excentré".' What is at stake, rather, is the refusal to find in self (or the world) the other (hence emptying out the two terms such as the 'real' identity of the person or the person in the mirror), or to merge self in a like other (Hilarion). Antoine's solution is prayer, address to the self-in-God as beyond one's human self. For Flaubert the agnostic, this is the cry into the void, the voice ranting in the 'gueuleoir'. To return, then, to the awesome solitude and isolation of being uniquely a visionary, Flaubert ensures that his Antoine holds on, literally outside, at the end of *TSA* so that he can 'see' that he does stand in relation to a true Other. Acknowledgement of one faith, one Godhead, allows for knowledge of oneself, of truth in the inner man, of giving up a false self to find a true one. Antoine can make this leap of faith because he embodies it. The Father of Monasticism can do no less than be, true to himself (in history or hagiography), or subsequent intertextual re-representation.

Flaubert's *TSA* none the less refuses to rewrite an apology in the manner of Athanasius' original *Vita Antonii*, imitation used as an authority or as a vehicle of proselytism (see Orr, 2000). The text withdraws ultimate endorsement of the nature of Antoine's 'victory' at the end. The *deus ex machina* of Christ's face can equally be read as a send-up of such an apparition, depending on where one stands as critic or reader *vis-à-vis* faith itself. The Cartesian *cogito* tacitly sits in judgement on both Antoine's *Méditations* and Hilarion's post-Cartesian science, his *Discours de la Méthode*. *TSA* furnishes much evidence that there may be more magic in miracles than in necromancy, more reason in ecstatic revelation than logic or numerology, more unity in the Trinity of one God who is also triune than in the adversarial singularity and vaunting pride of the devil who is also Legion. Ultimately the value of *TSA*, be this its sacred, ethical, or aesthetic worth, is less its erudition and complexity as polemic (see Bowman, 1986: 2), than its quest to 'perceive and image the spiritual in a world voided of its traditional sacred'.

Brooks's words quoted at the beginning of this chapter formulate the case for an anti-religious but none the less sacralized 'Écriture'. Flaubert, is then, more than a martyr to the cause of high art as desacralized form of the sacred, or a recherché collector of myths, mysteries, and mysticisms whose meanings ultimately cancel one another out and refuse meaning itself.[5] *TSA* represents art as properly part of the scriptural, a writing for the soul of a nation whether or not this also includes transcendence towards a sublime. In his Antoine, Flaubert has created the 'm(h)ystérique'—an ethical, aesthetic, mystical, spiritual figure of no small prophetic import to the age of science and progress in a secular, syncretist, and materialistic France post-1870. Through the strictly theological refiguration of the saint/martyr Antoine, Flaubert challenges the spiritual redundancy and irrelevance of Catholic theology calqued onto a now obsolete Cartesianism, the hypocrisies of a State bolstered up by

[5]   For two different views on Flaubert as martyr for art, see Lombard (1934: 56): 'Un homme tel que Flaubert a été vraiment le martyr de son siècle. Les questions que le romantisme avait laissées sans solution, les idées philosophiques de son temps, avec toutes leurs contradictions et leurs lacunes, l'ont préoccupé jusqu'à l'angoisse. La pression exercée par le spinozisme a été très forte chez lui'; and Séginger (1987: 83), 'La sainteté est la capacité de s'ouvrir à l'infini; aussi à la générosité éthique (ne pas s'occuper de soi-même), s'associe à un désintéressement philosophique. L'artiste ne cherche pas la Cause, la Conclusion—paradis métaphysiques . . . L'Art est une foi sans fond.' For the best overview of Flaubert, myth, and comparative religion, see Bowman (1986: 21–2), '[Flaubert] comptait parmi ses amis personnels trois "mythologues" importants, Renan, Alfred Maury, Frédéric Baudry: à travers eux il a dû connaître les travaux des deux Müller, de Bréal, de Louis Ménard. Comme il a dû être conscient des nouvelles découvertes érudites: la révision de la datation des Védas, les travaux archéologiques . . . la découverte de textes tels que la *Didache des Apôtres* en 1854, le *Pasteur d'Hermès* en 1856, et pour le gnosticisme, la *Pistis Sophia* en 1851. Pour le schéma du débat, il faut remonter d'abord à Creuzer, et à son interprète français Guigniaut'; and 'Selon Guigniaut . . . le mythe alors embrasse histoire, philosophie, religion, art, s'exprime par la tradition populaire et sa fille aînée la poésie. Pour comprendre la mythologie, il faut une conscience à la fois historique et philosophique capable de "se transporter, par sa puissance de l'imagination, dans une sphère de faits et d'idées" fort différent de la nôtre. Le fond du mythe peut être une idée, une croyance, un fait, un phénomène du monde physique ou du monde moral etc.: sa force est celle d'un récit, dont la loi fondamentale est la personnification' (24); 'Renan conclut même que le polythéisme est plus favorable au développement de la science que le monothéisme, mais quand la culture s'affaiblit le polythéisme s'ouvre à la superstition.' (34) ; and: '[in *TSA*] le syncrétisme est perverti au point où les ressemblances entre dieux leur permettent de s'entretuer. La mythologie chez lui fait souvent partie d'un arsenal antichrétien ou du moins anticatholique' (51).

religion as institution and the real spiritual vacuum in a syncretist (Hilarion) age. As Bowman (1990) puts it:

the lack, in the church and elsewhere, of any clear distinction between natural and revealed truth; indeed, the proper theological sense of the word, 'mystery' was . . . unknown at the time. . . . It also coincided with Romantic historicism and with the general desire to perceive the harmonies of the divine beneath (or beyond) the appearances of nature, of languages, of myths and beliefs, even in the very forms of intelligence, seeking . . . to discover the transcendent. Flaubert was to raise grave questions, not only about syncretism, but about all these intellectual activities. Finally, Catholic theology during the July Monarchy was intensely concerned with differentiating itself from Victor Cousin's Eclecticism (185) . . . [*TSA*] does not substitute for traditional religious beliefs the creeds of Spinoza or of psychoanalysis, it destroys the significance of religion in general. (195)

As a writer, Flaubert's own temptation would have been to improve upon the tradition of Antony as exemplar of Orthodoxy or the hagiography or imitation *à la Vita* which is constantly present in *TSA*. The faithfulness to intertextual and erudite sources, because they are modestly hidden from the average reader, creates the tensions which dynamize and discipline the text. Not least of these is the development of Hilarion from Jerome's *Vita Hilarionis*, which indicates Flaubert's wide-ranging knowledge of much early, and specifically ecclesiastical, sources for his work. In the guise of modern, rational, tempter, Flaubert's Hilarion is a touchstone for unorthodox approaches to Orthodoxy and its representations. To show, not preach orthodoxy, the heretical other who deviates from some of the truth but not all is the benchmark of discernment and place whereby judgement between the two can be made. Hilarion is the mocker-fool imparting Flaubert's critical verve against western theology and philosophy and western representations of eastern thought, but couched in the language of nineteenth-century French scientific discourse of logic, reason, and comparative religion. Flaubert's *TSA* demonstrates his place in a tradition of writer-visionaries, but in modern, secular, prophetic mode. His Antoine resoundingly voices the author crying in the many anti-spiritual wildernesses of his age, where all he can do is return to his desk and muse upon the crisis in positivist, empiricist ideologies and the all-too-male versions of cultural and economic-material values. It will be in *BP* that he takes up not an allegorically 'equivalent' epoch, the Alexandria of Antony's times, but the challenge of his own France with its heterodoxies masquerading as truth.

5

Trois Contes

IN Chapter 3 on *ES*, the concluding discussion on genre focused on the problems of intertextual degeneration and descendancy combined with the freedom to experiment with a syncretic collusion of forms—the historical novel, the realist novel, and the *Bildungsroman*. *TC* has a more obvious plurality of related subgenres all clustered under the term 'conte': depending on how each is classified in relation to the others, they represent variously in critical opinion the legend, the hagiography, the moral tale, the fairy story, the fantastic tale, the imaginary adventure, the Bible story. The consequence of this strange trinity of tales is that critics have argued for a sacred or a profane exploration of themes and genres, a sum of parts read through an allegorizing screen to voice truths about history, psychoanalysis, myth, or theology.[1]

I have begun this chapter with a comparison to *ES* not to be perverse, but to reframe *TC* in the context of 1870 and its aftermath, that is, the semi-prophetic import of the eternal return and derivative nature of war and defeat. Positivism and historical 'truth', progress and greater civilization, could no longer hold as predominant ideological tenets in the wake of the Franco-Prussian War. Therefore *TC* allows Flaubert to turn his

---

[1] For categorization of the tales by genre see e.g. Bart and Cook (1975); Biasi (1986). For a reading of *TC* as sacred or a profane, see *inter alia* Bargues-Rollins (1988); Bonnaccorso (1990); Debray-Genette and Huston (1984); Lytle (1984); Neefs (1982); Raitt (1991); Reish (1984). For *TC* as allegory of history, see Beck (1977); Hausmann (1984); M. Lowe (1981–2); Peterson (1983); as psychoanalysis see Felman (1981); as myth see Czyba, (1997); Lehmann (1979); Vierne (1992); or as theology see Borot (1992), and Wise (1993). Daunais (1998) is among many critics to interpret the tales as cameo extensions of the 'related' earlier novels: *CS* with *MB*; *LSJ* with *TSA*; *H* with *SAL*. Other critics have emphasized speech as important in *TC*: Frølich (1988); Killick (1993); Murphy (1992); Scrogham (1998).

back directly on the genres related to political ideology, such as the historical novel or the *Bildungsroman*, to concentrate on three kinds of 'histoire invraisemblable et mensongère' (*Petit Robert*: third definition of 'conte' and linked to 'chanson', 'fable', 'sornette'). It is oral, rather than literary, history as leit-motif throughout the tales, a return to previous forms of narration and representation, that this chapter will highlight.

In the crisis of values of 1877, and in a move similar to the one I outlined with Arnoux's path through the aesthetic, Flaubert turns to prior religious forms such as stories in icons and stained glass (see Masson, 1993*b*; and Orr, 1995). In *TC*, this is however not a vulgarization (as Arnoux) either of the novel form, or of moral and aesthetic topics as a path to re-tran-scendentalization (as elucidated by Sachs, 1970; Selvin, 1983; Strike, 1976). In the same manner as I uncovered in Chapter 3 earlier etymologies of 'bachelier' incorporated into Frédéric's anachronistic and clichéd ideals, I argue here for a Flaubert melding the grotesque with the sublime, the kitsch-cliché with imitation in the Renaissance sense, the decadent with irony and parody; the last theme has been well worked in critical studies (for example Beck, 1990; Desvaux, 1992; Erickson, 1992; Haig, 1991). What results in *TC* is a rather writerly chap-book.

Flaubert's novels are everywhere moral but not moralizing. The *conte* obviously implies not only a moral, the 'right' ending, the victory of good over evil, but an overcoming in a variety of senses. First there is the 'heroic' kind (as in *LSJ*), overcoming enemies, obstacles, temptations. Then there is the triumphalist mastery and dominance of order (*H*), with equally strong oppo-sitional emotions such as anger and hatred to restrain. Finally there is the passive sense of being overcome (as in *CS*), by powers, forces, or emotions stronger than oneself. In its extreme form, such a response may render the person transfixed, mute, paralysed: whether by a natural cause such as cold, tiredness; negative emotions such as fear, grief, shock; or by magic and the supernatural. Overcoming speaks a transcendence and its oppo-site, dehumanization. At all junctures it investigates states which separate man from other animals (angels or the gods), to define his (in)humanity. The very old debate surrounding animals having souls for example, strikes right at the heart of *TC*, for not only has Loulou, as 'Paraclet', more than a soul:

Hérode and Hérodias questionably have none. Julien falls neatly between the two. The moral, spiritual, and aesthetic dimension is therefore something which separates man from the natural world of animals, plants, or stones. *TSA* meditated on this body–soul question from a theophilosophical position. *TC*, I will argue is quintessentially about morality, meaning the body put in various extreme positions by other extreme bodies. In this, *TC* moves outside the parameters of both the hierarchization of the cosmos or élitist society I discussed in *SAL* and the median, political, polemics of the 'fraternities' explored in *ES*. I will argue for Flaubert's *conte* as a study of nature versus culture, of what it is that makes one human rather than animal or superhuman, for the genre automatically provides a vehicle for an investigation of the world of the monstrous, of monsters inside and outside man. The main protagonists of *contes* then can be larger than life (or smaller); magic worlds, curses and blessings, miracles and interventions of fate are part and parcel of what is, so that causality may have nothing to do with logic or effects. And underlying the fairy-tale are taboo social relationships such as incest, parricide, rape, all moral subjects *par excellence*. Thanatos and Eros, the two antagonistic forces which undergirded *SAL* as delineations of patriarchal power and domination, recur in the bodies, souls, and emotions of the characters in *TC*, pitted against forces in the natural and supernatural worlds, in similar and different ways.

The three rhetorical figures examined in *SAL* in Chapter 2 — hyperbole, *pars pro toto*, synecdoche — will be put into the hyperbolic language of the tale, where concepts and mythic structures are given bodies saturated with recognized cultural significance. I will provide an anatomy of each story, in the senses of both close analysis and dissection, by separating out the parts of this strange *corpus*, to argue for Flaubert as a moral vivisectionist who has cut out three body-metaphors of life and death. I build on Donato and his study of death in *CS* (1993: ch. 5) and the 'crypt' of writing more generally (ch. 9, 'Bodies: On the Limits of Representation in Romantic Poetics'). This chapter discovers the preoccupation with *cœur* throughout *CS*, not only in its title. In *LSJ*, there is a fixation with *corps*; and in *H* there is the obvious meditation on *tête*, not least in the final image. I will take these (metaphysically male-valorized) body-parts in reverse order, because it seems to me that in this interpretative move (as I demonstrated in Orr, 1992), there is another reading of the whole awaiting discovery. By taking the tail of the tales about a head, first, analysis of the two more commentated tales can be respun to reveal the paradoxes which lie at the centre of fairy-tale logic and Flaubert's *œuvre in toto*.

The ending(s) form the second part of my investigation. Rather than seeing them as optimistic 'happy ends' as Israel-Pelletier (1991: 1–2), this chapter views *TC* as tales quintessentially concerned with the forces of life over death. The overwhelming number of deaths Flaubert had faced by the time he was writing *TC* is well documented but, interesting biographical note apart, he had been oppressed by death even from earliest childhood in his father's dissecting room. Flaubert crystallizes in *TC* the mortuary leitmotif of his three earlier novels and their pseudo-saintly heroes—Charles, Mâtho, Antoine—but in three remythifying versions—Loulou, Julien, Ioakanann. All these transformations will turn out also to be 'abrutissements'. The indignities each suffers lie at the heart of Flaubert's indictment of his times. The gratuitous mutilation, infamy, obscenity, take *TC* beyond the sacrifices and brutalities of sex and war in *SAL*, and beyond traditional fairy-tale traumas and their resolutions. What is being represented in these three excessive, grotesque, and macabre ends?

Flaubert's *TC* will, then, finally be read as 'adult' fairy-tales that examine morality in terms of the human or inhuman. Unlike in many fairy-tales, it is the adult protagonist who is central, not the child or youth, although children play catalytic and nefarious roles (Salomé in *H*, the young Julien in *LSJ*, Victor and Virginie in *CS*). Thus I will move away from rereading *TC*'s moral body from the point of critical *idées reçues* under the dual aegis of the sacred and profane which would frame morality either theologically (good versus evil), or as the law (good versus bad). Some insights then emerge about the crisis of values *TC* describes in syncretic 'picture' language. It is in the all-male and unmanly composite of peculiar male protagonists—parrot, stag, and headless man—that Flaubert's version of late nineteenth-century masculinity is revealed as a story of Frankenstein and his monster.

H closes *TC* by focusing on the head of Ioakanann borne off towards the horizon, its heaviness requiring that three men share the task 'triumvirately'. The stopping of the voice of the prophet opens the story to prophetic time; the brutal 'transport' of death allows the disembodied voice to leave its earth-centred locale to 'speak' in others; the end of the 'festin' marks the end of an epoch of history, the imperial Roman empire, as Lowe and Burns (1953: 13) note. This empire is the very one which would have ended Carthage and Hamilcar in *SAL*. The beginning of a new epoch will here again pronounce the beginning of the end of the political and personal history of the man, Hérode. While Hubert (1982: 250) has remarked on the similarity in shape between the citadel and Ioakanann's head, his is not the only heavy head in the story. From the outset of *H*, in its very title, it is Hérode's headship and position that are constantly in question as *Tét*rarque. We see him looking down from the tower of his citadel (the 'capitole'), in the same manner as Hamilcar in *SAL*, on the 'mer Morte' and the various regions of the Middle East which represent a question mark over his headship and author-ity (the 'capitale'), over Arabs, Romans, Syrians, Jews, Parthians, Samaritans. The main cause of his headache is, however, Ioakanann, who 'l'empêchait de vivre' (*H*, 146) in spite of the fact that figuratively the head is the 'partie vitale', the 'siège de la pensée' (*Petit Robert*). There are several reasons why Hérode's pretensions ('avoir la grosse tête') are punctured by Ioakanann. The prophet broadcasts his incestuous relations with his sister/wife Hérodias who, by wearing the trousers, also has him 'en tête.' In many ways she is similar to Madame Bovary *mère* who rules the roost because her irascible and feckless husband refuses to assert himself in society (Orr, 1999*b*). Throughout *H*, Antipas is constantly caught as 'chef' between conflicting loyal-ties and political (dis)empowerments ('capitulation') coupled with highly charged and conflicting traits within himself. His obstinate nature ('têtu', 'tête de mule', 'entêtement', 'capiteux') sits with doubly incestuous eroticism ('sensualité capiteuse') not only because he has had sex with his sister ('amour collatéral'), but, by extension, because it is at his birthday feast that the request is made, through Salomé's sexualized dancing body on her mother's behalf, for Ioakanann's severed head ('décollation') on one of the plates from the meal ('collation'). It is truly here that his head and Ioakanann's come unstuck.

In fairy-tale terms, Flaubert has made Antipas (note the double negative of his name) into a superembodiment of the wicked stepfather-king. Roman history is repeated: Hérode echoes Caligula, who also married his sister and indulged in orgiastic killings arising from mad internal rage towards any who would oppose him. Intertextually, Flaubert extracts Hérode from the New Testament gospel of Luke, but I would suggest more importantly from the Old Testament first book of Kings, the story of Ahab and Jezebel. His fictional John speaks to Hérodias directly as 'Iézabel' (*H*, 167). Ahab's wickedness is the accumulation and epitome of all wickedness: 'Ahab son of Omri did evil in the sight of the Lord more than all who were before him' (1 Kings 16: 30). Ahab's line and genealogy of wickedness goes back through his father Omri, who ruled after conspiracy and schism in the time of Zimri, who had himself conspired against Baasha, who also did evil in God's sight. Baasha conspired against the previous wicked king, Nadab, whose wicked father was Jeroboam. Jeroboam marks the moment of schism of Solomon's rule between Israel and Judah. His failed coup against Solomon resulted in his later rule of Israel after Solomon's death. What marks out Jeroboam as shorthand for 'terrible wickedness' until Ahab comes along is his setting-up of two golden calves to be worshipped in Bethel and Dan at the altar of God. This prefigures the Baal worship Jezebel institutes in greater measure. In *SAL* (see Chapter 2), Flaubert's exploration of Baal—Moloch, the bull-god, offers a direct parallel to Hérode's heritage, ancestors, and psychic defences in *H*.

What is so striking about *H* is that Flaubert puts Hérode's side of the New Testament version, and from Hérode's point of view, so that the true nature and context of his appalling judgement and 'immorality' (and Hérodias's) come through only via Ioakanann's well-known prophecy and indictment of his lifestyle. This contra-Christian perspective may be a reason why Flaubert hesitated over the title, between 'La Décollation de Saint Jean-Baptiste' and 'Hérodias', or 'Hérodiade', as Raitt (1991: 58) notes. Not only has Flaubert rewritten Ahab-like supreme wickedness back into this figure, he has done so by means of Catholic terminology. If careful count is kept, Hérode commits all seven of the 'péchés capitaux' (pride, envy, sloth, intemperance, avarice, anger, and lust). The real horror of *H*, then, is that someone of Hérode's political and moral standing has such an unopposed position of leadership and can execute orders, judgements, and people on a whim. *Candide*-like, the tale's compressing of horrors into one protagonist in such a small space glosses the real impact of corrupt autocracy and its inherent moral anarchy. This matches the early narrative report at the beginning of the tale: 'Les Juifs ne voulaient plus de ses mœurs idolâtres, tous les autres de sa domination' (*H*, 139). It is then up to astute readers to judge either from their own Christian or secular justice-systems the real import of the crimes being committed before their very eyes.

The full import of this headless headship is made evident in the climate of justice in which Hérode rules in *H*: decapitation is the normal mode of punishment (*H*, 141, 156); rulers expect an order of internecine murder (*H*, 143); prophet political prisoners are locked up in dungeons. Again, the last is no exotic detail from Flaubert's imagination, but further underscores the Old and New Testament intertexts. In 1 Kings 18 the prophets of God are kept alive by Abdias in caverns, and in Luke 3: 20 the emprisonment of John is seen as more terrible than the incest with Hérodias. What *H* maps out pre-Kafka is a trial of macrocosmic import, with the death sentence paradoxically also falling on the council for the prosecution as it pronounces on the council for the defence (Ioakanann). The grand jury in this 'procès capital' (Hérodias, Mannaië) face, in the mirror of the 'perpetrator' of crimes against them, their own sins. This mirror is made from words, the various strategic *têtes-à-tête* which mark the progress of the trial to the final judgement scene, the banquet, and the physical confrontation of severed and unsevered heads. The various dialogues highlight male voices in the act of evaluation. However, instead of logical and rational arguments, negative and defensive modes and moods are most frequently used, such as anger, threats, vociferations, accusations, harangues, invectives, and, of course, curses.

The first *tête à tête* in *H* is between Hérode and Mannaië, 'son corps ayant la souplesse d'un singe, et sa figure l'impassibilité d'une momie' (*H*, 140). A Samaritan who hates the Jews, he sides easily with Hérode's terror of Ioakanann because his desecration with friends of their temple led to his escape but their decapitation. He is a man of hand gestures and curses: 'indiquant avec son pouce un objet derrière lui' (*H*, ibid.), 'il étendit les bras du côté de Sion . . . les poings fermés, lui jeta un anathème' (*H*, 141–2). As executioner (Mannaïe first appears wearing a very phallic cutlass in a bronze scabbard on his thigh), it is he, again by the force of his arms, who lifts the lid off Ioakanann's prison when the Roman officials are inspecting Hérode's treasuries. He, like Hérode, is in a quandary when he fears one of the lictors will cut off John's head with his axe and thereby steal his thunder. He is thus the means by which the 'lid' comes off Ioakanann's voice-box and hence Hérode's secrets. He will do the eventual decapitation, but only after meeting his divine double, the 'Grand Ange des Samaritains, tout couvert d'yeux et brandissant un immense glaive, rouge et dentelé comme une flamme' (*H*, 188) and thus fluffs his first execution in forty years. Cursed and shamed himself, the black humour of his meeting with his divine alter-ego here only makes his 'victory' over his fear, and the build-up to the final scene, more intense. '*La* tête entra;—et Mannaïe la tenait par les cheveux, *au bout de son bras*, fier des applaudissements' (*H*, 188–9, my emphasis). Critics have most frequently blamed Hérodias in their interpretations of *H*, for her trickery of Hérode, and argue the *idée reçue* of the 'dégradation de l'Homme par la Femme' (Czyba, 1997) because, 'Not only has he committed a heinous crime for no valid reason, he has been tricked into it by a woman he hates and who despises him' (Raitt, 1991: 70). There is no doubt that Hérodias is the most powerful figure in *H* worthy of her eponymous status. However, if we consider the passage of the head round the hierarchy of the company, it is Hérode's ultimate responsibility that is at stake. There is undoubted mysogyny in *H*, but the male reaction (even impotence) may be more crucial. Mannaïe's arms speak more anathema than his voice, for he puts the head on its platter and shows it to all the different factions and guilty parties in, I would contend, reverse order of blame: Salomé, Hérodias, Vitellius, the Roman captains, the Pharisees, Aulus the glutton, and finally Hérode. This is the ultimate *tête à tête* and not its removal into the distance.

Ioakanann's actual words in *H*, a dense biblical intertextuality from the gospels of Luke and John, are perhaps less important than Flaubert's fictional recontextualization of him, and the form of their delivery, which resembles stage directions. 'Voice off' in semantic, theatrical, and ideological terms, Ioakanann is the catalyst of contention and contestation throughout *H*. Everywhere he provokes hostility (between Hérode and Hérodias), shame (Hérodias, Mannaïe), a challenge to pride and human dominion (Hérodias). As Flaubert has cast Hérode as indirect commentator of his own injustice, Hérodias is primarily the figure and mouthpiece of secular triumph, necessarily her own, against all odds. Silent in her first appearance (*H*, 142), a touch, quivering nostrils, triumphant joy on her face are expressed before her 'voix forte' shakes Hérode. She fills in all the background history, politics, and religious context as in the opening scenes of a Greek or French classical tragedy of which she is a major protagonist. Ends (often literally) for her justify the means, regardless of any maternal, uxorial, or political censure this will evoke. What has touched her to the quick is Iaokanann's essential challenge to her power, and to worship of power *per se* (hence idolatry), as no one has stood in her way. Her humiliation (being made small) when her carriage is stuck in the sand and she is forced to hear out Ioakanann, is doubled by her repeated paraphrase of the event to Hérode (whom she despises). Later the interpreter doubles Ioakanann's humiliation of her 'omnipotence' with Hérode, in translation, to the assembled Romans. It is through her position of authority and greatness that she paradoxically gives the greater authority to her enemy and to the kingdom which is not of this earth or under her calculated sway. It is she who describes Ioakanann's unlikely appearance, 'une peau de chameau autour des reins, et sa tête ressemblait à celle d'un lion' (*H*, 146), a kind of new Samson to herself as Delilah, with unusual prolixity and uncharacteristic vagueness (there are no controlling commands or short counter-arguments). She outlines his prophetic qualifications: 'Dès qu'il m'aperçut, il cracha sur moi toutes les malédictions des prophètes. Ses prunelles flamboyaient; sa voix rugissait; il levait les bras, comme pour arracher le tonnerre ... ces injures qui tombaient comme ne pluie d'orage' (*H*, ibid.). The words circulate like the wind: 'cette force plus pernicieuse que les glaives, et qu'on ne pouvait saisir, était stupéfiante; et elle parcourait la terrasse, blêmie par sa colère, manquant de mots pour exprimer ce qui l'étouffait' (*H*, 147). This claustrophobia replicates the space of her rooms, as Wetherill (1994) points out. It has not been noticed how often she is on terraces, on the final 'tribune', but how much she is also 'terrassée' by Ioakanann.

When the prophet is eventually allowed his own, not reported, 'voix caverneuse' at the pivot-point in *H*, the divine and secular nature of the copy is revealed (and foreshadows the question of the copy as speech-act in *BP*). Prophecy is special reported speech, of God's words in human form. The writer then copies the written testament to the divine original. First, direct quotation from the Old Testament from a number of prophets (the curses) is followed by a change of tone, the blessings, which are from the final book of the Bible, the Revelation of Saint John. The final section via the metaphor of the 'Fils de David' returns Revelation to the 'Church history' of the story of Jezebel in 1 Kings 16, passing through Luke 3 and Isaiah. It is *la voix* as supreme medium across time which 'grossissait, se développait, roulait avec des déchirements de tonnerre, et, dans l'écho dans la montagne la répétant, elle foudroyait Machaerous d'éclats multiples' (*H*, 167). Not only does the message end with the supreme humiliation and death-sentence of Hérodias as double of Jezebel ('Crève comme une chienne!' *H*, 168), but high and low are put in their divine context by implication: 'L'Eternel exècre la puanteur de tes crimes!' (ibid.). This further prefigures the ultimate justice and judgement of the tale, the vindication of Ioakanann as prophet to end all prophets, even Elijah: 'Pour qu'il croisse, il faut que je diminue' (Ioakanann's final words as reported by the Essene, Phanuel). The double curse concludes what has been a double prophecy (and doubles fictionally the curse of the 'grand cerf' in *LSJ*). The echoes and reverberations of these words are then also framed in poetic justice. Flaubert's usage and departure from Renan's *La vie de Jésus* as source, and alienation techniques through the use of Semitic names, underline what Scrogham defines as the divorce of 'action from understanding' (1998: 783). Flaubert's sense of the spirit and the letter also divorces words from understanding, for more intertextual 'casse-têtes' are curtailed as Mannaïe puts the lid back on the prison. The prophet necessarily has to be a 'casse-cou' and live out the literal and figurative consequences this entails. His cries, 'à tue-tête', lead from here to his own beheading and representation as the 'tête de mort'.

Like the scene in the Club de l'Intelligence in *ES*, where republican confronted republican, Ioakanann's actual final words are triggers for representation of the religious factionalism and schism among those who were opposed to Caesar, but were also opposed to splinter groups such as those who held to the Messianic promise. The question of how to interpret, accept, or validate prophecy is not only for those under its curse, but for those who are its potential advocates. Phanuel throughout *H* plays this support role. In an initial *tête à tête* with Hérode, he becomes a sort of emissary of John the Baptist, precursor of Jesus, by announcing that 'Le Très-Haut envoie par moments un de ses fils. Ioakanann en est un. Si tu l'opprimes, tu seras châtié' (*H*, 150). His viewpoint is totally Essene, for the Essenes upheld a religious and moral value-system at odds with the pomp of the Caesars; however, unlike the Pharisees or Sadducees, they were not interpreters of the Torah but of the stars. Interrupted by the arrival of the Roman Vitellius, Phanuel has to wait until after Ioakanann's prophecy to validate what he has seen predicted in the stars, like one of the Magi, in a second aborted *tête à tête* with Hérode (*H*, 169–71). His augury defines the death of 'un homme considérable'. The question is who, and in earthly or heavenly terms? Because of his superstitious fears that it might be himself, and personal worries that Hérodias will laugh at him again, Hérode plays the role of 'la tête de Turc' and as ever takes the safe option and throws his party to appease and quell, as he thinks, all political oppositions. It is ironically Phanuel himself who is allowed to interpret his own prediction, and thus he distances himself from Hérodias's counterfeiting 'sorcelleries' and 'divine' magic (Hanquier, 1994: 36). This interpretation not of tongues but of signs occurs only in the final double *tête à tête* with the severed head itself. Phanuel's 'ravissement' is first visual, then aural. The understanding and interpretation of diminution and ascendancy for himself and for his religious community is reiterated in astronomical verbs referring to the waxing and waning of the moon: 'Pour qu'il croisse, il faut que je diminue'. The head thus reveals mysteries about itself and its symbolism, but ultimately, in the hands of the religious, it transfigures in fairy-tale terms the ritual entry of the calf's head in *ES*, symbol of the fall of foreign monarchs.

Hérode's and Hérodias's pent-up 'emportements', their violent bursts of anger because they want to have supremacy ('l'emporter') over Ioakanann, are negative human enactments of divine and justified anger. This is even framed in *H* by the manifestation in nature of the drought-ridden land (*H*, 142), a further hint back perhaps to 1 Kings and the frame of the Ahab–Jezebel story. Elijah's prophetic curse on the land also meant that there was no water. Phanuel's personal transport and the physical transport underlined by the weight of the prophet's head are a double demystification of figurative language or any supernatural vindication of events. The tale refigures all kinds of 'emportements' absolutely literally, and hence fittingly offers the 'flat' and supremely banal end to *H*. For those wishing supernatural justice, the 'known' is left suspended over the landscape, but unwritten onto this crucial moment of absolute human horror. More than a classical tragedy in form and unities (Raitt, 1998: 186), the questioning of divine and earthly justice make the bathetic and absurd end the only possible one in this theatre of supreme cruelty.

Now that the capstone has been taken off the edifice of *H* as the 'unreadable' story in *TC* (Genette, 1984: 201; Raitt, 1991: 74; Robertson 1982: 171), through a meditation of the head at its tail and the *têtes à tête* which punctuate it, *LSJ*'s equally edifying embodiments and disembodiments of maleness can be read through a meditation on the various *corps à corps* around which the narrative is incarnated. Killick is one of few critics to remark on the 'compassionate body language of the exploited servant . . . increasingly replaced [in *LSJ*, *H*] by displays of physical violence and sensual self-indulgence' (1993: 320). I want to read more into the 'body language' of *LSJ*, for, in the manner of a stained-glass image or legend, the play with insubstantiality and incorporation comes from the shedding of new light on familiar images and critical *idées reçues*.[2] As with *H*, I want to

---

[2] For readings of *LSJ* as new hagiography or medieval tale, see e.g. Bart and Cook (1975 and 1977); Biasi (1986). For two excellent psychoanalytical readings, see Berg, Moskos, and Grimaud (1982) and Felman (1981). The body has been

read the moral import of this tale outside either its religious–profane frame or the psychodynamics of the Oedipus complex, with their concomitant genre debates: *LSJ* is neither fictionalized hagiography, medieval tale, nor refabulation of Oedipus, depending, on how the dual prophecy is interpreted. Because it is fixated with bodies, particularly male bodies, I propose a reading of *LSJ* as 'légende' in the sense of folk-tale, part of a corpus of oral, regional, traditional narrations, which the final words of the story 'dans mon pays' (as explanation to a picture) suggest. The anthropological, rather than theological, dimension of folk-tales then offers a different way back into the question of morality as behaviour, custom, or tradition in *LSJ*. It seems to me that the two main circumstances of *corps à corps* in this context focus on the extremely ancient rules for hunting and hospitality, both strict codifications of the licence to kill or spare from death.

The lengthy introduction to Julien's story prior to his birth is one of Flaubert's key elaborations of the Julien of legend and of the fairy–tale genre; the orgy of killing in the fateful hunt, the lengths he pursues to atone for this, the gruesome and macabre details of the killing of his parents and of the leper's final demands comprise the others. It is in these excrescences, developed edges and margins of the typical conventions, settings, plot-structures, and developments of the folk-tale that the raw mortality and morality of man is made visible, as Propp 'morphologizes' (1988, especially appendix 1: 119–27). If *H*'s opening frame was looming disaster, shaky containment of fear, and oppositional forces, *LSJ* oozes peace, contentment, oneness. Castles are run like monasteries; nature and agriculture are husbanded; Lord and Lady, fief and liegelord, operate an intersecting, mutual order. Hedges and fences, moats and overflowing armouries betoken separations but constantly emphasized is their symbolic, not utilitarian, nature. The idyll of peace and plenty is replicated by Julien's bountiful parents, who dispense

assessed by critics variously but not literally: the stained glass symbolizes the 'opposition between flesh and spirit' (Marston, 1986: 344); Czyba (1994) reads *LSJ* as a metaphor of regression into childhood and concludes that 'Corps et sexualité sont fontamentalement mauvais' (168); Bart considers that '[Julien] must integrate his body, his soul and accept his own place in a nature no longer conceived as inanimate, but rather understood pantheistically as one and all animate' (1973: 336).

favour with fairness in their demesne or domestic domain. They are paragons of 'noblesse' to which hospitality is central, embodied in the codified welcome and protection of strangers, the poor, even potential enemies at one's hearth. Both seers of Julien's future receive such a courteous welcome and acceptance; a merchant-stranger goes on his way 'sans avoir enduré aucune violence'; pilgrims feast and recount their terrifying and hostile journeys to the Holy Land; his father's friends are regally received and similarly 'pay' for their board in tales of war (*LSJ*, 83). Paradoxically, then, it is Julien's parents who are first and foremost the 'hospitaliers' of the story, for they welcome strangers without regard to caste or class (even supernatural guests), and demonstrate charity in their liberal entertainment to an almost eucharistic degree.

Such ultra-civil behaviour to fellow men is matched by their regard for fellow creatures more generally. Their compassionate humanity is covered and enhanced by the signs of their respectful co-existence with the animal kingdoms: we first see the fox-fur cloak of Julien's father while the white presence of Julien's mother heightens animal adornments: the 'cornes de son hennin' and the 'queue de sa robe de drap traînait de trois pas derrière elle' (*LSJ*, 79). A son given in answer to prayer elevates the natural fruit of union and unity to a higher level. Hence, the doubly violent son they produce seems some kind of monstrous joke, for neither genes nor cultural influences can be blamed for his bloodlust against animals or his murderous irreverence for other humans.

The frame of *LSJ* is the medieval code of honour, which 'traditionally regulated relations between men, summed up the prevailing ideals of manliness, and marked the boundaries of masculine comportment' (Nye, 1993: p. vii). This is not so much the codification of hierarchies of submission and domination in male–male relations, as Zants (1979: 37) among others argues. Rather it is the training in 'noblesse' that the 'chevalier' undertakes either as crusader or huntsman. Obviously in Julien, Flaubert represents the harmonizing into one person of what would appear to be two contradictory paths to honour, exemplified in his namesake Julien Sorel's unresolved conflict between Church and Army, the red and the black. Stendhal's *Le Rouge et le Noir* may indeed be a heavily ironic intertext in *LSJ*.

Kelen (1994: 29) takes the three emblems of sword, book, flower to represent the trinity of virtuous ways to heroism: the active, contemplative, and amorous lives of the nobleman who expands all three on his solitary but 'exaltant' quest-journey. Flaubert's Julien pursues the sword above the book and the book above the flower, whereas Stendhal's Julien would valorize these in reverse order. As the son of a nobleman in *LSJ*, Julien's primary training at the magic age of 7 combines in equal measure horsemanship and letters founded on knowledge of Scripture. Surrounded by exemplary teachers in the form of a wise monk and his father's former fellow-crusaders, Julien, however, breaks the codes of honour and hospitality in about the most sacrilegious way possible: when his impoverished parents lodge at his castle, he kills them in their bed. His un-welcome, of a magnitude of deepest disgrace to *noblesse*, honour, and hospitality, can only be recompensed when he has learnt to give and to welcome to a 'superhospitalier' degree; he gives his *body* itself, to the leper at the end of the tale, once everything else pertaining to being a 'reasonable' 'hôte' has been offered. The mutual reciprocities of 'hôte' to 'hôte' in the corpo-real embrace sum up a cancelling-out and a transcending of hospitality itself as welcome: the embrace of the stranger, the succour of the beggar at the gate. Flaubert's Julien outdoes any saintly or indeed scriptural precursor by giving not just cloak and coat but also his body as cover to the leper. The further intertextual ramification is the reversal of outcome of Elijah's healing of the widow's son, who is resurrected by the body of the prophet upon him. In *LSJ*, the 'emportement' and 'ascension' of Julien is strongly orgasmic, for the 'petite mort' and death coalesce in this bizarre return to naked truth: the mortal-ity and immortalization of man through encounter with repre-sentations of his unrecognizable, because seemingly opposite, alternative self. Is this a male–male version of the flayed 'naked' truth of Mâthô's body and Salammbô's clothed one at the end of *SAL*?

Flaubert's Julien further elaborates confrontation of male 'alter ego' by this incorporation alongside his namesake Julien (patron saint of innkeepers, boatmen, and travellers) of the 'secularized' saint of hunting, Saint Hubert. The *Oxford Dictionary of Saints* (1992) notes the borrowing of this legend from the 'Acts of Saint Eustace'. This further layering upon apocrypha decentres the sources of *LSJ* to an even more incredible degree, so that its anti-hagiographic import returns, especially at the end. The most famous episode in Hubert's life is his conversion while hunting on Good Friday, when he sees the image of the crucified Christ between the antlers of a stag. Julien's confrontation with the prophetic stag and its triple curse is the crux of his secular 'salvation'. This noble animal, ('prodigieux', 'comme un patriarche et comme un *justicier*', *LSJ*, 93, my emphasis) is the only fitting creature who can check or judge Julien. This is because it has the authority over the order Julien has not as yet recognized, the rules and rights fundamental to the natural law of life and death. Hunter and hunted, human and animal exchange places here, for the curse that issues from the stag strikes at the heart of Julien's moral turpitude against the natural law by addressing him as a 'cœur *féroce*' (*LSJ*, ibid.). The *Petit Robert* not only exemplifies this word from this very sentence of *LSJ*, it clarifies the etymology and point that is being made: '(1468, «farouche» (V. **Fier**, etym.); lat. *ferox*, de *ferus* «bête sauvage»). 1. Qui est cruel par instinct (animaux) . . . 2. Cruel et brutal.' Julien is so inhuman that he has sunk *lower* that any animal could. Therefore the stag pronounces the most fitting punishment, to underpin natural-law justice, that Julien commit the most ignoble crime of all; putting to death in cold blood the very people who gave him life in the first place, a life he has totally abused. While patri-matricide has a psychoanalytical-Oedipal implication, it is the animal–inhuman distinction which the hunting confrontations, the *corps à corps* with animals, most emphasize in Julien's fate. Hunting is itself a codified male sport with strict rules about the culling of animals and fair-play between prey and hunter. However, it finds its most elevated form in *LSJ*, as befits the *noblesse* of Julien, as 'la grande vénerie'. This 'poetry', quite distinct from 'la chasse', its prosaic version, has a complexity of rules especially concerned with the use of other hunting animals, falcons and hounds. This hierarchy of hunter through hunting animal to hunted is precisely the path Julien has himself to experience, triggered here by confrontation as hunted, instead of assuming that he has an absolute right to kill anything because he is the hunter. The stag's words open up the chiastic, reverse, process of the order of Julien's slaughters. From the church mouse, defenceless and unprotected even by the sanctity of its surroundings, and the pigeon, wounded by his stone and then strangled for daring to be alive, he progresses to the highly 'sophisticated' orgy of wanton destructive killing (*LSJ*, 90–2). Here, Julien harnesses all the skills of trapping and 'grande vénerie' as means to further his uncontrolled and debased 'humanity' beyond animality ('Il devint comme elles', *LSJ*, 88), to a completely gratuitous carnage beyond sense or instinct. The stag causes the necessary shock of disgust by his 'magic' powers of speech (like Balaam's ass), to render Julien the inhuman protagonist human and confront him with his most ignoble fate beyond the 'simple' mass murder, done to the forest creatures. Animals rarely kill their parents, whereas Julien is doomed to do just that.

The reversal process puts hunting and hunted back into the human frame in the second part of *LSJ*. 'Brute' power and will are rebalanced to prevent the near-miss of both parents, before Julien creates an army to protect the defenceless (the mouse) and the slaves (the trapped pigeon), and seeks justice through a positive, not a negative use of dexterity at arms. The mouse's needless sacrifice on the altar steps is transposed into the later 'just wars', and the Crusades on which Julien embarks. In fact it has escaped critics' notice that the mighty deeds he undertakes in interstate politics replicate the prowess and biography of the historical and legendary *El Cid*, although in true legend fashion also he is awarded the emperor's daughter. The idyll they build, and Julien's subsequent passivism, smack of the opening scenes with his parents. However, the fetters of fate and blood, life and death, are stronger than the reformed volition of Julien as defender of the faithful and the anti-hunting lobby. He glimpses the connections now between hunting and homicide: 'il lui semblait que du *meurtre des animaux* dépendait le sort de ses parents' (*LSJ*, 102).

It is only when the animals themselves turn the tables on Julien after he agrees to his wife's suggestion to return to hunting, and hunt him down with all their natural weaponry of hoof and horn, claw and beak, that Julien can curse himself (take the blame for his nature) because he is ready to perform the patri-matricide *contra* nature and his noble upbringing. Hospitalier kills those who were first hosts giving hospitality and are now 'hôtes' receiving it. Their model reversal from hospitaliers to beggars, their gratuitous death, will however open a way to Julien in the final part of *LSJ*: they are the hinge couple in their sacrificed bodies of the two beggar-seers at the beginning of the story, and the final reincarnations at the end of the all-male couple, Julien and the leper. Having stoned animals, Julien is stoned by people and even rejected by animals, made to diminish on the scale of the human and animal to a point of willed self-abnegation. It is in the final giving of his own flesh that Julien's humanity is 'sanctified', but read through the law of nature. His life finds its life-affirmation only when he understands the humanity central to knowledge of death. Existentialist before his time, Flaubert's Julien questions the moral import lying behind the codes of hunting, war, and hospitality. The will not to kill cannot prevent killing, but is none the less the only moral frame which separates the human from inhuman beingness. Sainthood can then only be that suprahuman dimension of self-giving even to death (so like many animal species), rather than any altruism dressed up as the law of perfect hospitality. It is the constant corporeality of body-languages betwen man and beast which allows Julien access to some transubstantiated experience of flesh to atone for his innate monstrosity.

As the 'emportements' of Hérode and Hérodias unleash the final transportation of Ioakanann's head, so the climactic 'rage' (*LSJ*, 108) against the unharmed animals opens Julien's desire to 'massacrer les hommes' (*LSJ*, 110) before 'Éclatant d'une colère démesurée' (*LSJ*, 111) in the murder of his parents. 'Rage' is then translated in the final scene into literal and figurative tension. The leper's disease ('maladie infectueuse et contagieuse') is like the animal-carried rabies; he almost 'rabidly' takes possession of Julien's body. Thereby, Julien is released by propulsion and energy ('faire rage') like that of a mighty storm, heavenwards. Sanctity or ascension (as Elijah or Jesus) are framed in the story only in nature; it is culture of religion which elevates Julien and sets him in the window at the end of *LSJ*. Nothing, however, alters the full horror of the final *corps à corps* to match, the awful *tête à tête*. Instead of reading this terror as a kind of pantheism—'[Julien] must integrate his body and his soul and accept his own place in a nature no longer conceived as inanimate, but rather understood pantheistically as one and all animate' (Bart, 1973: 336)—we are left with Julien's and the leper's bodily relics, subject to the 'mortal coil'. Like a Herculaneum asphyxiation, the final embrace is completely *pro* and, for some, *contra* nature.

Same-sex embrace seals a rare moment too in *CS*. It is Virginie's death, not life, which joins Madame Aubain with her maid, 'satisfaisant leur douleur dans un baiser qui les égalisait' (*CS*, 42). This almostly uniquely female environment and moment in Flaubert's work, lying as it does at its heart-point, is key to the expansion of the word 'cœur' whose beat is the tale's alternative body-language. And it is Félicité's, not Madame Aubain's, 'unsacred' heart which expands, not unlike Julien's at the end of *LSJ*:

Félicité lui en fut reconnaissante comme d'un bienfait, et déshormais la chérit avec un dévouement bestial et une vénération religieuse.

La bonté de son cœur se développa. . . . elle se mettait devant la porte avec une cruche de cidre, et offrait à boire aux soldats. Elle soigna les cholériques. Elle protégeait les Polonais.   (*CS*, 42)

Care of Père Colmiche's cancer follows this charity, an outpouring of 'cœur' which is both religious and non-religious in its expression of selflessness and concern for others. His death is the almost ironic prelude to Loulou's arrival as 'gift' and the allfamous, reciprocal relationship that bird and deaf woman, both bereft and abandoned by all human care or comfort, commence.

Like the 'point capitale' of *H*, its headlessness, the 'cœur du sujet' of *CS* is heartlessness, simple or double. Where Ioakanann's prophetic head provided the touchstone to judge other 'entêtements', it is the servant's heart that is the nonverbal indictment of her society and times by mere comparison and contrast. While Hérode incarnates the deadly sins and Félicité embodies the person of the beatitudes (as Beck, 1990: 297 notes), more important for my exploration of morality, as both non-religious and non-legal in *TC*, is the question of how action, if we want to call it human, has moral significance. This morality is even more 'basic' than a code of conscience, reason, or even the morality of the Golden Rule ('Do as you would be done by'), or a proto-existentialist authenticity. There is a prospective overlap between Félicité's *absurdité* and her *surdité* with the notion of the Absurd. However, her uncalculating and almost motiveless life of acceptance runs contrary to the tenets of this modern philosophy. Félicité's unthinking, but totally heartfelt and spontaneous acts, are the mirror back to the 'civilized' France which surrounds her. As in *H* and *LSJ*, it is the actions of the male protagonists in *CS* that chiefly demonstrate the cruelty, murder, destruction, callousness, selfishness, and abuse of natural morality. In a word, this is response to the imperative 'Be!' with 'human' understood in brackets. Félicité's obedience is remarkable in her role as 'good servant', but more remarkable is her unquestioning but non-passive obedience to this call to be herself whatever her limits and whatever the circumstances. Her stature comes from this present-tense beingness, not from any of the higher states or lifestyles which intersect her world.

CS is a world, both religious and secular, which cares nothing for its outcasts: the widow, the fatherless, the orphan, or the unwanted 'foreign' parrot. Charity does not even begin either at home, or in society, except among women; Madame Aubain does leave her house literally to Félicité to inhabit until her death. It is utility and economic self-interest that predominate in the behaviour of all those with the most power to enhance their lot—men. As in *MB*, and because of the restrictions of women's access to money or the public world laid down by the *Code Napoléon*, even butcher boys like Fabu at the bottom of the hierarchy, or farmer's sons like Théodore, have and use power. This 'natural order' is more than a pattern of domination and submission in *TC*, as Zants (1979), among many critics, has read. In its simplest and raw form, power is everywhere visible and economically valorized by the *Code Napoléon*; it stems from the fact that men take, because women have to do the giving. This 'law' of priority and status, importance and value, subject and object, places men in a hierarchy of takers, with varying degrees of force, and in a relationship of non-reciprocity with women and each other. Some men like Père Colmiche have to take, because illness limits them, but it is not men who succour or display charity, only a woman servant. Most of the other male protagonists actively take because their sex gives them the right to expect this, such as Paul Aubain, brought up to believe that he, the 7-year-old boy, is 'd'une manière précieuse' (*CS*, 11). The centre of attention at home until he is sent to school in Caen, he only learns more about taking or taking things out on defenceless others. His cruelty to Loulou when he blows cigar smoke into the sick parrot's face (68) is symbolic of such wanton superiority. He continues to gain (almost at the expense of others' lives— Virginie's, Loulou's) until, married and at the height of his success, at the age of 36 he finds his vocation as the recorder of (others') gains: 'Après avoir été d'abord clerc de notaire, puis dans le commerce, dans la douane, dans les contributions, et même avoir commencé des démarches pour les eaux et forêts, à trente-six ans, tout à coup, par une inspiration du ciel, il avait découvert sa voie: l'enregistrement et y montrait de si hautes facultés qu'un vérificateur lui avait offert sa fille, en lui promettant sa protection' (*CS*, 54).

In an ironic repetition of the heroic pursuits of Julien as *El Cid* figure gifted with a princess because of the father's gratitude for his services, Paul is given the chief of customs's nameless daughter as bride. She acts the 'princesse' with her mother-in-law, but remains the prize, not a person. Théodore, too, demonstrates the male right to take his pleasure of women, first with an attempted rape after having paid for Félicité's evening, and then for self-gain in his marriage to the old rich woman, Madame Lehoussais. While Heep (1996) among other critics has compared Théodore's act to the raging bull that Félicité confronts both for herself and for Madame Aubain and the children, it is not this 'animal', brutishness that most controls Théodore. The tale makes it quite clear why he treats Félicité even more ignominiously when he takes her human feelings for granted and sends a surrogate to tell her of his marriage. It is the same law of take (or give) which suddenly threatens him: 'ses parents . . . lui avait acheté un homme; mais d'un jour à l'autre on pourrait le reprendre; l'idée de servir l'effrayait' (*TC*, 9). Hence, to ensure his position of taker, he marries only for money. His heartlessness contrasts vividly with Félicité's 'serrements de cœur'. If one requires more evidence of the contrasts between 'heartfelt' and 'heartless' response in this scene, various idioms in French centring on 'cœur' are put in opposition here.

For Félicité, for example, this relationship has been 'pris à cœur' whereas for Théodore, 'le cœur lui manque'.

It is Bourais, former man of the law ('avocat') and manager of Mme Aubain's estate, and the most powerful man in *CS* who is, however, also its most 'écœurant'. (*Petit Robert*, '1. Qui écœure, soulève le cœur. V Dégoûtant, fétide, infect, nauséabond, répugnant. . . . 2. *Fig.* Moralement répugnant, révoltant . . . 3. Qui crée une espèce de malaise, de découragement.') A combination of Guillaumin the barrister and Lheureux the merchant-moneylender in *MB* (see Orr, 1999*b*), he abuses his power and position. Acting as surrogate 'father' in his role as head of Madame Aubain's affairs, he chooses a 'collège' for Paul, blocks Félicité's view at Virginie's confirmation, and then is among the chief mourners at her funeral. These roles of supporter and adviser (he informs Félicité too, witness the mocking laughter of her naïvety about Victor's house when he shows her Havana on the globe), are, however, of the same order as Théodore's 'investment' in small things in order to reap the larger reward. Obviously, as Madame Aubain discovers to her cost, when news of his suicide breaks, he has used one widow's money to finance other relationships: 'des doutes s'élevèrent sur sa probité. Mme Aubain étudia ses comptes, et ne tarda pas à connaître la kyrielle de ses noirceurs; détournements d'arrérages, ventes de bois dissimulées, fausses quittances, etc. De plus, il avait un enfant naturel, et "des relations" avec une personne de Doluzé' (*CS*, 55). The inner cost of Bourais's infamies, like Théodore's betrayal of Félicité for a wealthy widow, is Madame Aubain's chest-pain and death nine days later. Madame Aubain has given more than she ever thought, thus experiencing the double trap of the male sexual double standard. Men can have their cake and eat it.

Two male figures do, however, give; and give moreover to the character who gives her all throughout the tale. The first is Félicité's nephew Victor, who brings his aunt gifts from his sea voyages, but who leaves for Havana and death by yellow fever. The second figure is Loulou, who comes as a kind of surrogate Victor both in his exotic origins and as loyal companion until his own 'departure' in death. As unwanted 'gift', as unwanted as Victor ('Ses parents l'avaient toujours traité avec barbarie (*CS*, 35)), he none the less fills an equally major space in

Félicité's mind in those places outside her physical world. Critics frequently explore the symbolism of Loulou—for example, this 'oiseau "mite" (mythe)' (Vierne, 1992: 18), or the 'posible lectura psicoanalítica' (Prado, 1992: 38). Loulou in my reading is a 'real presence', who simply is, being neither giver or receiver. Havana and the realms of the Holy Spirit are as one and the same. Loulou signifies the possible and the imaginary for Félicité, a non-economic token of exchange from being to noth-ingness at a time in Félicité's life when there is no one else upon whom to lavish her beingness. Her gift of him for the 'reposoir' is her token acceptance and understanding of the mortal coil. The 'restes' she has contemplated of others who are dead in the mausoleum which is Madame Aubain's house, and now of Loulou, stuffed and rotting, prepare her for her own death. Loulou, like the bull, only acts within a natural order which she is now going to follow. Beyond giving or taking, but merely being, Félicité, in pre-Sartrean terms, comes to authenticity at the point where her immanence, matching the parrot's, becomes transcendence in the death which takes her. Like Victor and Loulou before her, it takes her through illness. This is a very different process and path from Bourais's, who takes right to the end, including his own life. Félicité therefore gives up the ghost at the end of *CS* by giving up to death and to the pseudo-Holy Ghost. Her 'surdité' finds fullest expression in her ending as 'absurdité', the bringing to Félicité of her felicity, as Loulou has found his last site on an altar of adoration ('louer', Loulou), outside Félicité's window in the procession and inside her heart.

The endings of each of the tales, therefore, disembody and embody, literally as well as metaphorically, the head, the body, the heart. These three synonyms for life are returned to nature at that point where transcendence through death transports them into either a cultural or a religious icon (Orr, 1995). This nature–supernature dichotomy has mock supernatural import at the end of each tale in order to underpin the unrepresentable nature of death itself. However, by reading backwards through the collection to *CS*, arguably the tale with the most supernat-ural ending, from the most intensely banal and flat *H*, this, if considered as ending to the whole work, must surely hold a collective key to the moral of the stories. In each one, in various ways, Eros and Thanatos have met and shaped the central human protagonists to force them up against the parameters of their humanity, or lack of it. The animals and monsters of *TC* are not so much the magic stag, Loulou, the raging bull, but the truly brutish creatures who inhabit the tale without animals, *H*. The life-force so visibly snuffed out in each tale returns paradoxically as Ioakanann's head is borne off. New life is born as others carry on the banal act of living. Huge weights of circumstance load Félicité, Julien, and Ioakanann with undue *fatalité*, but it is in this that they realize their humanity by overcoming with grace. When the moralities of giving and taking, of life and death as hospitality and hunting, of absolutist force, are all considered, the only moral possible is: 'Be human!' Strangely situated in the cusp of critics' polarization between reading the tales as religious or as anti-religious, this moral and its depiction requires three very inhuman or unhuman insignificant and marginal figures to represent it. Good and evil, right and wrong pale before these explorations of the human–inhuman dimensions of civilization, not least the times in which Flaubert was writing. Taking up the 'civilization' and barbarity debate as political or psychic structure in *SAL*, *TC* expores the moral impact of being human.

These three adult tales, a chap-book for contemporary times, speak directly to the crisis of values of progress and civilization that Flaubert experienced at the end of his life. They speak a moral message in three different, but complementary keys. In *CS*, the *inter*dictions of the *Code Napoléon*, those prohibitions by men on the power of women to be, have as a consequence the immoral double standards of a Bourais in a society of self-interest. In *LSJ* the *male*dictions of the stag decree the outcome of extreme human instinct which sinks below the depths of animal killing to annihilation (the killing of parents). In *H* the *pre*dictions of Ioakanann voice the call to humanity as community, not dictatorship of progress as symbolized by the decadence of Hérode's court. Crass materialism is being lambasted in favour of some return to the senses, these being neither the rational nor the instinctual, but the ethical and aesthetic parts of man which render him human. Czyba (1997: 92–3) would see the head as the locale of creative genius and of the fears in Flaubert the writer of having this vital organ 'castrated' by woman, who decapitates the imaginary. Leaving biography aside, to return to the figurations and transfigurations in *TC*, Flaubert inadvertently uncovers in *CS* the missing parts to bring forth the human: the unleashing of women and an unmale energy. This potential fullness and reharmonization is overwritten by the Jezebel in Hérodias most to be feared by men, so that, in the end, the male head and male bearers of the future endorse the old morality-play Flaubert has sought throughout the tales to undo. The theatre of man's inhumanity to man which makes 'countless thousands mourn' is the theatre of cruelty, brutality, oppression in *TC* with few glimmers of humanity left alight at the end to bring in the ray of hope of all classical tragedies. The monsters more monstrous than the stag, the mouldy parrot, the headless man, or their combination like some Greek half-man, half-beast, are everywhere apparent in the mutilations of manhood that *TC* depicts in Bourais, Julien, and Hérode. These images do indeed repudiate 'any notion of vertical ascension' of the mock endings, or of 'man's historical progess' (Peterson, 1983: 251 and 255 respectively). The apotheoses of man in each tale as Paraclete, stained-glass saint, or prophet of revelation are fantastical images proper to the fairy-tale genre. Alongside is the more terrifying 'merveilleux' (as elucidated more widely by Palaccio, 1993 with specific reference to the *fin de siècle*), the monstrous that lurks within man and which flouts truly 'civilized' behaviour at every juncture. It is the profanity in each tale of society's sacralization of those who have commited murder, incest, or exploitation which Flaubert overwrites, over-rights, and over-rites in *TC*. It is therefore the supreme folly of the ending of *H* that brings the shock warning to positivism and obedience to its dictats. Requiring a group (three men, not one), to bear the brunt and the weight of the head into the future, these tales ultimately suggest as their moral that without the awareness of the absurdity of death, of decrease not increase, of the value of life, and potentially of the need for interhuman engagement, (male) humanity will disappear in the grim world of 'bêtise', which simply means to be terrifyingly inhuman.

6

Bouvard et Pécuchet

BECAUSE *BP* is in many ways as unreadable a text as *TSA*, critics compare the 'bibliothèque fantastique' nature of both.[1] Focus on the erudition, however, has occluded some of the properly apocalyptic explorations in *BP* as a story of ends, ironically itself unfinished, which raises the question of whether ends are (un)justified by means. If *TSA* showed the necessary position of spiritual retreat from the world as the only place to find integrity and a final stand against the joining of causes, in spite of constant bombardment by the world and its ideologies, including religious doctrine, then *BP* describes two figures, in secular retreat on the other side of the Cartesian watershed, who have neither cause nor effect. Where *TSA* also shows the difference between informed faith and other conflicting faiths, Bouvard and Pécuchet at every turn re-enact a blind leap of faith in their belief that the written word and its scientific authority

---

[1] See e.g. Greene (1981: 112) and Bowman (1986: 51), 'Or le traitement de savoirs chez Flaubert, et surtout des 'savoirs érudits' est notoirement nihiliste: toute théorie de la connaissance dans *BP* est mise en doute par sa juxtaposition avec d'autres théories . . . Mais il prend comme cible préférée, surtout dans *BP*, le syncrétisme et le traditionalisme.' For an example of the comparative approach, see Guedes (1984: 101), 'La dimension grotesque de l'orgueil dans l'autosuffisance du savoir est introduite dans *BP* comme antithèse complémentaire du sublime dans *TSA*'; 'l'ambition dernière de Saint Antoine . . . a comme le revers complémentaire d' "être tout" dans une intégration cosmique, dans le collectif, l'anéantissement de l'être individuel, somme existence humaine' (ibid. 107); and 'Pourtant la conclusion des deux œuvres suggère une ascèse authentique, par le "guérison" du désir métaphysique, symtôme du mal ontologique' (ibid. 111). Séginger more recently highlights the 'bibliothèque' and the 'fantastique': 'Mais à la fin de sa vie, dans *BP*, il édifie un nouvel enfer. Les personnages sont alors tour à tour croyants et avocats d'un Diable transformé en une vaste Bibliothèque. Ils ne voyagent pas sur les cornes d'un Tentateur comme Antoine, mais la lecture de Spinoza leur donne l'impression d'être emporté dans l'espace par un ballon' (1997: 13).

match truthfully the reality of the world around them.[2] The hallucinations of *TSA* return in *BP* in equally monstrous forms, as 'expériences', lived by the eponymous heroes, and in the sense of 'scientific' experiments in those subdisciplines of science which are all vying for precedence in the rational world. Modern sorcerer's apprentices, autodidacts, and pedagogues, Bouvard and Pécuchet are revisionaries of Antoine's gifted discipling and exemplary knowledge in both spiritual and earthly matters. Theirs is, however, no amiable buffoonery or harmless mediocrity. Bersani puts it in a nutshell: 'The relationship of Bouvard and Pécuchet to knowledge is highly practical; if Flaubert has satirical intentions towards them, it is not because they are intellectually mediocre, but because they would put knowledge *to use*' (1990: 161). Lethal when there is no supervision or check on their activities, Bouvard and Pécuchet herald, in quite prophetic ways, modern cloning, experimentation in alternative medicine, unregulated puericulture, all because they are free agents with books at their disposal. This chapter will argue that they push to the limits the logic that has been unfolding in Flaubert's *œuvre* concerning the dangerous territories of the masculine under republicanism and post-revolutionary

---

[2] For critical appraisal of the theme of the blindness of faith, particularly in science and the written word, see *inter alia* Guedes (1984: 104), 'Dans les deux textes, le livre est le lieu de la tentation, où les connaissances amènent la perte de la connaissance'; Neefs (1990: 73), 'La toute confiance en la description systématique rejoint la croyance au surgissement empirique du système. Flaubert construit son texte dans le jeu permanent d'adéquations défaites, de rubriques vides ou rhétoriques, d'applications manquées et de théories contredites. Glissements des choses entre leurs noms ou leurs classes possibles, destruction des classes par les choses, il y a un brouillage propre à Bouvard et à Pécuchet, qui tient à une sorte de croyance aveugle en la puissance de la nomination, des classements et des systèmes'; Starr (1984: 1092), 'What matters in temptation is that the structure of temptation itself be preserved, that desire itself persist. . . . By their very action Bouvard and Pécuchet show that the truth of science is a will to believe in it, a resolve to say . . . that the lack of an infallible method is actually a precondition of that truth'; and Colwell (1987: 874), 'the protagonists . . . are constantly deceived by words into believing that the external world is knowable'; 'From the emphasis Flaubert lays on the fallibility of language in the novel . . . *BP* is not simply a satire of two inept figures in search of knowledge or a critique of different aspects of pseudoscientific activity in the nineteenth century' (ibid. 859). Language as 'truth' is taken further by Bernheimer (1974: 144), 'Flaubert himself termed *BP* a "philosophical" novel and it is so in the most modern, post-Wittgensteinian sense of the term: it constitutes an investigation into the nature and status of language in respect to reality and to truth.'

democracy. It is the logic of enlightenment cutting itself off at each crisis in history from those territories it deems 'other', thus reinforcing a heightened importance for those that remain and hence need shoring up. Figure 1 (p. 20) represented such evaluations in schematic grid form. Figure 2 traces the logic of male values across western philosophy (in capital letters), with, below the line, the daemonized other. The spectrum is held at each end by *TSA* and *BP*, but as with the polarities explored in *SAL*, this chapter again questions the differences of such delineation, and the nature of 'progress'.

'Bouvard et Pécuchet incarnent, de façon caricaturale ... le mal du rationalisme moderne, qui ne trouve que contradictions partout, désespère de connaissance absolue, et conclut cyniquement qu'on ne peut rien affirmer'; 'Avec Roquentin et le *nouveau roman*, Bouvard et Pécuchet sont les enfants malades du rationalisme moderne' (Fournier, 1974: 78, 81) Not only does *BP*'s very inception and logic illustrate what I can only call an 'ontologie mâle' as continuity from *TSA*; it also pronounces the 'mal ontologique' of the late nineteenth century as its secular apotheosis. Free will, individual autonomy, and individuality in a democracy of equals, as was demonstrated in Chapter 3 concerning the concept of 'fraternité' in *ES*, are contradictions in terms. The question in *BP* centres less on political than on epistemological equalities—Bouvard and Pécuchet's average mediocrity. Theirs is the law of the mean, the middle term, the *non-lieu* of the *lieu commun*. Hence, the repetitive, iterative, digressive, enumerative episodes, enacted by puppets whose

MEN'S HISTORY				
Pre-1789 ⟶			Post-1789 ⟶	
TSA				*BP*
spirit	mind/matter	aristocracy	democracy	progress
v.	v.	v.	v.	v.
nature	dark continent	barbarism	homicide	madness
WOMEN'S TIME				

FIG 2. The logic of male values set along the continuum of western philosophy, showing the positions of *TSA* and *BP* at opposite ends of the spectrum.

actions or failures are forgone conclusions, take up in peculiar harmony the aimlessness of Frédéric's and Deslaurier's return to adolescent memory and Antoine's return to his hut after various experiences with the world, the flesh, and the devil. However, the new twist is the none the less gruesome development in Bouvard and Pécuchet's epistemological 'progress' as regress, in spite of the uncompleted Sottisier and *DICT*. Colwell (1987: 859–60) is among few critics to note this paradox. Not only do Bouvard and Pécuchet uncover philosophical aporias—in Figure 2 it is they and not Antoine who fuse together the previously delineated reason as progress and madness. And it is not merely the madness of writing as Barthes suggests: 'Flaubert . . . devient le premier écrivain de la modernité parce qu'il accède à une folie. Une folie qui n'est pas de la représentation, de l'imitation, du réalisme, mais une folie de l'écriture, une folie du langage' (1995: 437). *BP* reveals the illusion of mimesis by presenting fiction's distorting mirror through interreflecting but non-communicating characters.[3] The double-edged legacy of the Cartesian *cogito*, so blatantly personified in its double protagonists in *BP* in an-all-too-male world, is therefore not only the madness of reason and the reason of madness; it is quintessentially the unbearable likeness of being. Taking the political concept of 'confrérie' as discussed in Chapter 3 into a philosophical domain, the nightmarish familiarity of the reflective vortex that this chapter will uncover constitutes the secular apocalyptic nature of *BP*. Indeed, with comic frequency, Bouvard and Pécuchet as men of science are constantly the butts of 'acts of God'. These are often also the means by which

---

[3] The question of the exploration of *mimesis* in *BP* has been taken up variously by Barthes (1995: 435), 'personne ne s'adresse à personne . . . Eux-mêmes, les deux personnages forment un bloc amoureux, mais ils sont en rapport de miroir: on a d'ailleurs beaucoup de mal à les distinguer . . . Et ce couple, ce bloc amoureux . . . est lointain, glacé, et ne s'adresse pas au lecteur. . . . Le psychotique, quand il parle, ne s'adresse pas et c'est pourquoi *BP*, sous un habillage tout à fait traditionnel, est un livre fou'; and Gothot-Mersch (1981: 15): 'Ce "nouveau tour" fait passer les bonhommes de l'apprentissage à l'enseignement—mais il faut remarquer qu'ils continuent d'apprendre, eux-mêmes, ce qu'ils vont enseigner'. Later Gothot-Mersch states that 'ce parcours inlassable du même circuit me paraît relever, elle aussi de la Mimésis. Mais ici le livre, au lieu d'imiter les autres livres s'imite lui-même; si bien que, paradoxalement, cette encyclopédie critique est aussi un "livre sur rien", qui fonctionne en s'appuyant sur soi-meme qui se nourrit de sa propre substance. Qui, nouveau Catoblépas, se développe en se dévorant' (ibid. 22).

Flaubert ends a section: with a '*deus absconditus ex machina*'. For example, in the middle of chapter II there is the fire which destroys the haystacks and finishes off Bouvard and Pécuchet's agricultural experiments, while the alambic explodes at the end of the chapter and heralds in their desire to study chemistry. Yet no angels appear with scrolls; rather, books arrive on order to the Chavignolles world and open up 'miracles' and 'mysteries', revelation in consumer terms.

> Ce livre des livres se nourrit des volumes qu'il démantèle, défigure, en même temps qu'il les représente . . . Flaubert nous fait assister à la perversion intertextuelle inhérente à toute lecture . . . les textes rapprochés produisent une irréductible cacophonie, parodie de polyphonie . . . [B&P] ne savent pas régler le dialogue entre les textes. Ils sont incapables du travail de l'encyclopédiste ou de l'écrivain, de P. Larousse ou de G. Flaubert. . . . Ils demandent à cette nouvelle image du livre total qu'est l'Encyclopédie d'apporter la même révélation que l'on attendait auparavant de la Bible.   (Gleize, 1992: 195)

BP undoubtedly is this virtuoso intertextual recycling—a collection of delicious satires of issues and writers contemporary to Flaubert himself. Excellent critical articles have concentrated on one episode or butt of Flaubert's satire, for example Ripoll (1993, on the Gaulois); Gayon (1998, on agriculture and agronomy); Meyer (1995, on gymnasts); Green (1980, on Flaubert's satire of Salgues); Lacoste (1997, on Flaubert's satire of Hugo). It is not the bookish that will be the focus of this chapter but rather the principal 'characters' who have never really been seen as more than cardboard cut-outs, possibly because they are so 'impossible' as models for male readers. I will look first at Bouvard and Pécuchet as 'êtres en retraite', both in terms of masculinity faced with the post-work world of early retirement (beyond 'mid-life crisis' but before old age) and 'en retraite' as a secularized religious retreat in the manner of a new monasticism. Kliebenstein (1991: 449) is the nearest critics have got to old age seen as second childhood in *BP*: 'A aucun moment le roman n'entrera dans le réalisme de la sénescence. Du *puer senilis* . . . il est un *senex puerilis* perdu dans l'autodidaxie éternelle.' Second, there is the related construct in *BP* of a dystopian society run by these men set within the official society (also run by men). Third, the novel is a transcrypt [*sic*] of dead writing, a testimony and testament to the fallibility of science's definitions of the world because it issues from the hands of its two copyist protagonists, whose 'new' experiences are always already 'de seconde main' (second-hand, copied). How far this ultimately sterile environment is embodied in these copycat characters will be the final question. Nowhere else in Flaubert's œuvre is there such an obsession with the body sexual as in *BP*. Jacquet (1987) has discussed the theme of sexuality with regard to *DICT* but not *BP*. Heads, hearts, and bodies figured large in *TC*. It is on the public and private parts of Bouvard and Pécuchet that Flaubert can turn his attention because, as with Charles Bovary, the average male reader will distance himself through mockery and scorn: 'Eux, c'est pas moi!' Does their embodiment of unvirile masculinity as codified by social roles and stereotypes actually speak of and to a deeper crisis in masculinity generally? And to current masculinity in the age of Viagra?

There are very few works of French literature which examine retirement, even less early retirement, as the concept has only recently come into being. The term has a strongly gendered implication because the world of work has mainly been male and public, whereas women are expected throughout their lives to be carers and nurses of children and elderly relations at home. Work in the home is not classified as work. 'Le mot "économie" vient du grec "oikonomia" et signifie organisation d'une maison domestique! Or aussi paradoxale que cela puisse être, les économistes n'ont jamais eu de théorie du "ménage domestique" ' (Lemennicier, 1988: 17). The impact of early retirement is therefore of particular interest as a threshold experience of the masculine, and as an opportunity for potential transformation or sublimation of self-evaluation, not least with respect to the ageing process and the degeneration of both the mind and the body.

The world of work also has strong class implications. One is either a blue-collar or a white-collar worker, a working-class or a bourgeois employee. Gorju, discussed below, is a highly significant representative of the former whereas Bouvard and Pécuchet are firmly in the latter category. However, Flaubert confuses the distinctions by demonstrating the ironies of the appellation *main-d'œuvre*. Their inane life as bureaucrats has harnessed Bouvard and Pécuchet in the democratic public machine as human cogs, part of a State *main-d'œuvre* in the form of a self-regulating body of paper valuations. Their work differs very little from that of the industrial factory making endless copies of objects. Although critics have noted the similarities between Frédéric and Deslauriers as couple and Bouvard and Pécuchet (for example Kelly, 1989: 142; Cogny, 1981: 39; Gleize, 1992: 154; Smith, 1984: 96), in counterpoint to Frédéric and even Deslauriers in *ES*, Bouvard and Péchuchet are petit-bourgeois—copyists, civil servants, and clerks with little opportunity to advance in the pecking-order and hence to become individuated from the herd. Their ubiquity and functionality in the civic and urbanized world of work none the less make the petit-bourgeois the thermometer of social change and class-movement of the period. The copy clerk of the period is also a thermometer of gender: 'A crisis in masculinity is precisely what many male office clerks experienced in the late Victorian period, as they saw their somewhat ambivalent occupational status undermined still further by the recruitment of female clerks' (Graham in Roper and Tosh, 1991: 19). As Buisine states:

Fondamentalement le petit-bourgeois du xixe siècle est copiste, attelé à un incessant labeur de duplication qui va manifester les représentations où il se reconnaît. Il devient le papier, calque de toute une société qui a de plus en plus envie de se voir. Car la copie dépourvue des assises financières et des fondements sociaux économiques de l'original, faux-semblant d'une illusoire appartenance de classe, plagiat social réalisé aux moindres frais par celui qui n'en a pas réellement les moyens, révèle en les singeant les représentations bourgeoises: copie exagérée . . . démodée . . . souvent caricaturale . . . Ainsi le petit-bourgeois, ce perpétuel imitant, rend imitable ce qu'il imite . . . le petit-bourgeois est éminemment représentable car il est la mimésis en action dans le social . . . [Bouvard et Pécuchet] réalisent le rêve de tout petit-bourgeois: l'indifférenciation qui témoignerait d'une parfaite réussite de l'imitation, du triomphe d'une altérité. Et quand Bouvard et Pécuchet se découvrent de minimes différences, la joie s'accroît encore car les variations mineures sont une preuve supplémentaire d'une fondamentale similitude . . . Il fallait donc un couple pour que Flaubert puisse représenter *le* Petit-Bourgeois.   (1977: 52–3)

Their voluntary withdrawal from the world of work, key site of male evaluation and designation of one's place in society and its pecking-order (as I have explored in *MB* in relation to the terms 'success' and 'failure'—Orr, 1999*b*), takes the notion of autonomy and free will into a completely secular province, figuratively and literally. Life at Les Chavignolles after the 'decision' of voluntary severance from their workplaces will raise the question of how much freedom from the world of work which they have left they can actually exercise. The 'copie salariée devenue odieuse', they actively turn to 'la Copie qui donne du plaisir' (Leclerc, 1988: 8). What has not been recognized is the all-important interim step. In Les Chavignolles, they become self-employed and at the same time employers. Their 'work'— completely voluntary, all-absorbing, outside office hours— combines both physical labour and desk activity. Ironically this double change and exchange in status is all brought about through Bouvard's surprise inheritance. As with Frédéric Moreau, the inheritance buys leisure or withdrawal from the world of employment. The differences in Bouvard's case are many. The gift of money discharges the all-essential petit-bourgeois condition, the need to earn, work and earnings being the 'currency' by which their status is guaranteed against non-status, unemployment. There is a second corollary for the petit bourgeois, education: 'A proprement parler, Bouvard et Pécuchet ne font pas partie de la société; ils n'y exercent aucune fontion ni responsabilité. Grâce à leur héritage, ce sont des hommes libres qui sont *en position d'étudier*' (Adert, 1996: 123, my emphasis). The case of Bouvard and Pécuchet is even more provocative because they transcend the stereotype of the man of fortune or unfortunate background making his way in love and life, precisely because they are not young men. The other irony concerning the gift-inheritance is that, normally, the illegitimate son is not entitled to inherit unless there is specific failure of filial duty in the legitimate line. 'La Loi règle l'ordre de succéder entre les héritiers légitimes: à leur défaut, les biens passent aux enfants naturels, ensuite à l'époux survivant; et s'il n'y en a pas, à la République' (*Code*, Art. 723). Thus Flaubert underlines the illegitimacy of the situation both through the person of Bouvard and through the lucky strike of Fate that plucks both men out of the humdrum, petit-bourgeois order and catapults them into the dis-order of pseudo-landed gentry.

The maladjustment of their lives only begins to show when the two Parisians try to apply in the private, provincial setting, methods learned in their urban world of copying. The problem is not so much their use or abuse of method, but rather their failure to see that definitions, labels, figures, and diagrams as universals do not match individual signifiers or signifieds in the way that, comically, they themselves did in the city. As Schehr (1997: 233–4) notes, on the boulevard Bourdon, person and hat are correctly labelled so that 'recognition' of reality takes place when one labelled hat-wearer meets another of the same order. 'Flaubert ajoute au conformisme bourgeois des traits supplémentaires. Car il assume deux rôles à la fois, un rôle social, celui du bourgeois, et un rôle professionnel, celui de copiste. Et le rôle professionnel ne fait que redoubler le rôle social' (Baron, 1994: 36). The recognition of this doubling is not merely the double in Bouvard and Pécuchet or their personification perhaps of bureaucracy itself. It is the *civic* nature of the copy and codification of the democratic compilation of 'reality' encapsulated in the Encyclopaedia as Enlightenment *summa*. Kempf describes this project as 'la démarche encyclopédique, telle que l'Occident l'avait consacrée, acte civique, de collecte, d'inventaire, de révérence, Flaubert la tourne en dérision, raflant pour les détruire, sous le tablier de *BP*, les objets fixés par la culture et l'idéologie de son temps' (1990: 40). This is derided first on the pavement, cityscape *par excellence*, when, as individuals, both set out to *combine* and define meaning, *agree* criteria, name parts, construct systems. Their fabrication of codes and practices overdo, yet undo, any individual expert's contribution to the wealth of knowledge. Practical replication and duplication only leads to plagiarism; the alignment of several specialists (or even two non-specialists) in one subject community only leads to contradiction and argument. The ensuing novel maps the second misapplication of such book- and city-lore for it is necessarily the wrong frame for both the country and nature.

Les Chavignolles therefore epitomizes the mad and bad transcription and translation of terms and values. 'Transcription abolishes signification: linguistic realism destroys the possibility of spiritual discrimination' (Bernheimer, 1974: 158). Through near-equivalence of homophones, its name offers in its first syllable a linguistic, Norman, equivalent of 'Schah' as discussed in *SAL* and picks up the ironic headlessness of Bouvard and Pécuchet's leadership in their household. In many ways their lack of control over the servants and their foster children mirrors Hérode's lack of control over his domestic and national situations. Too far north to produce wine (*vignobles*), it can only produce those who are unfit to be there (*ignobles*). On the ideological front, it also represents the double and counter 'expérience' of the 'private' as opposed to the ideology of the 'public', industrialization and urbanization as outcome of Enlightenment values as well as from the city as workplace and value-system (*lieux communs*): 'L'urbanisme effréné à l'œuvre durant la seconde moitié du xixe siècle tend à supprimer l'espace privé, et le sujet ne peut s'incarner dans l'espace public décrit comme un chantier permanent ou le vouant à un passage incessant. Les déplacements de Bouvard et Pécuchet se font dans des espaces d'articulation, de transition, lieux vides voués au seul passage' (Malgor, 1995*a*: 323). The capital city is translated into private capital, not least by the link through the doubled number, '33' (*BP*, 1 and 48). The double figure meshes perfectly with the duo's twinning and brotherhood to form a community: initiation to the same degree to become master builders, or in Bouvard and Pécuchet's case, failed erectors. There may be a strong Masonic undertow in the significance of the 33 degrees. Their secular retreat into a world of their own making is doubled through their persons and their chosen situation. A province within provincial France, Les Chavignolles is demonstrably where Bouvard and Pécuchet's ends are justified by their means, both material and intellectual. Although the bonhommes eschew the city, *BP*'s end none the less returns its white-collar manifestation, bureaucracy, relabelled, Homaislike, as the *DICT* forged in a provincial and communal State. 'A cette lumière l'Opinion apparaît comme une sorte de monstre discursif, dont la prétention à articuler un universel dogmatique n'a d'égale que l'inanité verbale'; 'Dans le cours du lieu commun, la Communauté prétend se faire Sujet, et venir occuper la place de l'Absolu' (Adert, 1996: 101, 103).

Les Chavignolles is also the place of counter-exchange of values. Where critics have attempted themselves to classify the running order of disciplines and areas of knowledge Bouvard and Pécuchet cover by an alphabetical taxonomy from agriculture to puericulture (for example Leclerc, 1988: 68–9), the audiences sought provide a different method of evaluating the dystopian community which demonstrates progress as in fact ideological regress. Bouvard and Pécuchet 'recreate' a world by stripping away recent layers of post-revolutionary civilization, first science as medicine and archaeological understanding (chapters III and IV); then uncovering the Renaissance *scientia* of literature, arts, and history in chapters V and VI; before returning ultimately to the medieval world of superstition, magic, spiritism, and religion in chapters VIII and IX. Bouvard and Pécuchet have the unsuccess of their experiments in these respective areas judged by the representative expert in provincial remodelling, who speaks on behalf of these quantum leaps in civilization. Thus Vaucorbeil the doctor is later replaced by *l'abbé* Jeufroy as touchstone of value-judgement. *BP*'s progression therefore details knowledge as regress. We shall return to the interlude chapters, VII and X, which deal with questions of normal relationship, in the final part of this chapter.

But the second touchstone of exchange are the two characters who constantly recur and who present distorted others of Bouvard and Pécuchet themselves. The first is Madame Bordin, who represents increasing financial and economic success whereas Bouvard experiences only dwindling resources and territory. The latter's attempt to tie the knot with this widow-reflection of his widowerhood because of their shared initial, and, one suspects, because of shared interest in the other's very similar person, only underlines the failure of *both* protagonists *vis-à-vis* this female remake of Bouvard. Madame Bordin can take on all men: 'Quand elle l'eut complimenté, elle s'informa de son ami. Les yeux noirs de cette personne, très brillants bien que petits, ses hautes couleurs, son aplomb (elle avait même un peu de moustache) intimidèrent Pécuchet' (*BP*, 30). This telling detail to sum up the post-menopausal, 'masculinized', widow recurs when Bouvard gets somewhat closer to her in the mock love-scene in chapter VII: 'Mme Bordin, en dilatant les narines, trempait dans la soucoupe sa lèvre charnue, ombrée légèrement d'un duvet noir' (*BP*, 235). Older bodies in *BP*, male and female, are clearly on display.

The second 'mirror' is Gorju, largely overlooked by critics, with the notable exceptions of Lacoste (1997: 106), who sees this figure as a caricature of Hugo, and Leclerc, '[le trio Bordin–Mélie–Gorju] Gorju intriguant politique et sentimental, personnage insignifiant qui se charge de toute la signification politique des événements' (1988: 72). Like Madame Bordin, he is also partly a remake of Bouvard by a half-link of the first part of their names—a 'bouvet' is not only a bullock, it is also a kind of carpenter's plane, as is a 'gorjet'—and of Pécuchet by social status. Gorju we are first introduced to in chapter II as an 'ancien menuisier' (*BP*, 63), but he moves rapidly on from being an artisan, a worker with his hands, employed in chapter IV to make an 'authentic' *prie-dieu* for Bouvard and Pécuchet's museum, and to varnish a large chest. It is then that his entrepreneurial face—he will later set up a *prie-dieu* business and take communion in chapter IV—takes on a more sinister side as he becomes a saboteur under Bouvard and Pécuchet's roof. A runaway cow, he claims, knocked over the chest; it then becomes clear that Gorju is involved with the female servants, and he will later inveigle his way into Madame Castillon's affections (chapter VII). His success at transforming himself into a worker-revolutionary and transcending social class are, however, most evident in chapter VI, where in the 1848 débâcle, he represents the democratization of working-class France: ' "La charité? Merci!" s'écria Gorju, "A bas les aristos! Nous voulons le droit au travail!" ' (*BP*, 201). After imprisonment, he reappears, 'nippé comme un bourgeois' (*BP*, 224), thus delineating the very fine line between the petit-bourgeois and the worker, the class and status demarcation that Bouvard and Pécuchet want to preserve to ensure their own autonomy on the white-collar side of the *main-d'œuvre* divide. The delicious irony is that they, like Gorju who reappears on rungs of the carpentry hierarchy, do not change their spots. After all, their success as copyists as Leclerc notes (1988: 42) was altogether dependent on their 'belle main'.

Les Chavignolles, then, is a plural place. It is a new communal home in the legal sense of *communauté* for Bouvard and Pécuchet (*Petit Robert*, '1. Groupe social dont les membres vivent ensemble, ou ont des biens, des intérêts communs . . . 2. Groupe de religieux qui vivent ensemble et observent des règles ascétiques et mystiques'), and increasingly in *BP* the non-secular meaning applies, thus linking their retreat to Antoine's hut

in *TSA*—separated from the city, a refuge for these hybrid
workers. It rarely, however, serves them as private domestic
sphere, but inverts instead, constantly, into workplace and
public space. Laboratory proving the failure of laboratory
method, theatre (medical and dramatic), museum to the *restes*
of Enlightenment culture (crystallized by collection and classifi-
cation), even a church—it is opened to the public who are the
people on the other side of its walls, as well as to the servants
on the inside. While all the projects undertaken look strikingly
similar to those of the world they have left, Bouvard and
Pécuchet's real need is, like Homais's, for an audience, for verification of their attempted reconstructions. Rather than freeing
themselves from the shackles of conservative and outmoded
values, Bouvard and Pécuchet seem ironically to become
increasingly dependent on the other world and its constantly
encroaching moral opprobrium or dis-opprobrium, without
which they would have no concept of the extent of their licence
to experiment. Self-confirmation as two people is therefore not
enough because the mirror and its image, the sound and its
echo, may not be sufficient to ground reality. The disappearing
echo in their garden at the end of chapter II is just such a case
in point, for it is only when the Grand Tour takes place that the
iterability of the phenomenon they have tried out on each other
proves false in larger company. Flaubert's rewriting of the
Narcissus/Echo myth, but in double male reconfiguration, is a
coup in the face of theories of the mimetic. Bouvard and
Pécuchet are both Narcissus and Echo inhabiting a world which
only reflects back to them the male remnants of their second-
hand rationalist heritage: they can only copy, because the hierarchies of thought and value which make inspiration or
elevation or transcendence possible have been eradicated by
notions of positivism and progress—future-driven evolutions
which refuse the so-called dark ages of their heritage.

Les Chavignolles therefore proves a nightmare of unfreedom
from social constraints and debunks Rousseau's *Contrat social*
(in Bouvard and Pécuchet's bibliography of Utopian literature,
BP, 219), and *Emile* in the upbringing of Victor and Victorine,
but most of all it is quintessentially an anti-Clarens (*La
Nouvelle Héloïse* is cited in *BP*, 376). It lies outside the current
study, but the intertextual reworking of Les Chavignolles to

debunk the ideal mini-state of Clarens in *La Nouvelle Héloïse* is striking, especially Rousseau's descriptions in part four, letter X. It is the anti-Utopian, or, better, the deliberately dystopian environment that makes it the *mi-lieu par excellence* to investigate 'progress'. Surprisingly few critics have seen the Utopian facet of *BP*, an exception being Lalonde: 'Le monde qu'ils habitent est un monde à *construire* . . . semblable à cel[ui] qui fonde traditionnellement la cité utopique'; 'l'utopie ici, n'apparaît que sur le mode d'une déception. Ce que Bouvard et Pécuchet veulent fonder en fait, ce n'est pas un autre monde, une société corrigée, refaite sur des bases nouvelles; le monde qu'ils essaient de reproduire par leur expérience est celui-là même auquel ils croient appartenir' (1994: 44 and 53 respectively). The term dystopia is even more apt not least because Bouvard and Pécuchet discuss various Utopian models at length fittingly at the end of chapter VI, where they experience the 1848 Revolution and debate French democracy. Because Flaubert uses his bonhommes' reading to pronounce opposite ideological and experiential realities, this concentration on modern Utopias, *inter alia* those of Rousseau, Saint-Simon, Fourier, Blanc, Comte, constitutes the theoretical mirror to the distorted reality which is Les Chavignolles. The prefix 'dys-' is interesting in itself, for it is both the archaic form of 'dis-' meaning 'in twain' and it also connotes the bad, the unlucky. In parentheses, the *Petit Robert* emphasizes that it frequently signals medical conditions. Bouvard and Pécuchet could not be more the embodiment of 'dis-' and 'dys-', especially in their retirement as 'dysfonctionnaires' in a malfunctioning environment. Pertinent too are their various forays into medical science, using both themselves and others in their trials. In all cases, Flaubert treats them with humour, for they are the antithesis of medical *science*. For example, in chapter III their understanding of anatomy is the taking apart, but not the reassembly, of the (male) model. (This is the peacetime version of the dismembered male bodies examined in the context of war in *SAL*, but equally at the *hands* of other men.) In chapter VIII, they overdo their gymnastic exercise and diets, and in chapter X, their phrenological studies of others fail to demonstrate their own mental inadequacies. Les Chavignolles then provides a site for the literalization of medical ailments prefixed by 'dys-': for example, the 'dysenterie' when Bouvard's beer-making goes awry; and their 'dysphorie' (depressions) when their attempts fail—most notably the 'tristes jours' at the outset of chapter VII which culminate in chapter VIII in their suicidal feelings on Christmas Day. And Bouvard and Pécuchet themselves abundantly demonstrate the symptoms of 'dysgraphie', 'dislogie', and 'dyslexie', that is 'trouble de la capacité de lire, ou difficulté à reconnaître et à reproduire le langage écrit' in metaphysico-figurative senses. At all stages in their tour of disciplines, Bouvard and Pécuchet leave a trail of decay, disaster, destruction, the inevitable results of activity which lacks creativity because it is but a copy. Les Chavignolles is, then, the new sanctuary for their 'dyslogie', both as 'trouble du langage lié à une altération des fonctions intellectuelles' and as space in which to write the *DICT*. Their constant difficulty is with the figurative use of language itself. For example in chapter IX they literalize the euphemistic—'*nudus*, en latin, signifiant nu jusqu'aux hanches', and the metaphorical—'Ezéchiel dévorant un livre n'a rien d'extraordinaire; ne dit-on pas dévorer une brochure, un journal?'; but realize that fact and metaphor might not be clear-cut as in the case of Bible stories (*BP*, 322–3). Bouvard and Pécuchet become the clerk embodiments of clerics in a cult not of resurrections, but of failed erections. Because Les Chavignolles turns out to be the worst of all possible worlds, it offers a dystopian space which not only mirrors the wider male-organized society outside its walls. Les Chavignolles and its frame *BP* are also precisely a monument to the failures of the Enlightenment, a crypt of writing as either literal or metaphorical, a 'tombeau de livres' (Gleize, 1992: 165), a home by the end of the book that 'has become a kind of burial ground for deceased values' (Bernheimer, 1974: 150), or, as I prefer to see it, a mausoleum of masculine achievement both private and public. Thus Bouvard and Pécuchet's erections are explicitly 'only' monuments as failed constructions (as the mocking definition in *DICT* elucidates) and, implicitly, monuments to their obsession with the male member.

The main nexuses of failure, however, or its most extreme manifestations, are found in connection with relationships and concern the dichotomy between Nature and Culture, that is, between natural reproduction and production or artificial reproduction. Bouvard and Pécuchet as male couple raise crucial questions about the codification of sex and gender in nineteenth-century France and the legitimizing of 'other' relationships. That Flaubert sets this 'expérience' in the (un)controlled environment of Les Chavignolles rather than in the city takes further the explorations of same-sex community and bi- or homosexual lifestyles which I have discussed in relation to Frédéric and Deslauriers (Orr, 1992). *Dégénerescence* in a variety of ways may be more aptly investigated in the country so as not to elide it with the notion of *décadence* associated with the city.

There is much in Flaubert's writing that is violent, monstrous, and obscene as we discovered in *SAL* and *TC*, but there is a distinct coyness across the *œuvre* when it comes to writing about sex. Critics, too, have either discounted the physical or bodily aspects of *BP* and any hint that Bouvard and Pécuchet are sexual beings to concentrate on the metaphysical, or have sought to recuperate this strange pair within a normalizing heterosexual model of the couple so that their 'maleness' and 'femaleness' return a sum total.[4] While critics interested in

---

[4] For emphasis on the metaphysical as opposed to the physical see Starr (1989–90: 144), '[liberal] desire in the wake of 1848 and 1871 implied a bourgeois quest for social distinction that could not announce itself as such without ceding the rhetorics of liberty to the forces of popular revolution ... A response to the dilemma was to be found, however, in the liberal ideal of the cultivated mind, according to which social distinction was not the reflection of membership in a priviliged class as much as the simple result of individual effort and energy ... There is no question but that *BP* valorizes the injunction to cultivate one's mind. Yet it ironizes it as well'; Fournier (1974: 79), 'Bouvard et Pécuchet sont angoissés par le relatif ... Ils ont soif de l'absolu'; Crouzet (1981*b*: 64), 'sans cesse le roman revient au problème de l'identité des êtres. De là même le thème du monstre et du miracle'. For different, non-sexualized views on the couple, see Brochu (1996: 33), 'Ils forment un couple sur une base qui exclut la sexualité, mais non la vie en commun ni la formation de projets identiques ... dans l'intersubjectivité, le moi acquiert la densité de l'autre'; Malgor (1995*b*: 123), 'La dualité n'est pas dialectique chez Flaubert. Le *et* relie, met en équivalence, quelquefois pour la symétrie, à la manière des doubles, des copies, des ersatz traversant le texte. ... Il ouvre aussi par son ambiguïté à un espèce de diversité, de multiplicité ... Le *et* s'oppose à *est* ... Il semble, en effet, que la conjonction *et* n'instaure pas un clivage, ni une relation entre les éléments'; Leclerc (1988), 'Jamais couple flaubertien dans la vie ou dans les œuvres n'a été mieux assorti, ni union mieux scellée. ... L'archétype ou l'androgyne s'est scindé en deux ... Si "mille différences ... séparent" Frédéric et Deslauriers, mille ressemblances rapprochent Bouvard et Pécuchet' (55); 'Il faut pourtant marquer l'absolue égalité entre les deux hommes, la culture fournissait à Flaubert ... des couples hiérarchisés ... Bouvard n'est pas le maître' (49); 'Depuis que Thibaudet a écrit que "ce couple ridicule de vieux débutants" présente une

gender studies have, more recently, uncovered the strongly
misogynistic or homosexual relations of this couple, reference
to sexuality has been made in passing or has been explored with
reference to the *DICT*.[5] With Bouvard and Pécuchet, more even
than Frédéric and Deslauriers, there is an overriding interest in

parodie du "couple humain, le couple normal, celui de l'homme et de la femme", la
critique bouvardesque cherche la femme. L'opinion la plus commune, après
Thibaudet, voit en Bouvard "l'homme solide, l'homme à femmes . . . et l'autre . . .
c'est Pécuchet par défaut et par complémentarité" ' (57); and Barkni-Boutonnet
(1990: 184–5), 'Bouvard et Pécuchet vont essayer l'un de renouer, l'autre de
connaître l'autre sexe. Les résultats sont édifiants. Bouvard, déjà expérimenté, ne
tente rien de charnel avec la veuve Bordin, qui requiert une dot impossible, et
Pécuchet s'en tire . . . Y a-t-il matière à scandale dans une approche sexuelle qui
permet le lecture homogène de ce qui est reçu d'ordinaire comme une fantaisie encyclopédique? . . . *Le Dictionnaire des idées reçues* donne la pédérastie pour une
"Maladie dont tous les hommes sont affectés à un certain âge". La cinquantaine
dépassée il était temps qu'ils s'y misent.'

    5 See *inter alia* Leclerc (1988: 58), 'couple en plein sens du mot [scénarios très
clair, très crus, sous rature et censure]'; Seebacher (1976: 23), 'Flaubert parle d'eux
comme d'amants . . . L'unité de ce livre inachevé et en apparence désarticulé se fait
peut-être de cette nostalgie grotesque de l'androgyne primitif, éclaté, émietté dans
les saillies de la satire et l'infinité des savoirs'; Kelly (1989: 120), 'But . . . the categories of masculinity and femininity are undermined not only because both characters are male and hence are the same literal gender, but also because they are actually
more alike than different in many ways . . . Thus rather than finding the simple,
conservative route of biological gender in Flaubert's realism, we find again the
double trajectory of the presence of clichéd gender categories alongside the undermining of those very clichés'; (ibid. 142–3), 'the feminocentric *MB* moves towards
androgyny, but in the androcentric novels *BP* and *ES*, the protagonists renounce
their feminine modes of representation in the end . . . Androgynous gender in androcentric fiction seems to need to return to a homogeneous male mode as well as to a
mirroring reflection of sameness when two male characters face each other at the
ends of both novels . . . females can be bisexual, but males and desire must be
masculine'; Kempf (1969: 123), 'le roman d'une amitié réussie . . . un coup de
foudre suivi d'un établissement avouable (le "mariage", en dehors du mariage de
deux employés dont l'un est veuf et l'autre vierge), une fidélité à toute épreuve, le
bonheur de persévérer ensemble.'; Grauby (1991: 15–17), 'Dans *BP* . . . on trouve
cette phrase curieuse: "Ils voulurent tenter des alliances anormales" . . . le thème de
la création monstrueuse . . . une recherche assurément grotesque du savoir . . . Dans
ce couple étrange passe parfois l'ombre d'un désir homosexuel . . . Voulant réformer
la nature, dans un désir de lui suppléer et de la dépasser . . . Le message contenu
dans cette œuvre nous renvoie à un procédé de transmutation du monde qui
exclurait la femme de la manœuvre reproductrice et conduirait à une humanité
monstrueuse'; and (ibid. 20–1), '[use of own bodies] Faire naître à tout prix, se
scinder, accoucher de soi-même, à l'image du bureau à double pupitre que se feront
confectionner Bouvard et Pécuchet . . . Les romans de Flaubert et de Huysmans
décrivent un rite d'accession à la maternité destiné à combler les frustrations de
héros masculins . . . ils détiennent un savoir organisé en creux, reposant tout entier
sur l'absence de la mère. L'occultation remarquable de la figure maternelle dans ces
deux ouvrages . . . montre que le refus de se soumettre au réel donne lieu à des

the sexual male body. At the same time *BP* is the novel of unambiguous sex scenes in those important interlude chapters I signalled above, VII and X, but essentially from the outset. 'L'incipit, comme tout segment de son genre est *bifrons* boulevard ... *tabula rasa*. Hyperboliquement désert, il l'est aussi *cartesiano more*, provisoirement ... Ainsi, dès l'incipit, dans l'impunité, surgit un espèce d'obscène physico-métaphysique, autour d'une information "plate comme un trottoir" ... Est *obscensus* ce qui est de mauvaise augure' (Kliebenstein, 1991: 454, 459). I shall be showing that this is no ordinary *fabula rasa*. Both characters are cruising when they meet on the pavement. The heat of 33 degrees replicates current same-sex feeling, 'schwül', and Seebacher underpins the *lieu* of this encounter, 'Le Dictionnaire d'Argot de Lorédon-Larchy indique: Bourdon: Prostitué. Le récit qui commence sur ce trottoir s'organise selon une géographie d'apocalyse, où le "réalisme" se fait des symboles qui pullulent' (1976: 26). In the heat of this moment, Bouvard and Pécuchet enter a homosocial partnership leading to their setting up home together, and a homosexual relationship which is a 'coup de foudre' contracted as a marriage:

La vue de cette noce amena Bouvard et Pécuchet à parler des femmes, qu'ils déclarent étaient souvent frivoles, acariâtres, têtues. Malgré cela, *elles étaient souvent meilleures que les hommes*; d'autres fois elles étaient pires. Bref, il valait mieux vivre sans elles; aussi Pécuchet était resté célibataire. ... Chacun en écoutant l'autre retrouvait des parties de lui-même oubliées. Et, bien *qu'ils eussent passé l'âge des émotions*

manifestations chimériques incontrôlées et finalement dangereuses. L'expérience de la féminité (organisée selon un refus de s'accoupler avec le réel) qui s'y révèle, témoigne du désir d'une conception à un sens unique où le livre, la bibliothèque et le savoir joueraient le rôle de fécondants'. Jacquet's (1987) discussion of sexuality and *DICT* applies to *BP*: 'La sexualité qui est, par excellence, lieu de théâtralisation exacerbée des idéologies peut abordée dans *Le Dictionnaire* précisément à partir d'une entrée, femme' (144). Later she asks 'Mais que se passe-t-il du côté de la sexualité masculine? Au départ, l'homme est doté d'une forte potentialité sexuelle: quantité de symboles phalliques ponctuent le texte du *Dictionnaire*: de l'épée tant regrettée, au cigare ... bâton, fusil, lancette ... la barbe. ... Par conséquent, il n'est pas, dans le *Dictionnaire* de sexualité vécue dans la normalité: il y a un refus du sexe vécu comme violence, comme agression faite à l'autre ou même subie. Ainsi s'explique l'abondance même des aberrations sexuelles évoquées ... qui se révèlent une image multiple de la solitude de l'individu ... Pour la femme comme pour l'homme, le sexe est lié à l'anormalité, à la maladie ... le vécu du sexe ne peut être que le propre des marginaux' (158–60).

naïves, ils éprouvaient un plaisir nouveau, une sorte d'épanouissement, le charme des tendresses à leur début. . . . ils faillirent s'embrasser par-dessus la table en découvrant qu'ils étaient tous les deux copistes . . . *Ainsi leur rencontre avait eu l'importance d'une aventure.* Ils étaient, toute de suite, accrochés par des fibres secrètes. D'ailleurs, comment expliquer les sympathies? Pourquoi telle particularité, telle imperfection, indifférente ou odieuse dans celui-ci, enchante-t-elle dans celui-là? Ce qu'on appelle le coup de foudre est vrai *pour toutes les passions.* (*BP*, 3–10, my emphasis)

'Car l'union de ces deux hommes était absolue et profonde' (*BP*, 17). Because of the position and intensity of this affair, overheated like the exaggerated temperature, as well as the preposterous *destin* of the meeting, debunking fairy-tale encounters, the preposterousness of homosexuality as a viable socio-sexual lifestyle is hidden by being made extremely public. Naturally, Bouvard and Pécuchet will not encounter homosexuality in their vast and multiform readings in the human sciences, except *en passant* in literature, in the form of a re-enactment of *Phèdre* in the mid-point chapter V (in seventeenth-century drama, female parts were frequently played by young boys). Flaubert may well have chosen a Greek model to serve the homoerotic ends of *BP*:

Et, parlant au profil de Pécuchet, il admirait son port, son visage, 'cette tête charmante', se désolait de ne l'avoir pas rencontré sur la flotte des Grecs, aurait voulu se perdre avec lui dans le labyrinthe.
    La mèche du bonnet rouge s'inclinait amoureuesement, et sa voix tremblante, et sa figure bonne conjuraient le cruel de prendre en pitié sa flamme. Pécuchet, en se détournant, haletait pour marquer de l'émotion.   (*BP*, 172–3)

Throughout *BP* they not only find immense pleasure in the mutual activity of 'expériences' shared in society, they also spend time in each other's exclusive company, privately, and naked, which causes more than idle comment from their shocked neighbours. The key to the physical in their relationship is Bouvard's seduction of the timid Pécuchet, wearer of the male equivalent of a chastity belt, his 'gilet de santé'. The great moment of its removal comes in chapter III, which talks about sex albeit euphemized or disguised in the medical context of anatomy and hygiene. Sexology as such was not known, but moral tracts and early sociology explained and policed sexuality by emphasizing the links between prostitutes, the state of Paris's sewers, and the question of hygiene. Alexandre Parent-Duchâtelet's *De La Prostitution dans la Ville de Paris* (1846) is a good example. Measures to deal with prostitution were frequently discussed as social reform with the aim of increasing the number of legitimate and 'pure' births. It is Bouvard who moves their experimentation of the senses to 'la génération', which reveals Pécuchet's *pudeurs*, and leads to the confession of his virginity at the age of 52. Flaubert then turns up the sexual heat, by displacement, describing the couple's experimentation with the Sanctorius method whereby Bouvard undertakes his friend's sexual initiation, notably by a further attempt to generate heat (thus recalling the opening scene of *BP*).

Mais, comme leur balance ne pouvait les supporter tous les deux, ce fut Pécuchet qui commença.
   Il retira ses habits, afin de ne pas gêner la perspiration, et il se tenait sur le plateau, complètement nu, laissant voir, malgré la pudeur, son torse très long, pareil à un cyclindre, avec des jambes courtes, les pieds plats et la peau brune. A ses côtés, sur une chaise, son ami lui faisait la lecture.   (*BP*, 80–1)

Pécuchet's long, penile, body interestingly puts him in the so-called 'male' position to the 'feminized' Bouvard (the opposite of the roles normally assigned the two by critics). Reciprocity of nudity follows, with Bouvard jumping into a bath to warm its water as his temperature also rises. It is Pécuchet's turn to command: ' "Mais agite tes membres pelviens! agite-les!". . . . Bouvard ouvrait les cuisses, se tordait les flancs, balançait son ventre, soufflait comme un cachalot, puis regardait le thermomètre, qui baissait toujours' (*BP*, 81). While the scene ends with the comic intrusion of a dog who steals Pécuchet's trousers, the farce deflects the overt sexual innuendos which are picked up later in the chapter when their experiments on others arouse jealousy in husbands and most of all scandalize the *curé*, because their newly learnt method of temperature-taking is 'd'introduire des thermomètres dans les derrières' (*BP*, 88).
   Generation of human heat rapidly leads to their mutual curiosity in animals mating, and they combine reading with eye-witness accounts from farm labourers. The list ends with same-sex

copulation and the interesting elision of ideas through careful use of the paragraph:

[ils demandaient] s'ils avaient vu des taureaux se joindre à des juments, les cochons rechercher les vaches, et les mâles des perdrix commettre entre eux des turpitudes.
"Jamais de la vie." On trouvait même ces questions un peu drôles pour des messieurs de leur âge.
Ils voulaient tenter des alliances anormales.
La moins difficile est celle du bouc et de la brébis. (*BP*, 98)

Remember that the two bonhommes are called Bouvard (*bœuf*) and Pécuchet (*pecus*, 'animal') and while their own experiments on animals fail, the subject of male love does not cease to absorb them overtly, both in their reading or observations. In chapter IV their investigations of Celtic Gaul bring them face to face with the tumuli and menhirs said to symbolize the female and male sex organs, but only the male symbol counts: 'pour Bouvard et Pécuchet, tout devient phallus' (*BP*, 141). Their museum then replicates this view of the phallic importance of the real world by its new section devoted to phalli, which the *abbé* deems 'indécente'.

While the subject of investigation moves to more recent history in chapter IV, Bouvard poses the burning question in their research on the life of the duc d'Angoulême, 'Une chose me chiffonne . . . c'est qu'on ne mentionne pas ses affaires de cœur?' (*BP*, 159). No matter how solid and important are the facts about his public life and *curriculum vitae*, including his date of marriage, the 'real' includes the private. This is precisely the point, in my opinion, of the 'love' interest as central 'expéri-ence' of chapter VII. Pécuchet observes Gorju and Madame Castillon's heated encounter, which not only mocks Emma Bovary's protestations and declarations of love with Rodolphe, but also counterpoints the opening scene of *BP* itself: 'Il était midi. *Le soleil brillait* sur la campagne, couverte de blés jaunes. . . . *Une torpeur s'étalait dans l'air, pas un cri d'oiseau, pas un bourdonnement d'insecte*' (*BP*, 229, my emphasis). The opening of Perec's *La Disparition* (1969) parodies what is already a parody of the *incipit* of *BP*. Pécuchet's voyeurism leads to desire less for itself, perhaps, than for his sense of wounded masculin-ity: Gorju's body and 'air de conquérant' mock his person as much as the lack of emotional response from Bouvard, who leaves him every evening in what will prove to be fruitless courtship of Madame Bordin, but who is willing to give him advice on how to get his wicked way with Mélie. Bouvard's descriptions 'incendièrent l'imagination de Pécuchet, comme des gravures obscènes' (*BP*, 233), but are all debunked by Mélie's non-conformity to the romantic-virgin stereotype complete with swoons, and her obvious sexual experience which comes to light when Pécuchet has to confess that he has syphilis. Their combined failure with Mélie and Madame Bordin not only reunites them, it reveals the extent of their unflagging homo-erotic interest. The opening sentence repeats almost verbatim the final scene in *ES* which I have argued is the *locus* of revela-tion of homoerotic liaison between the two protagonists (Orr, 1992).

Ils ruminaient ... au coin du feu, Pécuchet, tout en avalant ses remèdes, Bouvard, en fumant des pipes, et ils dissertaient sur les femmes.
     'Etrange besoin, est-ce un besoin?' ... ils dirent tous les lieux communs qu'elles ont fait repandre.
     C'étaient le désir d'en avoir qui avait suspendu leur amitié. Un remords les pris. Plus de femmes, n'est-ce pas? Vivons sans elles! Et ils s'embrassèrent avec attendrissement. . . . Bouvard, après la guérison de Pécuchet, estima que l'hydrothérapie *leur* serait avantageuse. . . .
     Les deux bonhommes, nus comme des sauvages, se lançaient de grands seaux d'eau, puis ils couraient pour rejoindre leurs chambres. On les vit par la claire-voie; et des personnes furent scandalisées. (*BP*, 239–40, my emphasis)

The covert sexual innuendo of the bath scene in chapter III is now overt and sex is homosexual in orientation to suggest its 'higher' value above heterosexuality with its malign (sexually transmitted diseases) or procreative outcomes. None the less, the couple finally experiment with foster-parenting as a 'natural' outcome of their own edification and self-education. The arrival of Victor and Victorine, and the couple's abortive attempts to educate them *à la* Rousseau, are not only humorous as a further debunking of artificial techniques and attempts at reproduction (of knowledge or children). Engendering is central to patri-archy's self-validation. Flaubert uses Bouvard and Pécuchet in their properly legal capacity as guardians to question further the legitimacy or illegitimacy of men *in loco parentis*, given that this is the basis of all institutions in a democracy.

For very good reason, Flaubert ensures that Bouvard and Pécuchet have reached 50 by the time they decide to foster Victor and Victorine, both under 15. Their case fits the exact criteria for 'la tutelle officieuse' of the *Code Napoléon*:

Art. 361, Tout individu âgé de plus de cinquante ans, et sans enfans ou descendans légitimes, qui voudra, durant la minorité de l'individu, se l'attacher par un tire légal, pourra devenir son tueur officieux, en obtenant le consentement des père et mère de l'enfant, ou du survivant d'entre eux; Art. 364, 'Cette tutelle ne pourra avoir lieu qu'au profit d'enfans âgés de moins de quinze ans. Elle apportera avec soi, sans préjudice de toutes stipulations particulières, l'obligations de nourrir la pupille, de l'élever, de le mettre en état de gagner sa vie. Art. 450, Le tuteur prendra soin de la personne du mineur: et le représentera dans tous les actes civils. Il administrera ses biens en bon père de famille, et répondra des dommages — intérêts qui pourraient résulter d'une mauvaise gestion.   (*Code*, 67–8, 83)

Contrary to the bad upbringing the children have experienced as orphans either from institutions or female beneficiaries, the home life and education Bouvard and Pécuchet provide demonstrate care for their physical and intellectual needs far beyond what the average family could provide. The children could find no better 'fathers' from whom to learn to read and write (by copying). Furthermore, the two children receive rather avant-garde gender training because Pécuchet pays special attention to Victor, and Bouvard to Victorine. Pécuchet fulfils to the letter the end of Art. 364 above as he foresees Victorine's future:

Sa sœur, parasseuse comme lui, bâillait devant la table de Pythagore. Mlle Reine lui montrait à coudre, et quand elle marquait le linge, elle levait les doigts si gentillement que Bouvard, ensuite, n'avait pas le cœur de la tourmenter avec sa leçon de calcul. Un de ses jours, ils s'y remettraient. Sans doute, l'arithmétique et la couture sont nécessaires dans un ménage, mais il est cruel, objecta Pécuchet, d'élever les filles en vue exclusivement du mari qu'elles auront. Toutes ne sont pas destinées à l'hymen, et si on veut que plus tard elles se passent des hommes, il faut leur apprendre bien des choses.   (*BP*, 361)

The unfortunate and real irony is that Victorine's seductive 'calculs' lead to her precocious encounters with young boys and then to her defencelessness against Père Romiche. Bouvard and Pécuchet's parenting of the children's minds fails as spectacularly as do their attempts to include some sex education in the curriculum. Real life supersedes textbook conditions and good intentions, for Victor, too, prior to his sister's 'downfall', is manifesting 'mauvaises habitudes', to such a worrying degree that Bouvard thinks his masturbation will be cured by taking him to visit prostitutes (as Pécuchet had had to endure at the same age). The unfinished *BP* leaves the bonhommes with new pedagogical projects on adults, as if inheritance of minds is best after all, given that they have no progeny of their own. Ultimately, however, Flaubert's indictment of patriarchy's ability to bring up its children is the message of the ensuing plans. Bouvard and Pécuchet themselves are the illegitimate offspring of the Nation, born in Year 1 of the Republic: 'Ils ont 47 ans en 1838 . . . leur date de naissance remonte donc à l'année 1791–2, l'an 1 de la République. Ils sont nés avec l'histoire moderne' (Leclerc, 1988: 108).

In Chapter 1 on *MB*, I investigated the heterosexual couple as norm to evaluate male performance in the public and private spheres, and in Chapter 3 I discussed 'fraternité' as the false relationship of equals in *ES*. *BP* not only pushes the homoerotic implications of the couple and brotherhood into new territories, its homosocial society questions the stigmas and prejudices surrounding non-heterosexual *ménages,* most notably the bachelor and the homosexual couple, particularly when the partners are old.

Trahissant leurs devoirs envers l'humanité, dénués de sens civique, ils forment une race à part qui menace les fondements même de notre société. Dès les années 1850, les célébataires seront traqués par les hygiénistes, les législateurs et les littérateurs. Une pétition envoyée au Sénat en 1859 réclame un impôt spécial pour 'individus inutiles et improductifs' . . . Sans enfant, sans famille, sans postérité, sans propriété, sans références, le célibataire fait grincer les rouages de la nouvelle morale bourgeoise. Hors du couple, point de salut. Le bourgeois, c'est l'homme au sein de sa famille. Dans le foyer, la sexualité est réglée, propre, nettoyée, hygiénique. (Adler, 1983: 15–16)

While this question may have exercised Flaubert's own mind at the time of writing *BP*, it is through the illegitimate and orphaned men left bereft of carers except each other in their old age that *BP* takes on a poignancy about social outcasts. Perhaps the true repulsion the reader feels at Père Romiche's seduction of Victorine is a response to the age of the lecher. No hunchback, old man, or outcast ought to enjoy, or be able to have sex; and least of all with the greatest prize of all, a virginal girl. In the discussion with Girbal the lawyer at the end of chapter IX, the question of monstrosity or normality has already been raised in relation to Bouvard and Pécuchet's innate concerns about nature, their own proclivities, and what vice is:

Pécuchet prit la parole:
  'Les vices sont les propriétés de la Nature, comme les inondations, les tempêtes.'
  Le notaire l'arrêta . . .
  'Je trouve votre système d'une immoralité complète. Il donne carrière à tous les débordements, excuse les crimes, innocente les coupables.'
  'Parfaitement,' dit Bouvard. 'Le malheureux qui suit ses appétits est dans son "droit" comme l'honnête homme qui écoute la Raison.'
  'Ne défendez pas les monstres!'
  'Pourquoi monstres? Quand il naît un aveugle, un idiot, un homicide, cela nous paraît du désordre, comme si l'ordre nous était connu, comme si la Nature agissait pour une fin!'   (*BP*, 290)

The key question here is freedom to be, the basic principles of the rights of man—particularly lifestyle and the freedom to express how one is made. The remainder of the chapter is Bouvard and Pécuchet's full confrontation with social censure. The ironically named Foureau (one 'r', but read two), 's'en émut et les menaça de la prison, s'ils continuaient de tels discours'. *Liberté*, *égalité*, and *fraternité* are all therefore discovered to be relative terms, leading rapidly to Bouvard and Pécuchet's self-censure, self-sequestration, and consideration of suicide as ultimate 'freedom'. '*BP* subverts a constellation of traditional liberal values—particularly those of freedom, culture and individual distinction' (Starr, 1989–90: 137). The black criticism of *BP* not only allows Bouvard and Pécuchet a revelatory glimpse of their own solipsistic existence, 'une faculté gênante se développa dans leur esprit, celle de percevoir la bêtise et de ne plus la tolérer' (*BP*, 292), and hence existential confrontation with Death. Self-perspicacity becomes physiological at the moment when they might have otherwise hanged themselves among their papers and books. Heat and fire again re-emerge at this crunch point. Pécuchet, holding a torch, is ready to tie the noose when Bouvard, about to join him on the second chair says, ' "Mais . . . nous n'avons pas fait notre testament" . . . Des sanglots gonflaient leur poitrine. Ils se mirent à la lucarne pour respirer' (*BP*, 297). With delicious irony they are 'saved' by midnight mass, the warmth of the candles and the comfortable words of the Testaments. The real issue is that they have no offspring, and feel the total weight of their own legal 'status' outside any heritage, and thus the sterility of their physical position. This extends beyond any metaphysical impotence of *BP* and of *DICT* as a project: 'In *BP* style caresses an encyclopedic culture out of its project of mastery and into a liberalizing impotence' (Bersani, 1990: 164). Without blood or marriage-ties to confirm their proper citizenship and thus ensure that their property and line continue after them, their solution is to co-adopt and thus try to create a heritage of second-hand learning.

Bouvard and Pécuchet, therefore, are figures who constantly come up against the problem of the relative, and not merely in terms of ideas. They are without legitimate relatives, only 'uncles' who prove to be their natural fathers, and like Flaubert's other main male protagonists, they are without blood brothers. Les Chavignolles therefore provides a homosocial solution to the two kinds of problematic legal status they embody: illegitimacy and its bar to financial inheritance taken care of by the *deus ex machina* of the uncle's will; and their non-marital condition as bachelors. Single men were only deemed acceptable if young and actively seeking to change their marital status, thus conforming to norms. Old bachelors become 'dirty old men'. Thus the monstrous vegetables and monstrous matings that Bouvard and Pécuchet try to propagate and grow, revert or abort. Their own 'monstrosity' is saved by their togetherness as two of a kind; a new species within French society which it cannot recognize—the orphan and the bastard— and the 'bonhommes prennent les Modèles pour autant de Pères mais l'admiration cède vite la place à la dérision' (Leclerc, 1988: 157).

Les Chavignolles therefore contains Bouvard and Pécuchet as if in some asylum, separated from the other inhabitants of the region. Their presence and uncontainability, however, directly challenge prescribed definitions of the normal. Their self-sufficiency without women is a direct alternative response both to narrow, heterosexist modes of social formation and to the very patriarchy which will not legitimize masculinity in all its facets including those parts of itself which have been pejoratively named 'feminine' nature.[6] The so-called 'feminine' traits in Pécuchet, the orphan, such as his 'virginity', mark him out as unintegrated in society 'proper' until he meets the male other who complements his skills and talents without these necessarily having to be classified as 'male' or 'female' traits. As Lemennicier argues:

A priori, la spécialisation des rôles au sein de la famille n'est pas liée au sexe. Un couple d'individus de même sexe peut très bien saisir l'opportunité des bénéfices procurés par la division des rôles si leur temps et/ou productivité ne sont pas identiques . . . Si deux partenaires décident de vivre ensemble, *il est dans leur intérêt d'investir en capital humain et d'acquérir une formation ou un talent différent pour se créer un avantage comparatif.* Ces individus se donneront les moyens d'augmenter leur bien-être en profitant aux gains dûs à la division du travail. (1988: 23).

The dystopia which is Les Chavignolles mocks this male *ménage à deux* for trying to imitate patriarchy's bank of knowledge, but at the same time mocks patriarchy itself for its impossibly narrow and inappropriate definitions for the very sexuality and lifestyle this couple represent and for which they seek to find a name. Their testament to their cultural and natural exclusion is their preoccupation with their sex as male members of a new 'club', and the ways in which diverted and chanelled drives fulfil a need beyond the isolating, lonely, self-pleasure by their

---

[6] Wyly (1989) offers a Jungian interpretation of man's nature by distinguishing *phallos* 'the energy with which a man creates' from the inflationary, grandiose, and unrealistic postures of Priapic exaggeration so often manifest in patriarchy as compensation for impotence. 'Inflation occurs when strong defence against fear of being "feminine" effeminate or impotent' (24). For him it also leads to homosexual promiscuity. Later he argues that 'the form of the patriarchal masculine which runs our society's affairs must have an unsconscious powerfully adolescent tie to the mother archetype. This alone would be enough to start the priapus cycle on a cultural level, isolating *phallos,* causing male egos to make inflationary substitutes for it . . . the goal of reintegration of *phallos* is *coniunctio,* creativity, paternity' (113). Flaubert's works overtly eschew the latter solution, paternal procreativity.

own hand(s). Their combined knowledge may be copied, second-hand, but its mutual satisfaction provides the reason for their physical satisfactions *à deux*. One purse joins two similar male members, embodying in 50-year-old form the very anatomy of the male of the species as (impotent) little testers, 'testicules'.

BP is therefore both a vulgarization of the *Encyclopédie* as copy (Gleize, 1992: 185) and a scatological climax to Flaubert's *œuvre* just as it is an eschatological one. The ends of men are very clearly predicted as doomed to copies of copies, like Binet's napkin rings. The only 'élite' in this all-too-male world is the ironist, or *Übercopier*, copying the copy to show its nature as copy and setting it within a fiction which is itself the mongrel form *par excellence*. Bouvard and Pécuchet are virtuosi creations of paper men. Demotic in all that they do, their double desk and copying makes them incarnations of 'la main' as synecdoche, and their function as mirrors illustrates the reversibility of the chiasmus. The blotter and the ink, they are a testament to Flaubert's creative genius both as writer and seer of the ills of progress. '*BP* appears to be a defeat but it is actually a silent revolt, an act of sabotage that exposes and thereby undermines the dehumanizing patterns of contemporary thought' (Kovács, 1984: 41). That unlikely men litter the pages of Flaubert's works as mouthpieces of unconforming masculinity is nowhere better illustrated than in *BP*. 'Bouvard et Pécuchet, recto et verso de la même feuille de copie, vivent là leur stade du miroir' (Leclerc, 1988: 50) Their different similarities with the men outside Les Chavignolles leaves much cause for reflection on the definitions of what is male or masculine, and on democratic models of first-world societies and their failures to acknowledge the necessity to reintegrate women and all the amputated other parts of Being. Schahabarim the Eunuch, Antoine the sainted bachelor, the homosocial couples in counterpoint with failed heterosexual pairs, leave a legacy of the 'déshérités'. The equally applicable other reading is that such hypermasculinities will inevitably self-destruct. If nothing else, Flaubert has demonstrated in *BP* the perfect yet sterile logic of this. The futility of progress can only be written in the form of a dystopian parable without an ending.

BP offers multiple meditations on the false positivism of the empirical age, shoring up its actual fear of ageing, of impotence, of abnormal masculinities, by new scientific modes of rejuvenation. Flaubert's two male figures 'en retraite' in the hall of mirrors, trying to recreate themselves *ex nihilo*, push representations of mimesis embodied by the homunculus Homais to a double degree. Bouvard and Pécuchet set up 'une chaine de "tautégories", terme emprunté à Schelling' (Moussaron, 1981: 103) which is designed to 'interdire de discerner entre imitant et imité, copie et modèle, double et simple revient à attaquer l'ordre de la mimésis classique, qui s'instaure d'abord de la possibilité effective d'une telle séparation' (ibid. 105). Barthes (1995: 436) names this the 'atroce': '*BP* c'est un art elliptique . . . Flaubert a poussé ce travaille de manière démentielle . . . la catégorie de *l'atroce*. L'atroce représente un sacrifice total et obstiné de celui qui écrit.' I would suggest that it is their tautologous nature that makes Bouvard and Pécuchet the post-Enlightenment embodiments of the hyperbolic, excessive, figures in *SAL* and demonstrates the terrible sublime of *BP*. The novel throws down the gauntlet to future fictional progeny to come after it, but not in their turn to outdo this text as unique, a model in splendid isolation, like Bouvard and Pécuchet in Les Chavignolles. These figures are not simply or even doubly in and of writing, in an intertextual labyrinth with no Ariadne and her ball of string. Nor are they 'too inarticulate to share their thoughts, [and so] fall back on buffoonery to relieve their unacknowledged loneliness' (Smith, 1984: 110). They demonstrate the 'démentions' of fiction when reason and madness are joined and when the tautologous voice is, and is not, the impersonal 'on' caught between banality of the *status quo* (the bourgeois) and irony (Starr, 1989–90: 138). With all the 'authority' of the encyclopaedia, circular letters, and non-papal encyclicals, *BP* is also the laugh in the face of the void. Not two different halves of a totality, not two versions of the same, Bouvard *et* Pécuchet reassess the nature of the couple, or the *copula*—that all important link between subject and predicate, the very complements of the verb 'to be'.

Conclusions

THROUGHOUT this study, it has been abundantly clear that Flaubert's works are predominantly about men, and the vexed question of how being born male translates into becoming a man and maintaining a place in the social jungle of other men. Two very clear patterns for the masculine have remained constants in the shifting time-frames of Egypt, Carthage, or France in the nineteenth century. The first is the set of strong patriarch figures in private or public expressions of this authority in the home or the State (along lines which I delineated simply as 'the Fathers' in my study elsewhere of *MB*—Orr, 1999*b*). Chapter 2 of this book provides clear representation of this pattern in *SAL*'s Moloch empire. Hamilcar, its earthly embodiment of its god, rules the known world, and shares many of the same characteristics as Hérode in *H*. In *ES*, Dambreuse is the figuration of patriarchal dominance and survival in democratic key, amid not international but national political upheaval. His power to stay at the top stems from his position of financial control which is maintained throughout, even over the question of his inheritance. Essential to the maintenance of this kind of masculinity, however, is the sacrifice of the daughters of patriarchy—Salammbô, Salomé, and Cécile respectively—used in each case as pawns and hence dispensable, if need be. The stronger and more individual the daughter, the more she poses a threat to patriarchal laws, that is, the dichotomization of men from women. Her sacrifice is inevitable and not unusual in the male economy across the history of 'civilization'.

Chapter 2, however, also problematized this concept by demonstrating all its barbarities. What *SAL* and the other works studied have shown is that these also affect certain men, who are scapegoated, or made victims for their non-conformity to the criteria of ideal and proper masculinity as laid down by patriarchy. These too unmasculine or too masculine figures constitute the second pattern of masculinity across the chapters. In the negative as counter or rival figures to the predominant model, they offer clues to the 'dark side' of patriarchy (See Fig. 2, p. 170, and the negative terms opposed to 'positive' values). Lheureux, Hannon, Hilarion all offer images of this too masculine or sick masculinity. The positive, alternative, embodiments are the anti-patriarchal male figures in each of Flaubert's works, stumbling towards an identity true to themselves. Charles, Mâtho, Frédéric, Antoine, Ioakanann, Julien, Bouvard, and Pécuchet, all in their different ways represent this force for authenticity, even if it means death in the process. Regardless of the dominant ideological or metaphysical climate, they offer a challenge to patriarchy and the structures which it uses to maintain itself, whether political, institutional, philosophical, theological or, medico-symbolic validations of the male body. My diagram in the Introduction (Fig. 1), showing the redefinitions of the masculine at various stages of the development and maintenance of patriarchal power (Fig. 2), demonstrated that the power-base itself remains untouched. Self is delineated as against the amputated or daemonized Other, women. Flaubert's novels in fact trace the inexorable logic of the unfolding of these forms of patriarchy, from theocracy, through empire, autocracy, to revolutionary democracy and its aftermath. Figure 3 shows how the placing of Flaubert's novels according to the representations of the masculine uncovered on this continuum can now be mapped as a mirror figure of Figure 2.

MEN'S HISTORY					
Pre-1789 ————————→			Post-1789 ————————→		
TSA	TC	SAL	MB	ES	BP
spirit	mind/matter	aristocracy	democracy		progress
v.	v.	v.	v.		v.
nature	dark continent	barbarism	homicide		madness
	Ioakanann			Frédéric	Bouvard
Antoine		Mâtho	Charles		Pécuchet
WOMEN'S TIME					

FIG 3. Representations of the masculine on a continuum stretching from the pre-Renaissance to Revolution and its aftermath, with Flaubert's novels and their male protagonists placed according to the aspects of masculinity they reveal.

From left to right is traced the linear development of western metaphysics, politics, and history, as *TSA, TC, SAL* all belong essentially to a pre-Enlightenment world. I have mapped them over dichotomized pairs of terms, which represent the dominant expressions of the masculine at various moments in pre-Revolution history and philosophy (though elements of course overlap in each of these works). As before, however, the real divide is the realm of Woman, below the dotted line in the 'separate sphere'. I have placed the protagonists of anti-patriarchy from each of Flaubert's works studied above this line, because it can be argued that they plummet dangerously close to this territory, some more than others. Schehr (1997), and other male critics have described Fréderic, for example, as feminized. My reasons for refusing this terminology are twofold and are both based on the representations of the masculine as investigated by this study. The first is that the best men in Flaubert's fiction only ever come near, but can never top, his best women.

Stendhal, Balzac and Flaubert while they all are aware of the sexual disorientation in the times of which they write, while they all sense . . . the objectlessness of the energy that torments their female characters, never conceive of the solution to those problems as lying outside the conventional sexual roles or outside the one-sided culturation of 'sexual' attributes. They are more enclined to portray the malaise than to guess its cause, or prophesy its cure. None of them, not even Flaubert, can imagine the possibility that 'feminine' impulses might hold any promise for the future of mankind. (Heilbrun, 1982: 86)

Even the best of feminist criticism only goes some way here. If one reopens the issue of Emma's 'masculinity' and applies the discovery in Chapter 1 of her expressly feminized costumes of self to Salammbô, and the Queen of Sheba, it becomes abundantly clear that even when dead, these women have a stature and a splendour which will ever fascinate, haunt, or overshadow both the most worthy male protagonists in their respective fictional worlds and readers of both sexes. They blatantly step outside the roles allotted to patriarchy's women (wife, mother, muse) and express their sexuality, energy, prowess, and ingenuity around patriarchal circumstance. Even Félicité as carer *extraordinaire* in *CS,* or the wily Madame Bordin in *BP,* are in different ways forces that men have to reckon with. And in rather different mode in *ES*, Rosanette, the most maternal woman in an *œuvre* where babies are almost anathema, shows her true feelings about fathers and sons of the nation. She yawns openly at all the idols of male culture at Fontainebleau, while in the episode of the painting of her dead child, her feelings and the circumstances of failed paternity terminate any growth of an artist within Frédéric, who thereafter drifts parasitically in and out of male worlds of banking, travel, business, and politics. Flaubert does, then, acknowledge the power of the territory below the dotted line in all three Figures, and that it does provide a place to resolve some of the quandaries above the line. Emma and Salammbô even carry the double M in their names: the missing soul (*âme*), perhaps. And Félicité embodies the anchor, the 'at home' in oneself, in Flaubert's works as direct contrast to the restless public (hyper)masculinity around her. I have also suggested that the saga of Tanit is a narrative 'return of the repressed' with even greater import than the imminent overthrow of Carthage by Rome.

The second reason for eschewing the term 'feminine' when applied to Flaubert's unlikely male protagonists such as Ioakanann, Charles, Antoine, Bouvard, and Pécuchet, is that they remain quintessentially above the dotted line, in the masculine. Not only do their central places within their narratives save their day, even if they die, but they are always in a position of separation from the female or feminized by will and inclination. Even Charles, as male Cinderella, enthralled by Emma and desirous of union with her, is altogether other to her. Mâtho's fascination with Salammbô again requires her difference yet equality as worthy of him. At the two extreme positions of the continuum of Figure 3, Antoine's and Bouvard and Pécuchet's androcentricities outside patriarchy still require the other outside their relationships with men to exist, even in theory. The renounced feminine, weighted down under the impossible odds of being one form against the many male ones in *TSA* and *BP* respectively, demonstrates the extremes and monstrosities of masculinities in the conceptual space of the Mind–Body, Culture–Nature split.

Flaubert's figurations of the masculine, then, have no options but to explore other forms of homosociality outside mainstream patriarchy and the 'too masculine' or hypermasculine of a

Hilarion: the supreme temptation for Antoine of the joining of male equals, as Chapter 4 elucidated. The other unviable model is the Julien-leper couple, a union *in extremis*. It is the democracy side of Figure 3 that allows space for 'men in groups' and men in couples to be visible to an unprecedented degree in nineteenth-century France. 'The emerging pattern of male friendship, mentorship, entitlement, rivalry, and hetero- and homosexuality was an intimate and shifting relation to class and that no element of that pattern can be understood outside of the relationship to women and the gender system as a whole' (Sedgwick, 1985: 1). Frédéric and Deslauriers in *ES* exemplify these shifting territories as they negotiate public and private spheres to find expression for a more special relationship as yet without a name. They further illustrate the new state of personhood for men in 1848 across class and sex demarcations: 'l'homosexuel du xixe siècle est devenu un personnage: un passé, une histoire et une enfance, un caractère, une forme de vie: une morphologie aussi' (Foucault, 1984: 58). More radical is the later Bouvard-Pécuchet couple who turn their backs on the city (patriarchy) to retreat into their own world in the country. They do more, however, than turn 'traditional gender into a textual game' (Kelly, 1989: 119). Les Chavignolles becomes as much a purgatory as a paradise for male–male experimentations. Gender-doubling proves as troubling as remaining single. Neither total bisexuality nor radical homosexuality can solve the problem that they are in fact two faces of the same icon, coin, or page. The elusive unity is a repetition in *ES* at its close, as it is in the lifestyle, pursuits, and exploits of Bouvard and Pécuchet. The violent need to separate the *self* as such either through radical disagreement, discord, or secret action away from the partner in both novels reveals the essential egomania of Flaubert's protagonists. Attempts to clear androcentric space outside female economies of reproduction is nowhere better exemplified than in Bouvard and Pécuchet's 'abortive' attempt at fostering and child-rearing. The final bid to make child-*bearing* redundant in Les Chavignolles is terrifyingly portentous of current research in IVF and the cloning of humans. Throughout the whole of Flaubert's *œuvre*, this text gets closest to the catastrophes of genetic experimentation which are only a tiny step removed from Dolly the sheep and contaminated blood at the end of a different century. Mad-cow diseases of today are no different from 'bovarismes' and the gamut of 'bêtises' in *BP* striking back under the aegis of the current priests of Moloch, still intent to valorize gynophobic acts which ultimately only imitate the womb as a (phallic) glass test-tube or gas chamber. In a study of Jungian archetypes, Lauter and Schreier Rupprecht (1985: 168) note that the shadow of patriarchal gods 'is bull-like passion, raw desire and power: sadistic bull-dozing violence, demonic bullying'. Homais's bottled foetuses, the anarchic chaos created by the modern sorcerer's apprentices, the constantly destructive fraternities who expel, exorcize, and decapitate, are nowhere better confronted in their illogicality than in *ES* and the outcomes of *fraternité* after the meeting at the Club de l'Intelligence: the killing of Dussardier by Sénécal. This puts in 'new' world key the severing of Ioakanann's head from his hirsute and utterly male body so that the real masculine of his humility and authority cannot further challenge defensive and fearful patriarchy. Such 'bêtises' now have a new name: overarching masculinism. Therefore Flaubert's protagonists at the extremes or secondary extremities of Figure 3 demonstrate the paradox of patriarchal hierarchies once more. Setting oneself up as new model, as revolution from monarchy, entails a separation from and denunciation of the old forms. In this its paradoxical emasculation emerges, because it cuts off a previously valorized form of Self. By integration, not separation, Mâtho and Charles avoid this move. They also find their sexuality radically transformed. It is not this in itself which brings their deaths, but the overpowerful authorial intervention as both *deus* and 'déesse' *ex machina*. I would suggest that this reaction comes because Charles and Mâtho, the two characters on the brink of uncovering *phallos* masculinity (Monick, 1987), stripped of its phallic skins, lay bare the male heart revealed in all its fragility. Both these protagonists are then 'de-masculated' rather than emasculated, for daring to demask the false face of patriarchy.

Extreme separation also means staying intact, whereas the two texts in the middle of Figure 3 (*SAL* and *MB*) reveal the most broken bodies. Not only are their eponymous females' dead bodies splendidly and publicly in view, but broken male flesh is equally evident, or more so if one goes for quantity. In

SAL this decimation and dissection are the outcome of war or antagonistic orders and powers; the sacred rites, imperialism's holocausts, and the siege mentality are all extreme forms of ritualistic patriarchy defending its systems. 'Male rites and cults occur most commonly in patriarchal societies where the sexes are strongly segregated and ranked. These rites often lend a certain mystique to men that makes them "superior" to women, or they enhance male unity, which in turn can bolster their sense of superiority.' (Gilmore, 1990: 166–7). In times of peace, as in *MB*, democracy's medical science operates to correct male physical deformity while ignoring the psychic torture at work in male bodies unwilling or unable to conform to proper maleness and masculinity. The ultimate fragmentation of the male body occurs in the stories of *TC*: three male valorized body-parts cannot combine to reconstruct any holistic view of man, perhaps especially in the ultimately ironic 'unity' of male bodies, the *corps à corps* at the end of *LSJ*.

We have seen throughout this study that Flaubert always eschews the median, the middling, and the mediocre. His characters never stay in their socially constructed and allotted roles: 'La normalité, loin d'être un fait naturel, est une convention sociale' (Paz, 1993: 47). Flaubert's works display a masculinity that seeks this 'normality' at all costs as dangerous, ruthless, and in its own ways highly perverted. One thinks of the 'middle men' such as Homais and Lheureux in *MB* buying their way to middle-class acceptability either by 'family values' or economic acumen. Both are shown up by Flaubert to be amoral and sinister, opportunist and secretive, all qualities amply replicated in Spendius, Lheureux's mercenary counterpart as a jack-of-all-trades, and in Homais's wordmongering in his linguistic stock-broking with higher ranks than his own. These figures show up the banal iterability of the patriarchal imagination. Whereas those who care little for 'normality', the 'non-norm-formist' protagonists above the line (Figure 3), remain outside standard measure. This may, indeed, be a reason why they have been so misunderstood, especially Charles, because of their perceived 'failure' by critics to match up to 'acceptable' criteria. It is the limits that these figures investigate beyond their social 'place' which makes them transgressive and transcendent and consequently so much of a threat to bourgeois cultural and artistic standards. *BP* is a therefore a masterpiece in its writing of the story of two men of mediocrity. By merely intensifying, doubling, and exaggerating it, by presenting it through two protagonists, not one, Flaubert succeeds in rescuing the copy, or the copy of the copy; he writes an original which delights in all the fantastic and bizarre excesses normally associated with more extreme subjects, art forms, or value-systems. In every case, the protagonists closest to the territory of Women's time are transgressive figures in a variety of ways, for being too like or too unlike the norms of patriarchy. Transgression, then, is a central theme: testing norms at all levels, finding them wanting, and warning of the dangers of absorption, prescription, or false idealism. An extended reading of Flaubert through Foucault might uncover further emphasis on the place of transgression as moral and aesthetic category.

For Foucault, transgression is neither a denial of existing values and the limits corresponding to them . . . nor an affirmation of some new realm of values and limits. It is (and here Foucault employs Blanchot's term) a 'contestation' of values that 'carries them all to their limits'. In Nietzschean terms, transgression is an affirmation of human reality, but one made of the stark realization that there is no transcendent meaning or ground to that reality. 'To contest [transgress] is to proceed until one reaches the empty core where being achieves its limit and where the limit defines being' . . . Foucault sees transgression as essentially tied to intensity . . . Such intensity is the direct consequence of a transgression that by its very nature places us beyond the deadening and consoling certainties of conventional life.   (Gutting, 1994: 22)

Nowhere is transgression more evident in Flaubert than in the various limit-positions of male bodies—war (*SAL*), emotional pain (*MB*), spiritual anguish (*TSA*), moral confrontation of being human (*TC*)—or in the realm of male sexuality. *ES* and *BP* both experiment with 'high' and 'low' versions of male-only eroticism: 'Plato's model for spiritual begetting is the love of man for man, [but] surrender to physical desire reduces homosexual Eros to the status of the heterosexual or animal desire' (Fox Keller, 1985: 24). The overt exploration of male sexuality and ageing male bodies makes *BP* a 'steamy' novel in all senses. It all depends on whether one is prepared to read the bath scenes, thermometers, and temperatures within its pages as comic, but no less pertinent, expressions of male bodily life. 'La connaissance de l'érotisme, ou de la religion, demande une expérience personnelle, égale et contradictoire, de l'interdit et de la transgression ... La transgression lève l'interdit sans le supprimer' (Bataille, 1957: 42). Bouvard and Pécuchet, like Antoine, are not only in search of (head) knowledge (*savoir*, *scientia*) but carnal understanding (*connaissances*).

Across all six of my chapters, sex as theme interconnects with death. The most extreme deaths in Flaubert are of those protagonists who have most loved, raising the paradoxical nature of these two forces which counter-attack the ordering principles, control, rules, and classifications of patriarchy. In Lyotard's words, 'On désexualise Eros, on le mortifie, pour mieux resexualiser Thanatos' (1971: 121). The endings of Flaubert's works have all been considered as sites of the horror and fascination of this interconnection, particularly *LSJ*. Even the 'flat' endings of *SAL* or *H* are a concentrate of this cocktail. It may be why readers do not know quite how to respond to them. The latter especially offers an intense piece of realism—a severed head has to be got rid of—but transported into the horizons of meaning, idealism, symbolism, all those ingredients normally associated with Romanticism. As the direct 'love interest' is erased across Flaubert's works, so the death interest and this intensified will-to-death of the singular male subject becomes more striking in the late works. In this is offered a neo-Romantic vision of the male subject in Julian, Ioakanann, and Antoine, and an apocalyptic one through the projected deaths and attempted double suicide in *BP*. At the end of the *œuvre* these characters are the vehicles of secular prophecy. They foretell the end of Cartesian Man, that unfolding of the inevitable, terrifying, and irrevocable logic of patriarchy constantly cutting off forms of itself whilst adamantly pitted against Nature. Moreover, the fearful contingency of man is also revealed once moral limits are removed, or hierarchies based on (high) birth are replaced by egalitarian merit, utility, objectivity. All Flaubert's unlikely protagonists combine as prophets, sacred or profane, rejected by their generation for their cry to its real wilderness, the truth behind the comfortable bourgeois masks of competence and order. They stop short of prophecy as ultimate blessings to be won after the call to turn one's back on an unethical course, an act of repentance in religious terms, renunciation or apology in secular terms. Flaubert's novels and stories set out instead the bleakness of the curses, without respite.

The ends of Flaubert's works have rightly been read as ironic, paradoxical, bathetic. This study frames them in a morality which strikes at the false heart of hypocrisy—that is, the norms of uprightness, family values, virtue, the abiding by patriarchy's rules, Homais's *croix d'honneur* in a nutshell. It is the strange paradox of the intensity of emptiness which is the point of the endings in all Flaubert's works, the devastations of humanity. The endings all mark a secular apocalypse, *this* world without end. However, while these ends frame the masculine as proleptic force in their prophetic function pointing to the ends of man, they also frame aesthetic and moral imperatives calling a halt to forces out of control. Each of the endings connects moral disorder to artistic order through the active transgression of previous artistic norms and generic forms. 'Happy ends' are paradoxically the most sinister, and loose ends are tied up not as a *dénouement* but as a coda. Throughout I have highlighted the wilfulness of Flaubert's rewriting, such as the story of the after the 'happy-ever-after' in *MB*, the bad timing of inheritance or meetings with the 'beloved' in *ES*, or the numerous occasions when authorial control intervenes as a *deus ex machina* (or in *SAL*, a 'déesse' *ex machina*). The ends of each story and the collection which is *TC* intensify and earth the transcendent, defigure the figurative. Everywhere authorial objectivity and control, so carefully 'hidden' throughout in detached narration or the famous *style indirect libre*, in the end have to reveal his hand. Flaubert's writing itself is quintessentially and supremely 'masculine', not, I would argue because of its 'muscular style', but rather because of its phobic response to disorder even as it describes or circumscribes it. As the beautiful, but deadly, dissection of reality, Flaubert's writing in its 'objectivity' presents itself as the 'science' of art. I leave it to other critics to take this further or to reapply this term to his correspondence to both male and female addressees. Fox Keller's response to male science (1985) provides a starting-point to ground further discussion:

division between objective fact and objective feeling is sustained by the association of objectivity with power and masculinity, and its remove from the world of women and love. [p. 8] . . . An objectivist ideology prematurely proclaiming anonymity, disinterest, and impersonality and radically excluding the subject, imposes a veil over these practices, a veil not so much of secrecy as of tautology. Apparent self-evidence renders them invisible and hence inaccessible to criticism. The effort toward universality closes in on itself, and parochiality is protected. [p. 12] . . . The objectivist illusion reflects back an image of self as autonomous and objectified: an image of individuals unto themselves, severed from the outside world of other objects . . . and simultaneously from their own subjectivity. It is the investment in impersonality, the claim to have escaped the influence of desires, wishes, and beliefs . . . that constitutes the special arrogance, even bravura, of modern man, and at the same time reveals his particular sensitivity. [p. 34] . . . characterisation of both the scientific mind and its modes of access to knowledge as masculine [the latter connoting] autonomy, separation, and distance . . . a radical rejection of any commingling of subject and object, which are . . . quite consistently identified as male and female [p. 79] represents a miscarriage of development . . . that inhibits growth and perception . . . As such it leads to a state of alienated self-hood, of denied connectedness, of defensive separateness . . . Autonomy then takes on the familiar definition of free and unfettered self-government, of independence of others . . . but this requires constant vigilance and control [p. 101] They reflect not so much confidence in one's difference from others as resistance to (even repudiation of) sameness . . . not so much the security of one's ego boundaries as their vulnerability . . . it is primarily defensive response.

All the above has become abundantly clear throughout this study, through Flaubert's many representations of the masculine as different orders but the same ideology, patriarchal men and the few strange others. It can now include his own face in the mirror of 'impersonality', the artist 'like God, paring his fingernails'. The more ironic, allusive, and citational of the fathers Flaubert's later writing becomes, the more self-reflexive and hewn the style, the more worked and wrought in difficulty, the more it reveals its emptying copies, like Binet's napkin rings, turned endlessly on the lathe of definition of new items for dictionaries or *sottisiers*. These in *BP* are the ultimate stylistic and thematic coup, an 'écriture démasculée', a virtuoso mockery of manhood and his own endeavours.

There cannot be any doubt why Flaubert is thus canonized as a 'great writer' for sending back to male readers a reflection of the values that shape themselves, but which they refuse to see. To gender-sensitive critics, he offers a fascinating set of texts which are as much echoes of Fox Keller's 'defensive response' as an active attempt to represent alternatives. In this he is not perhaps the Father of Realism, but of 'Super-realism', his own sense of élite superiority as artist guarding against his depiction of several patterns of masculinities vying with one another. Flaubert's map of masculinity plots the continents, the cities, the battlefields, and the topographies of rising and waning 'civilizations' calqued onto one another in a never-ending cycle of conquest and defeat. What is not marked is nature, the reproductive, and regenerative forces of life. His is the plot of decay, degeneration, distinctive extinction, the effort to write the aporia of his generation as product of his times and place in society.

Does Flaubert's work, then, relegitimize the very power-structures for and against which he stands? Does Flaubert the misogynist stand in a pre-Darwinian position of advocacy of a survival of the male superfittest ? How far does Flaubert use art to fill the aporia of *re*productive creativity (the site of female otherness)? Is his master complex *vis-à-vis* his fictional creations (male as well as female) and his correspondants a phobic reaction about loss of authority, the puncturing of the very rational grounds on which he built his life's work? Is it true that 'Le roman masculin, du Nord au Sud et de l'Est à l'Ouest, a fait de la mère castratrice et mortifère l'un des thèmes les plus répandus de la littérature contemporaine' (Badinter, 1992: 96)? In response to these questions and to other excellent feminist criticism of Flaubert such as Czyba (1983), this study has made it clear that the very rigid, partisan, side of Flaubert should be made more evident, in keeping with his nineteenth-century sex and gender positionings. We need to look again through deconstructed deconstruction at determinisms rather then relativities, uncertainty, or indeterminacies at the heart of postmodern ideologies.

Our postmodern consciousness encourages a distrust of all determinisms and stimulates in us the conceit that we may refigure our selves infinitely, select new identities, slip in and out of roles in protean fashion . . . it seems perversely old-fashioned to consider sex, as our recent ancestors did, to be something that entails pre-ordained economic, social and familial roles, and dictates desires and personal comportment in keeping with biological sex.   (Nye, 1993: 3)

The writing of Flaubert, long before the postmodernists or the canonical modernists, T. S. Eliot, Joyce, Proust, was 'shaped by the contemporary turmoil in male gender and sexual identity and by disputes over masculine authority' (Lamos, 1998: 9). His writing of the masculine offers a complex base on which further theorizing and understanding of gender identity within given contexts can be built. The dual optic outlined in the Introduction—an understanding of Flaubert's socio-historical context and current theories addressing the very same 'crisis in masculinity' in a different key—calls for properly interdisciplinary approaches to be used when it comes to understanding complex literary figurations better.

Flaubert's work, as I have demonstrated, is full of paradox. By showing something of his representation of the orthodox and the heterodox in respect of the masculine, there remain other ways in which such study can be taken further, in respect both to Flaubert, to other canonical male writers in nineteenth-century France, and to current masculinities theory more widely. One avenue is the re-evaluation of 'value' and the ethics of postmodernity and modernity by investigating the roots of these ideologies. My reading of male body-parts in *TC*, 'de-transfigured', reveals a more fundamental morality and how value-judgements may be formed as reflections of those who make them. Showing up imbalanced valorizations of reason (the head versus the heart) or the phallus (Freud, Lacan) is not merely the work of feminist criticism.

When, symbolically, there is nothing left to destroy, the avant-garde is compelled, by its own sense if consistency, to commit suicide. This aesthetic thanatophilia . . . associated with the spirit of the avant-garde: intellectual playfulness, iconoclasm, a cult of unseriousness, mystification, disgraceful practical jokes, deliberate stupid humour . . . kitsch—for all its diversity—suggests repetition, banality, triteness. (Calinescu, 1987: 124–5, 226)

'Super-realism' *à la* Flaubert not only exemplifies all these tactics. Glimmers of what would make a path for reformation is also present in his works in the unlikely male protagonists. This opens up 'difficulty' to scrutiny not from its mirror theories of deconstruction, but from theories looking for underlying pattern as symbolic form in a different mode: reworking

Jungian archetypes through feminism or masculinities theory, for example. 'The great benefit of [Jung's] theory is that he does not presuppose that the unconscious is determined by any of the semiotic systems of culture. The unconsciousness is a generative system with its own energies that operate with some degree of independence from conscious mechanisms of the psyche' (Lauter and Schreier Rupprecht 1985: 224). Reading Flaubert through Jung or Jungian theory would be equally fascinating. Monick has investigated the negative effects of the stereotype and the distinction of *phallos* as against *phallus*:

Patriarchy is not the same as masculinity and must not be equated with it. It is not necessary to diminish or to subordinate masculinity as one draws away from patriarchy . . . Phallos is sacred to men as the manifestation of inner self . . . Phallos is co-equal with the feminine in origination *Phallos protos* . . . is the psychological equivalent of the maternal uroboros. (1987, 1)

A very different approach opened up by the political investigations of male power in *SAL* and in *ES* is further work in political theory and how far this too has been defined by the masculinist ethos it seeks to critique. Marx, or Mill's *On Liberty* outlining the liberal masculine subject, both set Culture and History against Nature, another politics of the phallocentric universes in Flaubert's works. Homosocial organizations of the public and private spheres is grist to any mill of gender studies' readings of history, and within this, gay studies' focus on male cultures. Boswell (1980: 58) advocates looking not so much at homosexuality as against heterosexuality as defining categories, but the minorities created by majorities. There is fruitful literary illustration of such revisioning of sex and gender differentiation in the dystopian worlds inside and outside Les Chavignolles in *BP*, perhaps especially its laying bare of the male (and homosexual) body politic. It seems no accident that the two bonhommes are as involved in mental gymnastics as in the physical kind, given that the Greek root, 'gymnos', means 'naked'. Male bodywork, Darwinian notions of the survival of the fittest, and human cloning outside the womb finally bring out mad science and gay science which Flaubert again pre-empted in *BP*. Masculinities theories have much work to do but could usefully take canonical male literary representations as a source.

But within modernity shaped by the terms of the Enlightenment and the scientific revolution of the seventeenth century, men have grown accustomed to take their reason and rationality for granted. Unlike our masculinity it is not anything that we have to constantly prove, for reason has been shaped within the image of the dominant form of masculinity. . . . There was a crucial sense in which masculinity occupied a central space within modernity and in which reason and progress were to be tied with the domination and control of nature. . . . the tendency to ceaselessly search for new ground . . . has long been a central impulse within modernity. It is also characteristic of a particular form of restless masculinity. We are looking for an escape and are unable to detect the crisis of values that has intensified in the post-colonial and post-communist world. . . . Supposedly we are to celebrate our fragmentation and discontinuity, for there is nothing beyond the realm of appearances.   (Seidler, 1994: pp. viii–ix)

In today's counterreaction against the Women's movement, the burning question is 'What is to become of men now that women are becoming like them?' In the androcentric fictions of French romanticism . . . the question is . . . 'What is to become of some men now that they have become like women? and when some men seem to be becoming more and more like women, what becomes of women? In other words, when are men's claim to feminization and their complaints of impotence a ruse that helps maintain patriarchal power?   (Waller, 1993: 3)

I have chosen to close *Flaubert: Writing the Masculine* against this classic of masculinities theory and in collaboration with the questions raised by feminist critics. Both speak about crisis. The response is to answer each with the other, in ways in which my readings of the representations of the masculine in Flaubert constantly refer to the feminine, and have been informed by both feminist and non-feminist criticism. This book suggests various ways in which study of writing the masculine can be undertaken. A focus on how the male characters in Flaubert's works interrelate with themselves, their peers, their culture, their ethos, and their epoch takes gender studies back into Flaubert using approaches different from, and complementary to, previous criticism. Male characters are mostly male in Flaubert, but it is precisely that 'mostly' which will be the key to unlock new ways of studying these rich and fascinating texts.

Bibliography of Works Cited

Adam, C. (1989). 'Le Rendez-vous manqué', in *Analyses et réflexions sur Flaubert*: L'Éducation sentimentale, *l'histoire*. Paris: Ellipses. 35–6.

Adert, L. (1996). *Les Mots des autres: Lieu commun et création romanesque dans les œuvres de G. Flaubert, N. Sarraute, R. Pinget.* Villeneuve d'Ascq: Presses Universitaires du Septentrion.

Adler, L. (1983). *Secrets d'Alcove: Histoire du couple de 1830 à 1930.* Paris: Galilée.

Agulhon, M. (1981). 'Peut-on lire en historien *L'Éducation sentimentale*?', in Agulhon *et al.* (eds.), *Histoire et langage dans* L'Éducation sentimentale. Paris: SEDES/CDU. 35–41.

Auerbach, N. (1982). *Woman and the Demon: The Life of a Victorian Myth.* Cambridge, Mass.: Harvard University Press.

Aurégan, P. (1989). 'Temps historique, temps narratif dans *L'Éducation sentimentale*', in *Analyses et réflexions sur Flaubert*: L'Éducation sentimentale, *l'histoire*. Paris: Ellipses. 45–52.

Badinter, E. (1992). *XY de l'identité masculine.* Paris: Éditions Odile Jacob.

Baker, D. L. (1990). '*L'Éducation sentimentale*: Figural Dimensions of Madame Arnoux'. *Symposium*, 44: 1, Spring. 3–14.

Bargues-Rollins, Y. (1988). 'Vertiges et vestiges de la danse macabre dans l'œuvre de Flaubert'. *Nineteenth-Century French Studies*, 16: 3 and 4, Spring–Summer. 329–43.

Barkni-Boutonnet, D. (1990). 'Bouvard et Pécuchet: Deux particuliers.' *Poétique*, 82, April. 179–85.

Baron, A.-M. (1994). 'La Bureaucratie flaubertienne du Garçon aux deux cloportes'. *Esprit créateur*, 34: 1, Spring. 31-41.

Bart, B. F. (1973). 'Psyche into Myth: Humanity and Animality in Flaubert's *Saint Julien*'. *Kentucky Romance Quarterly*, 20. 317–42.

—— and Cook, R. F. (1975). 'Flaubert's *Légende de Saint Julien*: Legend or Conte?'. French Literature Series, University of South Carolina II. 189–93.

Barthes, R. (1995). 'Flaubert et la Phrase', in *Œuvres Complètes*, iii, 1974–80. Paris: Seuil. 135–44.

Bataille, G. (1957). *L'Érotisme.* Paris: Minuit.

Beauvoir, S. (1949). *Le Deuxième Sexe.* 2 vols. Paris: Folio.

Beck, W. J. (1977). 'Flaubert's Tripartite Concept of History and *Trois Contes'*. *CLA Journal*, 21, September. 74–8.

—— (1990). 'Félicité et le taureau: Ironie dans *Un Cœur simple* de Flaubert'. *Romance Quarterly*, 37: 33. 293–300.

Beebe, J. (1989) (ed.) C. G. *Jung: Aspects of the Masculine*. London: Routledge (Ark Paperbacks).

Beizer, J. (1993). *'Rewriting Ophelia: Fluidity, Madness and Voice in Louise Colet's* LA SERVANTE', in L. C. Dunn and N. A. Jones (eds.), *Ventriloquized Bodies: Narratives of Hysteria in Nineteenth-Century France*. Ithaca and London: Cornell University Press.

Bem, J. (1979). *Désir et savoir dans l'œuvre de Flaubert: Étude de* La Tentation de Saint Antoine. Neuchâtel: La Baconnière.

—— (1980). 'Modernité de *Salammbô'. Littérature*, 40, December. 18–31.

—— (1986). 'L'Educ'centime: Recherches sur la significat dans *L'Éducation sentimentale'. RZFL*, 1–2. 102–15.

Benet, R. (1993). 'Clé de lecture pour *L'Éducation sentimentale*: Le Bal masqué chez Rosanette'. *L'Information litteraire*, May–June. 13–22.

Berg, W. J., Moskos, G., and Grimaud, M. (1982). *Saint/Oedipus: Psychocritical Approaches to Flaubert's Art*. Ithaca: Cornell University Press.

Bernard, C. (1996). *Le Passé recomposé: Le Roman historique français du dix-neuvième siècle*. Paris: Hachette.

Bernheimer, C. (1974). 'Linguistic Realism in Flaubert's *Bouvard et Pécuchet.' Novel*, 7: 2, Winter. 143–58.

Bersani, L. (1990). 'Flaubert's Encyclopedism', in M. Spica and C. McCracken-Flesher (eds.), *Why the Novel Matters: A Postmodern Perplex*. Bloomington and Indianapolis: Indiana University Press. 158–64.

Biasi, P.-M. de (1986). 'Le Palimseste hagiographique: L'Appropriation ludique des sources édifiantes dans la rédaction de *La Légende de Saint Julien L'Hospitalier'*, in B. Masson (ed.), *Gustave Flaubert 2: Mythes et Religions*, i. Paris: Lettres Modernes, Minard. 69–124.

—— (1989). 'Flaubert, *L'Éducation sentimentale'*, in Biasi, J. Body, and F. Hincker (eds.), *Un thème—trois œuvres, L'Histoire*. Baume-des-Dames: Éditions Belin. 59–121.

—— (1990). 'La Traversée de Paris de Gustave Flaubert', in D. Oster and J.M. Goulemot (eds.), *Écrire Paris*. Paris: Éditions Seesam: Foundation Singer-Polignac. 89–105.

—— (1994) (ed.). *Gustave Flaubert: Madame Bovary*. Paris: Éditions Imprimerie Nationale.

Biasi, P.-M. de (1995*a*). 'Gustave Flaubert: *L'Éducation sentimentale*, histoire d'un titre'. *Magazine littéraire*, 331, April. 45–8.

—— (1995*b*). *Flaubert: Les Secrets de l'"homme-plume*'. Paris: Hachette.

Bizer, M. (1995). 'SALAMMBÔ, Polybe et la rhétorique de la violence'. *Revue d'histoire littéraire de la France*, November–December 974–88.

Bloom, A. (1992–3). 'L'Agonie de l'homme moderne ou l'amour dans *Madame Bovary*'. *Commentaire*, vol. 15, 60. 785–97.

Bonnaccorso, G. (1990). 'Flaubert et le Sacré'. *Messana*, 2. 111–23.

Borie, J. (1976). *Le Célébataire français*. Paris: Le Sagittaire.

—— (1995). *Frédéric et les amis des hommes*. Paris: Grasset.

Borot, M-F. (1992). 'Agnus Dei, taureau, perroquet: La Vierge et les bêtes'. *La Méthode à l'œuvre*: Un Coeur simple *de Gustave Flaubert*. Actas I Simposio internacional. Barcelona: University of Barcelona. 161–74.

Boswell, J. (1980). *Christianity, Social Tolerance and Homosexuality*. Chicago: University of Chicago Press.

Bourdieu, P. (1992). *Les Règles de l'art: Genèse et structure du champ littéraire*. Paris: Seuil.

Bowman, F. P. (1986). 'Flaubert dans l'intertexte des discours sur le mythe', in B. Masson (ed.), *Gustave Flaubert 2: Mythes et Religions* 1. Paris: Lettres Modernes, Minard. 5–57.

—— (1990). 'Flaubert's Temptation of Saint Anthony', in *French Romanticism: Intertextual and Interdisciplinary Readings*. Baltimore and London: The Johns Hopkins University Press. 182–200.

Brady, P. (1977). 'Archetypes and the Historical Novel: The Case of *Salammbô*'. *Stanford French Review*, 1:3, Winter. 313–24.

Brochu, A. (1996). *Roman et énumération: De Flaubert à Perec*. Quebec: Bibliothèque Nationale du Québec.

Brooks, P. (1976). *The Melodramatic Imagination: Balzac, Henry James, Melodrama and the Mode of Excess*. New Haven: Yale University Press.

Buisine, A. (1977). 'Sociomimésis: physiologie du petit-bourgeois'. *Romantisme*, 17–18. 45–53.

Buisine, A. (1997) (ed.). *Emma Bovary*. Paris: Éditions Autrement (Figures mythiques).

Burton, R. D. E. (1996). 'Rosanette's Politics: History and Character in *L'Éducation sentimentale*'. *Romance Quarterly*, 43: 2. 93–108.

Busst, A. J. L. (1990). 'Epic realism and Pseudo-Epic. A Comparison of Flaubert's *Salammbô* with Zola's *Germinal*.' *Romance Studies*, 17, Winter. 67–82.

Butler, J. (1990). *Gender Trouble: Feminism and the Subversion of Identity*. London: Routledge.

Cabanes, J-L. (1991). *Le Corps et la maladie dans les récits réalistes (1856–93)*, vol. i. Paris: Klincksieck.

Cahiers de L'Hermétisme (1986). *L'Androgyne*. Paris: Albin Michel.

Cajueiro-Roggero, M. A. (1981). 'Dîner chez les Dambreuse: La Réaction commerçante', in M. Agulhon *et al.* (eds.), in *Histoire et language dans* L'Éducation sentimentale. Paris: SEDES/CDU. 63–76.

Calinescu, M. (1987). *Five Faces of Modernity: Modernism, Avantgarde, Decadence, Kitsch, Postmodernism*. Durham: Duke University Press.

Campion, P. (1991). 'Roman et histoire dans *L'Éducation sentimentale*'. *Poétique*, February. 35–52.

Castelain-Meunier, C. (1988). *Les Hommes aujourd'hui: Virilité et identité*. Paris: Acropole.

Champagne, R. A., and Daly, P. (1983). 'The Rhetoric of Passion: Narration and Ideology in George Sand's *Indiana* and Gustave Flaubert's *Madame Bovary*'. *Friends of George Sand Newsletter*. Fall/Winter, 13–20.

Cixous, H., and Clément, C. (1975) (eds.) *La Jeune Née*. Paris: UGE.

Le Code Civil 1804 des Français. (1974). Paris: Librairie Edouard Duchemin.

Cogny, P. (1987). 'La Parodie dans *Bouvard et Pécuchet*: essai de lecture du chapitre 1', in *Flaubert et le comble de l'art: Nouvelles recherches sur* Bouvard et Pécuchet. Paris: SEDES/CDU. 39–47.

Cohen, D. (1991). *Being a Man*. London: Routledge.

Collas, I. K. (1985). *Madame Bovary: A Psychoanalytic Reading*. Geneva: Droz.

Collier, R. (1995). *Masculinity, Law and the Family*. London: Routledge.

Colwell, D. J. (1987). 'The Deceptions of Language in *Bouvard et Pécuchet*'. *MLR*, 82, October, 854–61.

Connell, R. W. (1995) *Masculinities*. Cambridge: Polity Press.

Conroy, M. (1985). *Modernism and Authority: Strategies of Legitimation in Flaubert and Conrad*. Baltimore: Johns Hopkins University Press.

Constable, E. L. (1996). 'Critical Departures: *Salammbô*'s Orientalism'. *MLN*, 111: 4, September. 625–46.

Copley, A. (1989). *Sexual Moralities in France 1780–1980: New Ideas on the Family, Divorce and Homosexuality*. London: Routledge.

Cozea, A. (1990). '*Salammbô* dans une perspective romane: La Traduction d'Hannibal comme "survie"'. *Canadian Review of Comparative Literature*, September–December. 307–17.

Crouzet, M. (1981a). '*L'Éducation sentimentale* et le "genre historique"', in P. Cogny *et al.* (eds.), *Histoire et langage dans* L'Éducation sentimentale. Paris: SEDES/CDU. 77–110.

—— (1981b). 'Sur le grotesque triste dans *Bouvard et Pécuchet*', in *Flaubert et le comble de l'art: Nouvelles recherches sur* Bouvard et Pécuchet. Paris: SEDES/CDU. 49–74.

Crouzet, M. (1989a). 'Ecce Homais'. *Revue d'histoire littéraire de la France*, 6, November–December. 980–1014.

—— (1989b). 'Flaubert et l'égalité'. *Mesure*, 2. 29–40.

Culler, J. (1974). *Flaubert: The Uses of Uncertainty.* London: Paul Elek.

Curry, C. B. (1997). *Description and Meaning in Three Novels by Gustave Flaubert.* New York: Peter Lang.

Czyba, L. (1983). *Mythes et idéologie de la femme dans les romans de Flaubert.* Lyons: Presses Universitaires de Lyon.

—— (1994). 'Roman familial, sadisme et sainteté dans *La Légende de Saint Julien l'Hospitalier*', in Czyka and F. Migeot (eds.), *Texte, Lecture, Interprétation*, ii, Annales Littéraires de l'Université de Besançon, 519. Paris: Les Belles Lettres. 153–69.

—— (1997). 'Flaubert et le mythe d'Hérodias-Salomé', in *Literales: Mythe et littérature*, Annales Littéraires de l'Université de Besançon, 620. Paris: Diffusion des Belles Lettres. 81–93.

Danahy, M. (1991). *The Feminisation of the Novel.* Gainesville, Fla.: University of Florida Press.

Daunais, I. (1998). '*Trois Contes* ou la tentation du roman'. *Poétique*, 114, April. 171–83.

Debray-Genette, R., and Huston, S. (1984). 'Profane, Sacred: Disorder of Utterance in *Trois Contes*', in Schor, N., and Majewski, H.F. (1984), 13–29.

DeJean, J. (1984). *Literary Fortifications: Rousseau, Laclos, Sade.* Princeton: Princeton University Press.

Denommé, R. T. (1990). 'From Innocence to Experience: A Retrospective View of Dussardier in *L'Éducation sentimentale*'. *Nineteenth-Century French Studies*, 3–4, Spring–Summer. 424–36.

Derrida, J. (1984). 'An Idea of Flaubert: "Plato's Letter" ' *MLN* 99: 4. 748–64.

Desvaux, A. P. (1992). 'Pour une lecture "ironique' d'*un Cœur simple*', in *La Méthode à l'œuvre: Un Cœur simple de Gustave Flaubert.* Actas I Simposio internacional. Barcelona: University of Barcelona. 49–59.

Dethloff, U. (1989). 'Liberté et égalité: Gustave Flaubert et les acquis de la Révolution'. *Lendemains*, 55–6. 124–8.

Digeon, C. (1946). *Le Dernier Visage de Flaubert.* Paris: Aubier.

Di Stefano, C. (1991). *Configurations of Masculinity: Feminist Perspectives on Modern Political Theory.* Ithaca: Cornell University Press.

Dollimore, J. (1991). *Sexual Dissidence: Augustine to Wilde, Freud to Foucault.* Oxford: Oxford University Press.

Donato, E. (1993). *The Script of Decadence: Essays on the Fictions of Flaubert and the Poetics of Romanticism.* Oxford: Oxford University Press.

Doyle, N. (1991). 'Flaubert's *L'Éducation sentimentale*: 1848 as Parody'. *Australian Journal of French Studies*, 28. 39–49.

Duchet, C. (1969). 'Roman et objets: L'Exemple de *Madame Bovary*'. *Europe*, 47, September–November. 172–201.

Eliade, M. (1962). *Méphistophélès et l'androgyne.* Paris: NRF Gallimard.

Equinoxe. (1997). *Flaubert.* no. 14. printemps.

Erickson, K. (1992). 'Prophetic Utterance and Irony in *Trois Contes*', in B. T. Cooper and M. Donaldson-Evans (eds.), *Modernity and Revolution in Late Nineteenth-Century France.* Newark, Del.: University of Delaware Press. 65–73.

Fairlie, A. (1962). *Flaubert:* Madame Bovary. London: Edward Arnold Ltd.

Falconer, G. (1991). 'Le Statut de l'histoire dans *L'Éducation sentimentale*', in G. T. Harris and P. M. Wetherill (eds.), *Littérature et révolutions en France.* Amsterdam: Rodopi. 106–20.

Falconnet, G. (1973). *Le Prince Charmant ou la femme mystifiée.* Paris: Mercure de France.

Farmer, D. H. (1992) (ed.). *The Oxford Dictionary of Saints.* Oxford: Oxford University Press (3rd edition).

Felman, S. (1981). 'La Signature de Flaubert: *La Légende de Saint Julien L'Hospitalier*'. *RSH*, 181. 39–57.

Ferguson, P. Parkhurst (1994). *Paris as Revolution: Writing the Nineteenth-Century City.* Berkeley: University of California Press.

Feyler, P. (1991). 'La Révolution vue par Flaubert', in B. Cocula and M. Hausser (eds.), *Écrire la Liberté.* Bordeaux: L'Horizon Chimérique Éditions. 141–51.

Flew, A. (1971). *An Introduction to Western Philosophy: Ideas and Argument from Plato to Sartre.* London: Thames and Hudson.

Forrest-Thomson, V. (1972). 'The Ritual of Reading *Salammbô*'. *MLR*, October. 787–98.

Foucault, M. (1984). *Histoire de la sexualité.* Paris: NRF Gallimard.

Foucault, M. (1971) (ed.). 'La Bibliothèque fantastique'. *La Tentation de Saint Antoine.* Paris: Gallimard, Livre de Poche.

Fournier, L. (1974). '*Bouvard et Pécuchet*: Comédie de l'intelligence'. *The French Review* (Studies on the French Novel) 47: 6, Spring. 73–81.

Fox Keller, E. (1985). *Reflections on Gender and Science*. New Haven: Yale University Press.

Frier-Wantiez, M. (1979). *Sémiotique du fantastique: Analyse textuelle de* Salammbô. Bern: Peter Lang.

Frølich, J. (1977). 'Charles Bovary et *La belle au bois dormant*'. *Revue romane*, 12: 2. 202–9.

—— (1988). 'La Voix de Saint Jean, magie d'un discours: Lecture d'un épisode de *Hérodias*', in B. Masson (ed.), *Gustave Flaubert 3: Mythes et Religions 2*. Paris: Lettres Modernes, Minard. 87–103.

—— (1997). 'L'Homme kitsch au jeu des masques ou Flaubert au marché des vanités', in Frølich (ed.), *Des Hommes, des femmes et des choses: Langages de l'object dans le roman de Balzac à Proust*. Saint-Denis: Presses Universitaires de Vincennes. 51–83.

Gallina, B. (1992). *Eurydices fin de siècle: Emma Bovary et le roman naturaliste*. Udine: Aura Editrice.

Gayon, J. (1998). 'Agriculture et agronomie dans *Buvard et Pécuchet*'. *Littérature*, 109. 59–73.

Genette, G. (1984). 'Demotivation in *Hérodias*', in N. Schor and H. F. Majewski (eds.), *Flaubert and Postmodernism*. Lincoln, Nebr.: University of Nebraska Press. 192–201.

Gengembre, G. (1990). *Gustave Flaubert: Madame Bovary*. Paris: PUF, Études Littéraires.

Giddens, A. (1992). *The Transformation of Intimacy: Sexuality, Love and Eroticism in Modern Societies*. Cambridge: Polity Press.

Gilman, S. L. (1985). *Difference and Pathology: Stereotypes of Sexuality, Race and Madness*. Ithaca: Cornell University Press.

Gilmore, D. (1990). *Manhood in the Making: Cultural Concepts of Masculinity*. New Haven: Yale University Press.

Gleize, J. M. (1992). *Le Double Miroir: Le Livre dans les livres de Stendhal à Proust*. Paris: Hachette.

Gothot-Mersch, C. (1981). 'Le Roman interminable: Un aspect de la structure de *Bouvard et Pécuchet*', in *Flaubert et Le comble de l'art: Nouvelles recherches sur* Bouvard et Pécuchet. Paris: SEDES/CDU. 9–22.

—— (1986). 'Flaubert, Nerval, Nodier et la Reine de Saba', in B. Masson (ed.), *Gustave Flaubert 2: Mythes et Religions 1*. Paris: Lettres Modernes, Minard. 125–60.

—— (1996). 'Quand un romancier met un peintre à l'œuvre: Le Portrait de Rosanette dans *L'Éducation sentimentale*', in J.-L. Cabanes (ed.), *Voix de l'écrivain: Mélanges offerts à Guy Sagnes*. Toulouse: Presses Universitaires du Mirail. 103–15.

Grandpré, C. de. (1991). 'Sénécal et Dussardier: La République en effigie'. *The French Review*, 64: 4, March. 621–31.

Grauby, F. (1991). 'Comment naissent les monstres: Création et procréation dans deux romans fin-de-siècle. *Bouvard et Pécuchet* de Flaubert et *A Rebours* de Huysmans'. *Essays in French Literature*, 28, November. 15–22.

Green, A. (1980). 'Flaubert, Salgues et le *Dictionnaire*'. *Revue d'histoire littéraire de la France*, 5. 773–7.

—— (1982). *Flaubert and the Historical Novel: Salammbô Reassessed*. Cambridge: Cambridge University Press.

—— (1989). 'La Fin de *Salammbô*', in H. Cockerham and E. Ehrman (eds.), *Ideology and Religion in French Literature: Essays in Honour of Brian Juden*. Camberley: Porphyrogenitus. 165–72.

—— (1999). 'Flaubert and the Sleeping Beauty: An Obsessive Image', in T. Williams and M. Orr (eds.), *New Approaches in Flaubert Studies*. Lewiston, NY: Edwin Mellen Press. 65–80.

Greene, J. (1981). 'Structure et epistémologie dans *Bouvard et Pécuchet*', in *Flaubert et le comble de l'art: Nouvelles recherches sur Bouvard et Pécuchet*. Paris: SEDES/CDU. 111–28.

Griffin R. B. (1988). *Rape of the Lock: Flaubert's Mythic Realism*. Lexington: French Forum Publishers.

Griggs, C. W. (1990). *Early Egyptian Christianity: From its Origins to 451 C.E.* Leiden: E. J. Brill.

Guedes, T. M. (1984). '*Bouvard et Pécuchet*, le pendant de *La Tentation de Saint Antoine*'. *Ariane*, 3. 99–113.

Guillaumin, C. (1984). 'Masculin banal/Masculin général'. *Le Genre Humain*, 10, 'Le Masculin'. 65–73.

Guillemin, H. (1963). *Flaubert: Devant la vie et devant Dieu*. Paris: Nizet.

Gutting, G. (1994) (ed.). *The Cambridge Companion to Foucault*. Cambridge: Cambridge University Press.

Haig, S. (1991). 'Parrot and Parody: Flaubert', in E. J. Mickel Jr. (ed.), *The Shaping of the Text: Style, Imagery and Structure in French Literature*, Essays in Honor of John Porter Houston. Lewisberg, Pa.: Bucknell University Press; London and Toronto: Associated University Presses. 105–12.

Hanquier, M. D. (1994). 'Le Jeu des pouvoirs ou pourquoi *Hérodias*'. *Chimères*, 21: 2, Fall. 33–45.

Hausmann, F. R. (1984). '*Trois Contes*—drei Epochen, drei Gattungen, drei Stile—oder Gustave Flaubert und die "Trinität"'. *RZFL*, 1–4. 163–74.

Hearn, J. (1992). *Men in the Public Eye: The Construction and Deconstruction of Public Men and Public Patriarchies*. London: Routledge.

Heath, S. (1992). *Flaubert: Madame Bovary*. Cambridge: Cambridge University Press.

Heep, H. (1996). 'Degendering the Other: Objects of Desire in Flaubert's *Un Cœur simple*'. *Dalhousie French Studies*, 36, Fall. 69–77.

Heilburn, C. G. (1982). *Toward a Recognition of Androgeny*. New York: W. W. Norton & Co.

Hélein-Koss, S. (1991). 'Le Risible dans *La Tentation de Saint Antoine*'. *Romantisme*, 74. 65–71.

Hewitt, A. (1996). *Political Inversions: Homosexuality, Fascism, and the Modernist Imaginary*. Stanford, Calif. Stanford University Press.

Hilliard, A. E. (1993). 'Le Retour au préoedipien: *Salammbô* et le rejet du Patriarchat'. *Mosaic*, 26: 1, Winter. 35–52.

Hubert, J. D. (1982). 'Representations of Decapitation: Mallarmé's *Hérodiade* and Flaubert's *Hérodias*'. *French Forum*, 7: 3, September. 245–51.

Hutin, S. (1970). *Les Gnostiques*. Paris: PUF, 'Que Sais-Je?' Series.

Israel-Pelletier, A. (1991). *Flaubert's Straight and Suspect Saints: The Unity of Trois Contes*. Purdue University Monographs in Romance Languages, 36. Amsterdam and Philadelphia: John Benjamins Publishing Company.

Jacquet, M. T. (1987). *Les Mots de l'absence: Ou du* Dictionnaire des idées recues *de Flaubert*. Fascano-Paris: Biblioteca della Ricerca, Schena-Nizet.

Jameson, F. (1981). *The Political Unconscious: Narrative as a Socially Symbolic Act*. Ithaca, NY: Cornell University Press.

Jameson, M. (1990–1). 'Métonymie et trahison dans *L'Éducation sentimentale*'. *Nineteenth-Century French Studies*, 19, 566–82.

Jardine, A. and P. Smith (1987) (eds.) *Men in Feminism*. New York: Routledge.

Jay, B. L. (1972). 'Anti-history and the Method of *Salammbô*'. *The Romanic Review*, 63: 1, February. 20–33.

Jordanova, L. (1989). *Sexual Visions: Images of Gender in Science and Medicine between the Eighteenth and Twentieth Centuries*. London: Harvester Wheatsheaf.

Kaplan, L. J. (1991). *Female Perversions*. London: Penguin.

Karoui, A. (1974). '*Salambô* [*sic*] et la Tunisie punique'. *Les Cahiers de Tunisie*, 85–6. 135–46.

Kelen, J. (1994). *L'Éternal Masculin: Traité de chevalerie à l'usage des hommes d'aujourd'hui*. Paris: Laffont.

Kelly, D. (1989). *Fictional Genders: Role and Representation in Nineteenth-Century French Narrative*. Lincoln, Nebr.: Nebraska University Press.

Kempf, R. (1969). 'Le Double Pupitre'. *Les Cahiers du chemin*, 15, October. 122–49.

—— (1977). Dandies: *Baudelaire et Cie*. Paris: Seuil.

—— (1990). *Bouvard, Flaubert et Pécuchet*. Paris: Bernard Grasset.

Kennard, L. C. (1978). 'The Ideology of Violence in Flaubert's *Salammbô*'. *Trivium*, 13, June. 53–61.

Killick, R. (1993). 'The Power and the Glory? Discourses of Authority and Tricks of Speech in *Trois Contes*'. *MLR*, 88: 2, April. 307–20.

Kimmel, M. S. (1987). *Changing Men: New Directions in Research on Men and Masculinity*. London: Sage Publications.

Kliebenstein, G. (1991). 'L'Encyclopédie minimale'. *Poétique*, November. 447–61.

Knight, D. (1985). *Flaubert's Characters: The Language of Illusion*. Cambridge: Cambridge University Press.

Kovács, K. S. (1984). 'The Bureaucratization of Knowledge and Sex in Flaubert and Vargas Llosa'. *Comparative Literature Studies*, 21, Spring. 31–51.

LaCapra, D. (1982). Madame Bovary *on Trial*. Ithaca, NY, and London: Cornell University Press.

Lacoste, F. (1997). 'Bouvard et Pécuchet ou quatrevingt-treize "en farce"'. *Romantisme*, 95. 99–112.

Laforge, F. (1985). '*Salammbô*: Les Mythes et la révolution'. *Revue d'histoire littéraire de la France*, 85: 1, January–February. 26–40.

Lalonde, N. (1994). 'Flaubert, Verne, Huysmans: Trois bibliothèques utopiques'. *Les Lettres romanes*, 48: 1-2. 43–58.

Lambros, A. V. (1996). *Culture and the Literary Text: The Case of Flaubert's* Madame Bovary, New York: Peter Lang.

Lamos, C. (1998). *Deviant Modernism: Sexual and Textual Errancy in T. S. Eliot, James Joyce, and Marcel Proust*. Cambridge: Cambridge University Press.

Laqueur, T. (1990). *Making Sex: Body and Gender from the Greeks to Freud*. Cambridge, Mass.: Harvard University Press.

Lauter, E., and C. Schreier Rupprecht (1985) (eds.), *Feminist Archetypal Theory: Interdisciplinary Re-Visions of Jungian Thought*. Knoxville, Tenn.: University of Tennessee Press.

Leal, R. B. (1973). '*Salammbô*: An Aspect of Structure': *French Studies*, 27. 10–29.

—— (1990). 'The Unity of Flaubert's *La Tentation*'. *MLR*, 85. 330–40.

Leclerc, Y. (1988). *La Spirale et le Monument: Essai sur* Bouvard et Pécuchet *de Gustave Flaubert*, Paris: CDU/SEDES.

Leenhardt, J. (1992). 'Mythe religieux et mythe politique dans *Salammbô*', in J. Neefs and M. C. Ropars (eds.), *La Politique du texte: Enjeux sociocritiques*. Lille: Presses Universitaires de Lille. 51–64.

Lehmann, G. (1979). 'Flaubert ou les voiles d'Isis: Lecture d'Hérodias'. *NOK* 30. Odense: Romansk Institut.

Lemennicier, B. (1988). *Le Marché du mariage et de la famille*. Paris: PUF.

Lilley, L. A. (1981). '*La Tentation de Saint Antoine* de Flaubert: Hilarion, la clef du mystère'. *Nottingham French Studies*, 20: 2. 9–24.

Lloyd, R. (1990). *Madame Bovary*. London: Unwin Hyman.

Lombard, A. (1934). *Flaubert et Saint Antoine*. Paris: Éditions Victor Attinger.

Lowe, C. (1974). '*Salammbô*: Ou la question de l'autre de la parole'. *L'Arc*, 58. 83–8.

Lowe, L. (1986). 'The Orient as Woman in Flaubert's *Salammbô* and *Le Voyage en Orient*'. *Comparative Literature Studies*, 23, Spring. 44–58.

Lowe, M. (1981–82). 'Flaubert's *Hérodias*: "roman du Second Empire"'. *FSB*, 1 Winter. 9–10.

—— (1984). *Towards the Real Flaubert: A Study of* Madame Bovary, ed. A. Raitt. Oxford: Oxford University Press.

—— and Burns, C. (1953). 'Flaubert's *Hérodias*: A New Evaluation'. *Montjoie*, 1: 1, May. 9–15.

Lyotard, J.-F. (1971). *Discours, Figure*. Paris: Klincksieck.

Lytle, A. (1984). 'Three Ways of Making a Saint: A Reading of *Three Tales* by Flaubert'. *The Southern Review*, 20: 3. 495–527.

McEachern, P. (1997), 'True Lies: Fasting for Force or Fashion in *Madame Bovary*'. *Romance Notes*, 37: 3, Spring. 289–98.

McKenna, A. J. (1988). 'Flaubert's Freudian Thing: Violence and Representation in *Salammbô*'. *Stanford French Review*, Fall–Winter. 305–25.

Macherey, P. (1990). 'L'Irréalisme de Flaubert', in Machercy (ed.), *A quoi pense la littérature? Exercices de philosophie littéraire*. Paris: PUF. 155–76.

Madureira, L. (1996). 'Savages in the City: The Worker and the "End of History" in Flaubert's *L'Éducation sentimentale*', in C. F. Coates (ed.), *Repression and Expression: Literary and Social Coding in Nineteenth-Century France*. New York: Peter Lang. 65–72.

Maffesoli, M., and Bruston, A. (1979) (eds.). *Violence et Transgression*. Paris: Anthropos.

Malgor, D. (1995*a*). '*Bouvard et Pécuchet* ou la recherche du nom'. *Poétique*, 103, September. 319–30.

—— (1995*b*). 'L'Arbre, le coq et le forgeron'. *Littérature*, 99, October. 112–25.

Mangan, J. A. and Walvin, J. (1987) (eds.). *Manliness and Morality: Middle-Class Masculinity in Britain and America 1800–1940*. Manchester: Manchester University Press.

Marston, J. E. (1986). 'Narration as Subject in Flaubert's *La Légende de Saint Julien L'Hospitalier*'. *Nineteenth-Century French Studies*, 14: 3–4, Spring–Summer. 341–5.

Martin-Berthet, F. (1993). 'L'Expression "éducation sentimentale"', in J-P Saint-Gérand (ed.), *Mutations et sclérose: La Langue française 1789–1848*. Stuttgart: Franz Steiner Verlag. 107–21.

Masson, B. (1993*a*). 'La Forêt profonde: L'Épisode de Fontainebleau dans *L'Éducation sentimentale*', in Masson, *Lectures de l'imaginaire*. Paris: PUF. 99–115.

—— (1993*b*). 'Ecrire le vitrail: *La Légende de Saint Julien Hospitalier*', in Masson, *Lectures de l'imaginaire*. Paris: PUF. 116–30.

Matlock, J. (1994). *Scenes of Seduction: Prostitution, Hysteria and Reading Difference in Nineteenth-Century France*. New York: Columbia University Press.

Maugue, A. (1987). *L'Identité masculine en crise du tournant du siècle*. Paris: Rivages.

Mauran, H. (1996). *L'Aïeul, l'époux, la putain: Essai sur le mariage*. Nîmes: Lacour.

Mercier, J.-Luc. (1978). 'Le sexe de Charles'. *NRF*, 309, 1 October. 47–62.

Meyer, N. E. (1995). 'Flaubert's Gymnastic Prescription for *Bouvard et Pécuchet*'. *Nineteenth-Century French Studies*, 23: 3–4, Spring–Summer. 373–81.

Mitterand, H. (1984). 'Sémiologie flaubertienne: Le Club de l'Intelligence', in *Gustave Flaubert, i. Flaubert et après. La Revue des lettres modernes*. Paris: Minard. 61–77.

Monick, E. (1987). *Phallos: Sacred Image of the Masculine*. Toronto: Inner City Books.

Morgan, D. H. J. (1992). *Discovering Men*. London: Routledge.

Moussa, S. (1996). 'Signatures: Ombre et lumière de l'écrivain dans la correspondence d'orient de Flaubert'. *Littérature*, 104, December. 74–88.

Moussaron, J.-P. (1981). 'Une étrange greffe', in *Flaubert et le comble de l'art: Nouvelles Recherches sur Bouvard et Pécuchet*. Paris: SDES/CDU. 89–109.

Mullen Hohl, A. (1995). *Exoticism in* Salammbô: *The Languages of Myth, Religion and War*. Birmingham Ala.: Summa Publications Inc.

Murphy. A. L. (1992). 'The Order of Speech in Flaubert's *Trois Contes*'. *The French Review*, 65: 3, February. 402–14.

Nancy, J.-L. (1994). 'De l'écriture: Qu'elle ne révèle rien'. Collège Internationale de Philosophie, 10, June. Paris: Albin-Michel. 104–9.

Neefs, J. (1972). *Madame Bovary de Flaubert*. Paris: Classiques Hachette.

—— (1982). 'Le Récit et l'édifice des croyances', in P. M. Wetherill (ed.), *Flaubert: La Dimension du texte*. Manchester: Manchester University Press. 121–40.

Neefs, J. (1990). 'Noter, classer, briser, montrer: Les Dossiers de *Bouvard et Pécuchet*', in B. Didier and Neefs (eds.), *Penser, classer, écrire: de Pascal à Perec*. Saint-Denis: Presses Universitaires de Vincennes. 69–90.

Nieland, M. (1998). 'The Three Daughters of Lust: From Allegory to Ambiguity in Flaubert's *La Tentation de Saint Antoine*'. *Romance Studies*, 31, Spring. 57–68.

Nye, R. A. (1993). *Masculinity and Male Codes of Honour in Modern France*. Oxford: Oxford University Press.

Oakley, A. (1985). *Sex, Gender and Society*. Aldershot: Gower Publishing Ltd.

Ogura K. (1994). 'Le Discours socialiste dans l'avant-texte de *L'Éducation sentimentale*', in R. Debray Genette *et al.* (eds.), *Gustave Flaubert, iv: Intersections*. Paris: Lettres Modernes. 43–76.

Okita, Y. (1996). 'Le Droit de propriété dans *L'Éducation sentimentale*'. *Études de Langue et Littérature Françaises*, 68. 98–115.

Olds, M. C. (1997). 'Value and Social Mobility in Flaubert', in B. Cooper and M. Donaldson-Evans (eds.), *Moving Forward, Holding Fast: The Dynamics of Nineteenth-Century French Culture*. Amsterdam and Atlanta: Rodopi. 81–90.

Oliver, H. (1988–9). 'The Calves' Head Club Notes Sent to Flaubert'. *FSB*, 29, Winter. 5–7.

Orr, M. (1992). 'Reading the Other: Flaubert's *L'Éducation sentimentale* Revisisted'. *French Studies*, 46: 4, October. 412–23.

—— (1995). 'Trois Contes *et leurs identités intertextuelles: Figures, figurations, transfigurations*'. *French Studies in Southern Africa*, 24. 76–83.

—— (1995–6). 'Capes and Copes: Revealing the Veiled Man in Flaubert's *Salammbô*'. per*versions*, 6, Winter. 121–39.

—— (1996). 'Reflections on "bovarysme": The Bovarys at Vaubyessard'. *FSB*, 61, Winter. 6–8.

—— (1997). 'The Cloaks of Power: Custom and Costume in Flaubert's *Salammbô*'. *Nottingham French Studies*, 36: 2 Autumn. 24–33.

—— (1998a). 'Flaubert's Egypt: Crucible and Crux for Textual Identity', in P. Starkey and J. Starkey (eds.), *Travellers in Egypt*. London and New York: I. B. Tauris Publishers.

—— (1998*b*). 'Stasis and Ecstasy: *La Tentation de Saint Antoine* or the texte bouleversant'. *FMLS* 34: 4, October. 335–44.

—— (1999*a*). 'Reversible Roles: Gender Trouble in *Madame Bovary*', in T. Williams and Orr (eds.), *New Approaches in Flaubert Studies*. Lewiston, NY: The Edwin Mellen Press. 46–64.

—— (1999*b*). *Madame Bovary: Representations of the Masculine*. Berne: Peter Lang.

—— (2000). 'East or West? Flaubert's *La Tentation de Saint Antoine* or the question of orthodoxy.' in P. Cooke and J. Lee (eds.), *(Un)Faithful Texts: Religion in French and Francophone Literature from the 1780s to the 1980s*. New Orleans: University Press of the South.

Overton, W. (1996). *The Novel of Female Adultery*. Basingstoke and London: Macmillan Press Ltd.

Palaccio, J. de (1993). *Les Perversions du Merveilleux*. Paris: Séguier.

Paulson, W. (1992). *Sentimental Education: The Complexity of Disenchantment*. New York: Twayne Publishers.

Paz, O. (1993). *Un au-delà érotique: Le Marquis de Sade*. Paris: NRF Gallimard.

Pederson, L. E. (1991). *Dark Hearts: The Unconscious Forces that Shape Men's Lives*. Boston: Shambhala.

Pedraza, J. (1997). 'Le Shopping d'Emma', in A. Buisine (ed.), *Emma Bovary*. Paris: Éditions Autrement. 100–21.

Perera, S. Brinton. (1986). *The Scapegoat Complex: Toward a Mythology of Shadow and Guilt*. Toronto: Inner City Books.

Peterson, C. L. (1983). 'The Trinity in Flaubert's *Trois Contes*: Deconstructing History'. *French Forum*, 8: 3, September. 243–58.

Philippot, D. (1997). *Vérité des choses, mensonge de l'Homme dans Madame Bovary de Flaubert: De la Nature au Narcisse*. Paris: Honoré Champion.

Pleck, J. H., and Sawyer, J. (1974) (eds.). *Men and Masculinity*. Englewood Cliffs, NJ: Prentice-Hall.

Pliskin, F. (1994). 'La norme et l'exception', in R. Genette Debray *et al.* (eds.), *Gustave Flaubert*, iv: *Intersections*. Paris: Lettres Modernes. 99–113.

Prado, J. del (1992). '*Un Cœur Simple*: Un proceso destructivo'. *La Méthode a l'œuvre: Un Cœur Simple de Gustave Flaubert*, Actas I Simposio internacional. Barcelona: University of Barcelona. 31–59.

Propp, V. (1988). *Morphology of the Folktale*. Austin, Tex.: University of Texas Press.

Proust, M. (1987). *Sur Baudelaire, Flaubert et Morand*. Brussels: Éditions Complexes.

Pugh, D. G. (1983). *Sons of Liberty: The Masculine Mind in Nineteenth-Century America*. Westport, Ontario: Greenwood Press.

Raitt, A. (1982). 'La Décomposition des personnages dans *L'Éducation sentimentale*', in P. M. Wetherill (ed.), *Flaubert: La Dimension du texte*. Manchester: Manchester University Press. 157–74.

—— (1991). *Flaubert: Trois Contes*. London: Grant and Cutler Ltd.

Raitt, A. (1998). *Flaubert et le Théâtre*. Berne: Peter Lang.

Ramazani, V. K. (1993). 'Historical Cliché: Irony and the Sublime in *L'Éducation sentimentale*'. *PMLA* 108: 1, January. 1221–35.

Redfield, M. (1996). 'Aesthetics and History: *L'Éducation sentimentale*', in Redfield, *Phantom Formations: Aesthetic Ideology and the Bildungsroman*. Ithaca and London: Cornell University Press. 171–200.

Reff, T. (1974). 'Images of Flaubert's Queen of Sheba in Later Nineteenth-Century Art', in F. Haskell, A. Levi, and R. Shackleton (eds.), *The Artist and the Writer in France: Essays in Honour of Jean Seznec*. Oxford: Clarendon Press. 126–33.

Reichler, C. (1985). 'Pars pro toto: Flaubert et le fétichisme'. *Studi francesi*, 85, January–April, v. 29. 77–83.

Reid, M. (1995). *Flaubert correspondant*. Paris: SEDES.

Reish, J. G. (1984). 'Those Who See God in Flaubert's *Trois Contes*'. *Renascence*, 36: 4. 219–29.

Renaudin, A. (1979–80). 'Gustave Flaubert et Salammbô sur les chemins—égyptiens—de Carthage', in *Précis analytique des travaux de l'Académie des Sciences, Belles-Lettres et Arts de Rouen*. 211–32.

Rétat, L. (1990). 'Renan ou les testations de l'Absolu'. *Mesure*. Paris: José Corti. 125–38.

Reynaud, E. (1981). *La Sainte Virilité*. Paris: Syros.

Rincé, D. (1990). *L'Éducation sentimentale: Gustave Flaubert*. Poitiers: Éditions Natan.

Ripoll, R. (1982). 'Bouvard et Pécuchet à la recherche des Gaulois', in P. Viallaneix and J. Ehrard (eds.), *Nos Ancêtres les Gaulois: Actes du Colloque international de Clermont-Ferrand*, Fac. des Lettres et sciences humaines, 13. 331–7.

Robertson, J. (1982). 'The Structure of *Hérodias*'. *French Studies*, 36, April. 171–82.

Roper, M., and Tosh, J. (1991) (eds.). *Manful Assertions: Masculinities in Britain since 1800*. London: Routledge.

Rougemont, D. de (1982). *La Part du Diable*. Paris: NRF Gallimard.

Rubenson, S. (1995). *The Letters of Saint Antony: Monasticism and the Making of a Saint*. Minneapolis: Fortress Press.

Sachs, M. (1970). 'Flaubert's *Trois Contes*: The Reconquest of Art'. *Esprit créateur*, 10. 62–74.

Saïd, E. (1975). *Beginnings: Intention and Method*. New York: Basic Books Inc.

—— (1978). *Orientalism*. London: Penguin.

Sartre, J.-P. (1980). 'Entretien'. *L'Arc*. 33–7.

Schehr, L. (1989). 'Salammbô as the Novel of Alterity'. *Nineteenth-Century French Studies*, 17: 3–4, Spring–Summer. 326–41.

—— (1995a). *Alcibiades at the Door: Gay Discourses in French Literature*. Stanford, Calif.: Stanford University Press.

—— (1995b). *The Shock of Men: Homosexual Hermeneutics in French Writing*. Stanford, Calif.: Stanford University Press.

—— (1997). *Rendering French Realism*. Stanford, Calif.: Stanford University Press.

Schor, N. (1985). *Breaking the Chain: Women, Theory and French Realist Fiction*. New York: Columbia University Press.

—— and Majewski, H. F. (1984) (eds.). *Flaubert and Postmodernism*. Lincoln, Nebr.: University of Nebraska Press.

Schwartz-Salant, N. (1995) (ed.). *C.G. Jung: Jung on Alchemy*. London: Routledge.

Sckommodau, H. (1971). 'Un mot-thème de *L'Éducation sentimentale*: L'autre'. *Cahiers de l'Association internationale des études françaises*, 23.

Scott, J.W. (1988). *Gender and the Politics of History*. New York: Columbia University Press.

Scrogham, R. E. (1998). 'The Echo of the Name "Ioakanann" in Flaubert's *Hérodias*'. *The French Review*, 71: 5, April. 775–84.

Sedgwick, E. Kosofsky (1985). *Between Men: English Literature and Male Homosocial Desire*. New York: Columbia University Press.

—— (1991). *Epistemology of the Closet*. London: Harvester Wheatsheaf.

Seebacher, J. (1976). 'Le Réalisme de *Bouvard et Pécuchet*: Notes pour une topique de topographie utopique'. *Trentequatre/Quarante Quatre*, 1, Autumn. 23–6.

Segal, L. (1990). *Slow Motion: Changing Masculinities, Changing Men*. New Brunswick, NJ: Rutgers University Press.

Séginger, G. (1984). *Le Mysticisme dans* La Tentation *de Flaubert: La Relation sujet–objet*. Paris: Archives de Lettres Modernes, 215, no. 5.

—— (1987). 'L'Artiste, le saint: Les Tentations de Saint Antoine'. *Romantisme*, 55. 79–90.

—— (1988). 'Ontologie flaubertienne: Une naturalisation due sentiment religieux', in *Gustave Flaubert 3: Mythes et Religions 2*. Paris: Lettres Modernes, Minard. 63–85.

—— (1997). *Naissance et Métamorphoses d'un écrivain: Flaubert et* Les Tentations de Saint Antoine. Paris: Honoré Champion.

Seidler (V.) (1989) *Rediscovering Masculinity: Reason, Language and Sexuality*. London: Routledge.

—— (1994). *Unreasonable Men: Masculinity and Social Theory*. London: Routledge.

—— (1991) (ed.). *The Achilles Heel Reader: Men, Sexual Politics and Socialism*. London: Routledge.

Selvin, S. C. (1983). 'Spatial Form in Flaubert's *Trois Contes*'. *Romanic Review*, 74: 2. 202–20.

Seznec, J. (1945a). 'Flaubert historien des hérésies dans *La Tentation*'. *The Romanic Review*, October. 200–21.

—— (1945b). 'Flaubert historien des hérésies dans *La Tentation*', *The Romanic Review*, December. 314–28.

—— (1949). *Nouvelles études sur* La Tentation de Saint Antoine. London: The Warburg Institute, University of London.

Sherrington, R. J. (1965). 'Illusion and Reality in *La Tentation de Saint Antoine*'. *AUMLA* 24, November. 272–89.

Shillony, H. (1982). 'L'Art dans *L'Éducation sentimentale* et l'œuvre: (Re)production et originalité'. *Australian Journal of French Studies*, 19: 1, January–April. 41–50.

Showalter, E. (1997). *Hystories: Hysterical Epidemics and Modern Culture*. New York: Columbia University Press.

Sicard, M. (1980). 'Notes sur *Madame Bovary*, J-P Sartre'. *L'Arc*, 79. 38–43.

Siller, D. (1981). 'La Mort d'Emma Bovary: Sources médicales'. *Revue d'histoire littéraire de la France*, 81: 415, July–October. 719–46.

Sinclair, A. (1993). *The Deceived Husband: A Kleinian Approach to the Literature of Infidelity*. Oxford: Oxford University Press.

Slama, B. (1971). 'Une lecture de *L'Éducation sentimentale*'. *Littérature*, 2, May. 19–38.

Smith, P. (1984). *Public and Private Value: Studies in the Nineteenth-Century Novel*. Cambridge: Cambridge University Press.

Starr, P. (1984). 'Science and Confusion: On Flaubert's *La Tentation de Saint Antoine*'. *MLN* 99: 5, December. 1072–93.

—— (1985). '*Salammbô*: The Politics of an Ending'. *French Forum*, 10: 1. 40–56.

—— (1989–90). 'The Styles of (Post)Literal Desire: *Bouvard et Pécuchet*'. *Nineteenth-Century French Studies*, 18: 1–2, Fall–Winter. 133–49.

Steinberg, W. (1993). *Masculinity: Identity, Conflict, and Transfromation*. Boston and London: Shambhala Publications, Inc.

Still, J. and Worton, M. (1993) (eds.). *Textuality and Sexuality: Reading Theories and Practices*. Manchester: Manchester University Press.

Strike, W. N. (1976). 'Art et poésie dans La *Légende de Saint Julien l'Hospitalier*'. *French Studies in Southern Africa*, 5. 52–63.

Tabaki-Iona, F. (1989). *Le Personnage de Mme Arnoux dans* L'Éducation sentimentale *de Gustave Flaubert*. Athens.

Tanner, T. (1979). *Adultery in the Novel: Contract and Transgression.* Baltimore: The Johns Hopkins University Press.

Testa, C. (1991–2). 'Representing the Unrepresentable: The Desexualization of Desire in Flaubert's "Etre la Matière"'. *Nineteenth-Century French Studies*, 20: 1–2, Fall–Winter. 137–44.

Thomas, Y. (1990). 'La Valeur de l'Orient: L'Épisode de la Reine de Saba dans *La Tentation de Saint Antoine*'. *Études françaises*, 26: 1. 35–45.

Tondeur, C.-L. (1989). 'Gustave Flaubert—le désir, la fluidité et la dissolution'. *Neophilologus*, 73: 4, October. 512–21.

Toro, A. de (1987) (ed.). *Gustave Flaubert*. Tübingen: Gunter Narr Verlag.

Tricotel, C. (1978). *Comme deux troubadours: Histoire de l'amitié Flaubert: Sand.* Paris: CDU/SEDES.

Vargas Llosa, M. (1975). *L'Orgie perpetuelle*. Paris: NRF Gallimard.

Vidalenc, J. (1969). 'Gustave Flaubert historien de la Révolution de 1848'. *Europe*, September–November. 1–19.

Vierne, S. (1992). 'La Sainte et le perroquet ou le travail du mythique dans *Un Cœur simple*'. *La Méthode à l'œuvre:* Un Cœur simple *de Gustave Flaubert*, Actas I Simposio internacional. Barcelona: University of Barcelona. 13–30.

Walby, S. (1990). *Theorizing Patriarchy*. Oxford: Blackwell.

Wallen, J. (1989–90). '*Salammbô* and the Resistance of the Aesthetic'. *Romance Notes*, 30. 237–45.

Waller, M. (1993). *The Male Malady: Fictions of Impotence in the French Romantic Novel*. New Brunswick: Rutgers University Press.

Webster Goodwin, S. (1986). 'Emma Bovary's Dance of Death'. *Novel*, 19, 3, Spring. 197–215.

Weeks, J. (1989). *Sexuality and its Discontents: Meanings, Myths and Modern Sexualities*. London: Routledge.

Wetherill, P. M. (1993). 'Masculine and Feminine Voices in Conflict'. *New Comparison*, 15, Spring. 120–36.

—— (1994). 'L'Élaboration des chambres *d'Hérodias*'. *Orbis Litterarum*, 48. 245–68.

—— (1982) (ed.). *Flaubert: La dimension du texte*. Manchester: Manchester University Press.

Williams, D. A. (1973). *Psychological Determinism in* Madame Bovary. University of Hull Publications: Occasional Papers in Modern Languages, 9.

—— (1987). *The Hidden Life at its Source: A Study of Flaubert's* L'Éducation sentimentale. Hull: Hull University Press.

—— (1992). 'Gender Stereotypes in *Madame Bovary*'. *FMLS*, 28: 2. 130–9.

—— and Orr, M. (1999) (eds.). *New Approaches in Flaubert Studies.* Lewiston: The Edwin Mellen Press.

Williams, R. (1990). *The Wound of Knowledge.* London: DLT (2nd, revised edition).

Wise, C. (1993). 'The Whatness of Loulou: Allegories of Thomism in Flaubert'. *Religion and Literature*, 25: 1, Spring. 35–49.

Wyly, J. (1989). *The Phallic Quest: Priapus and Masculine Inflation.* Toronto: Inner City Books.

Yaeger, P., and Kowaleski-Wallace, B. (1989) (eds.). *Refiguring the Father: New Feminist Essays of Patriarchy.* Carbondale and Edwardsville, Ill.: S. Illinois University Press.

Zants, E. (1979). '*Trois Contes*: A New Dimension in Flaubert'. *Nottingham French Studies*, 18: 1, May. 37–44.

Zenkine, S. (1995). '*Bouvard et Pécuchet*: Un roman-brouillon' in A. Grésillon (ed.), *Les Manuscrits littéraires à travers les siècles.* Charente: Du Lérot Éditeur. 157–66.

—— (1996). Madame Bovary: *L'oppression réaliste.* Clermond-Férrand: Association des Publications de la Faculté des Lettres et Sciences Humaines.

Index